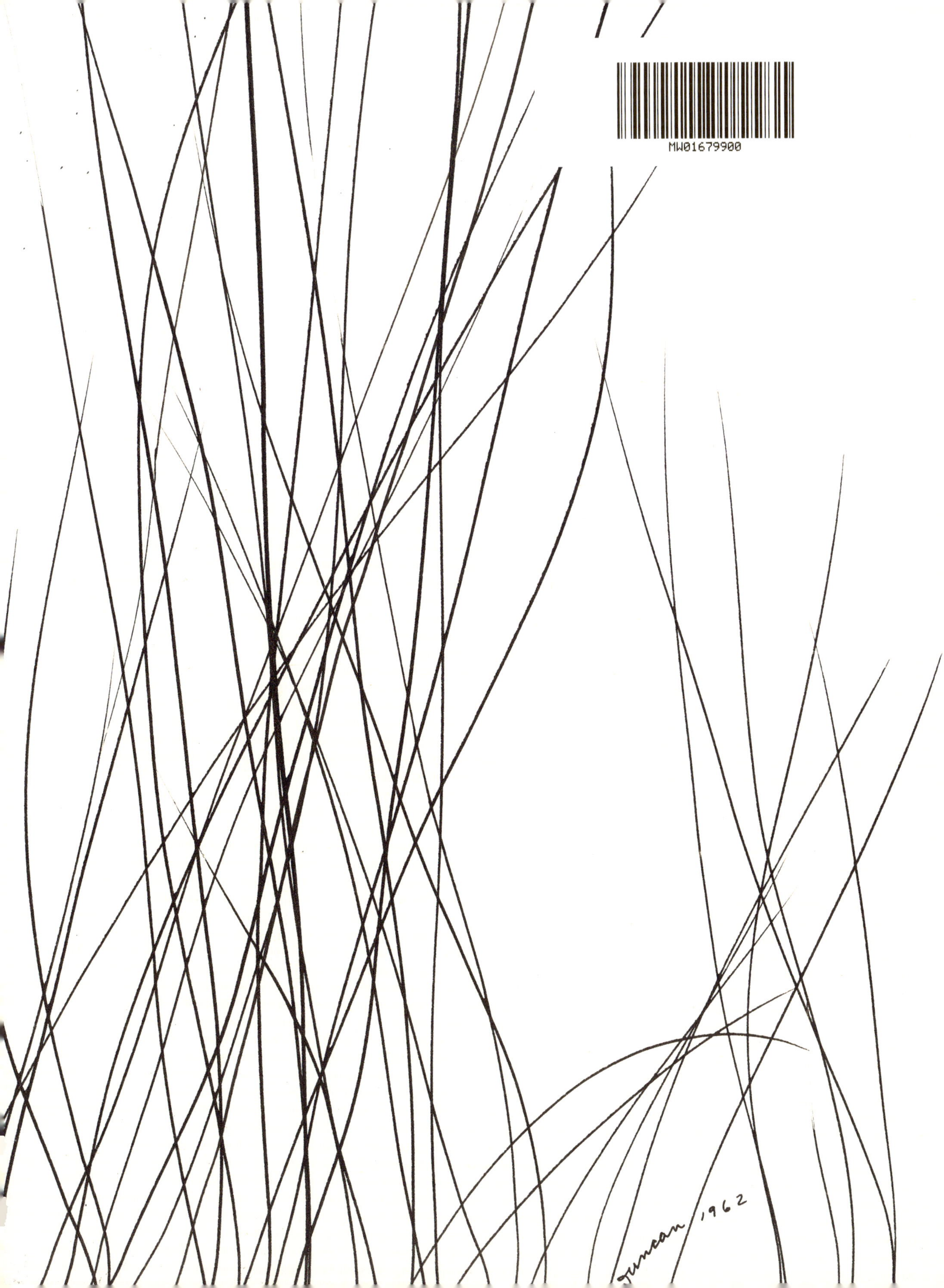
Duncan 1962

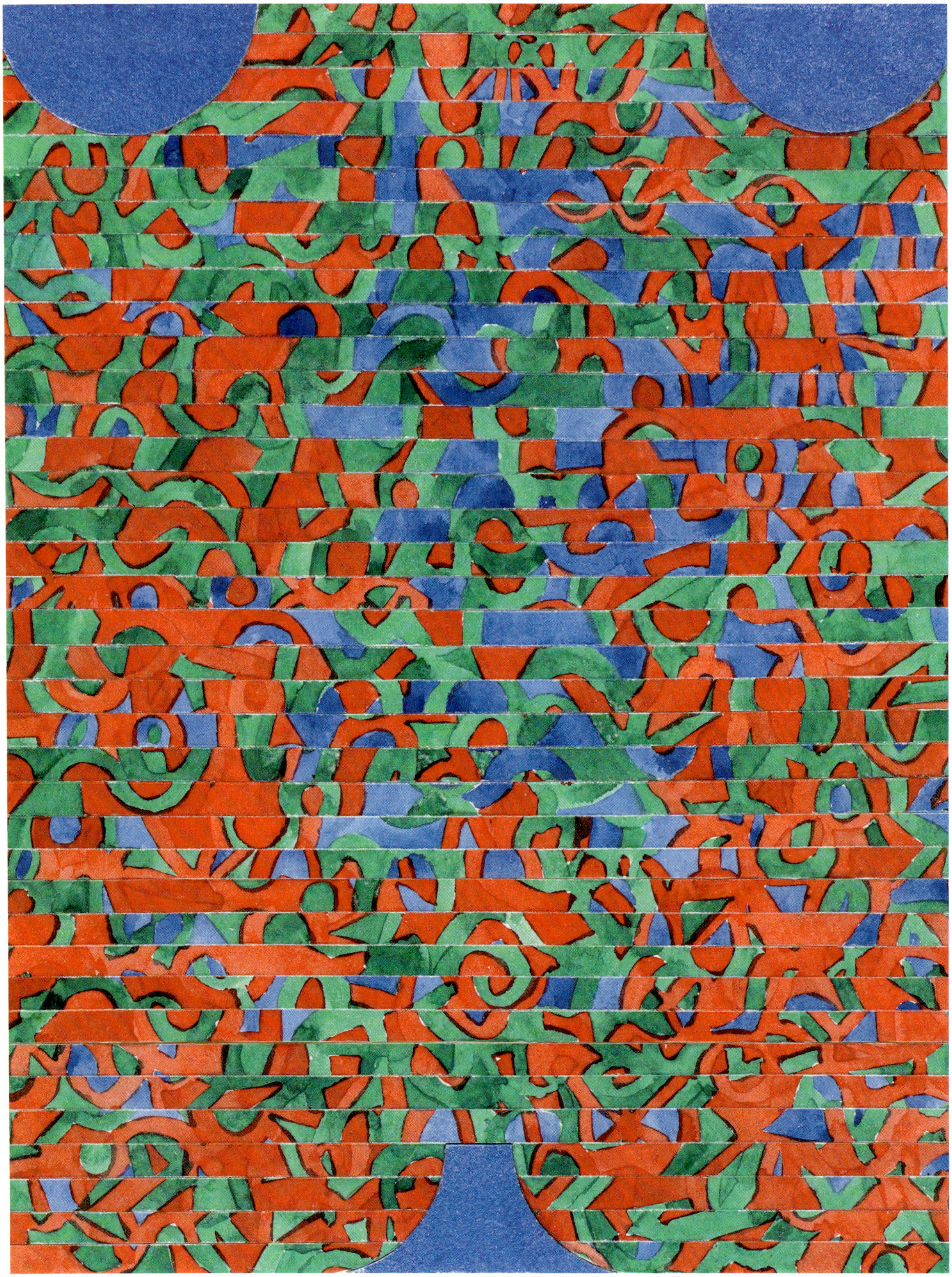

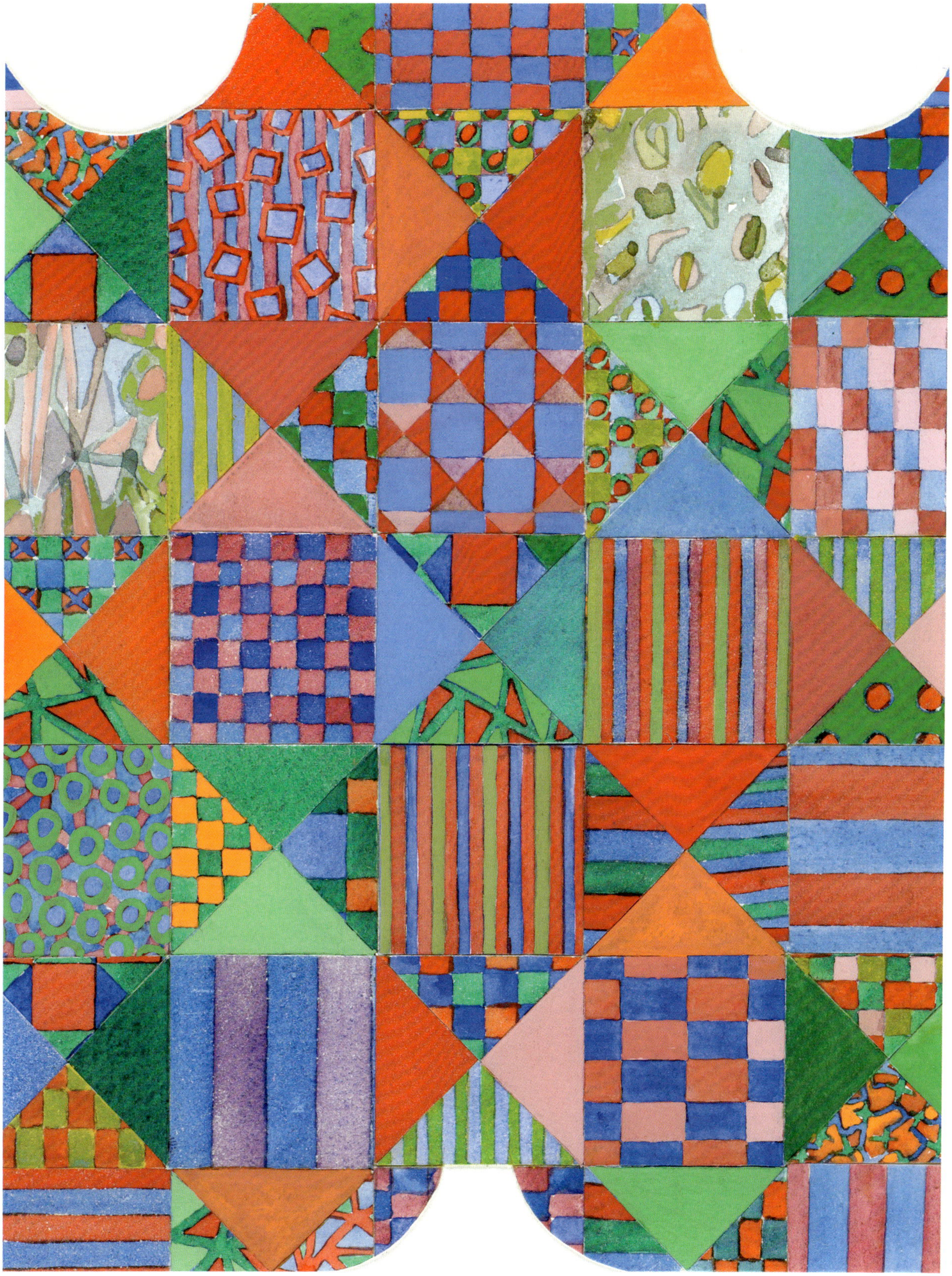

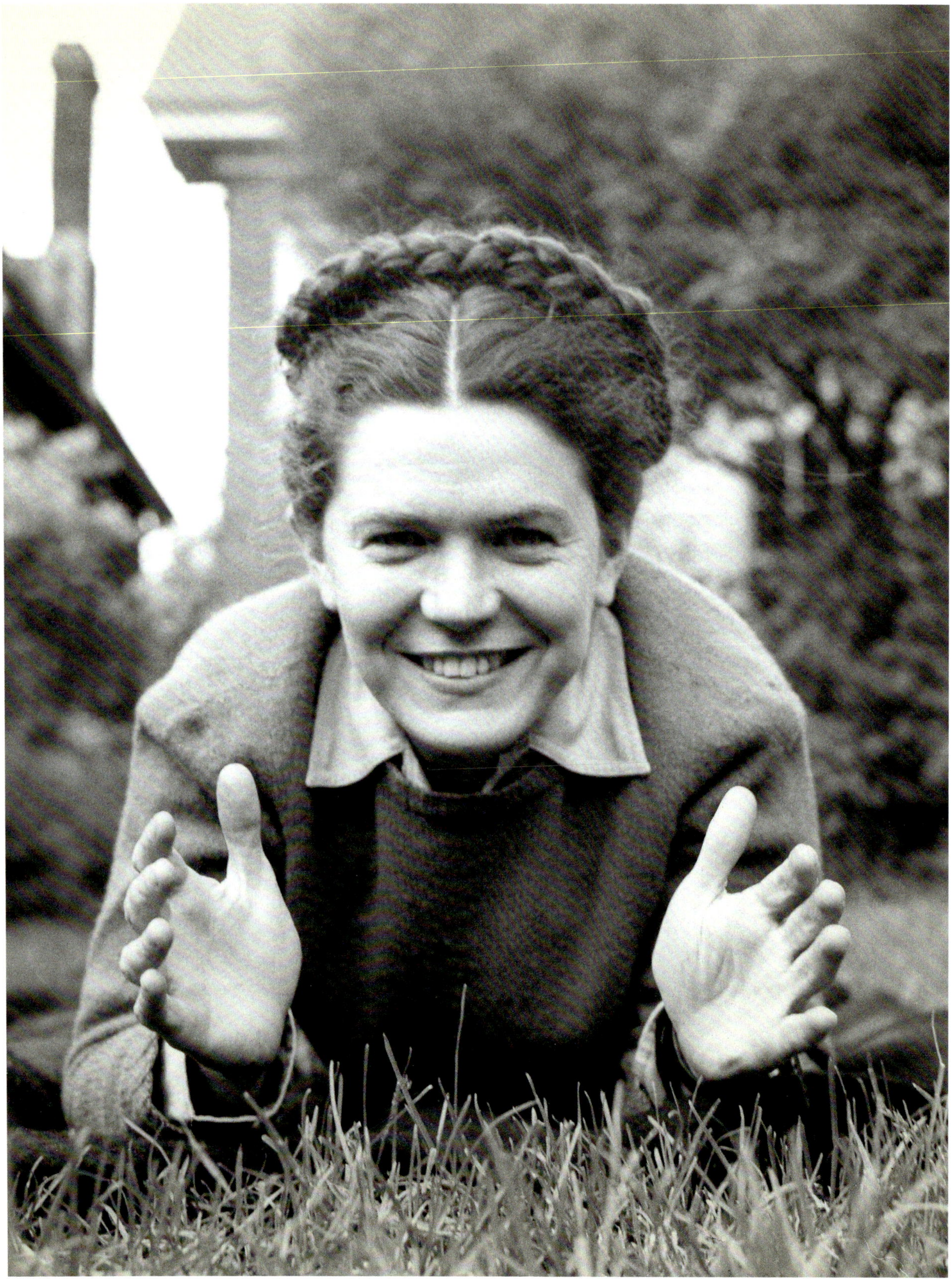

Tom McSorley | Anne Maheux | Jaclyn Meloche
Catherine Sinclair | Rosemarie L. Tovell

Alma

The Life and Art of Alma Duncan
La vie et l'œuvre d'Alma Duncan

1917–2004

Ottawa Art Gallery | Galerie d'art d'Ottawa
Judith & Norman Alix Art Gallery

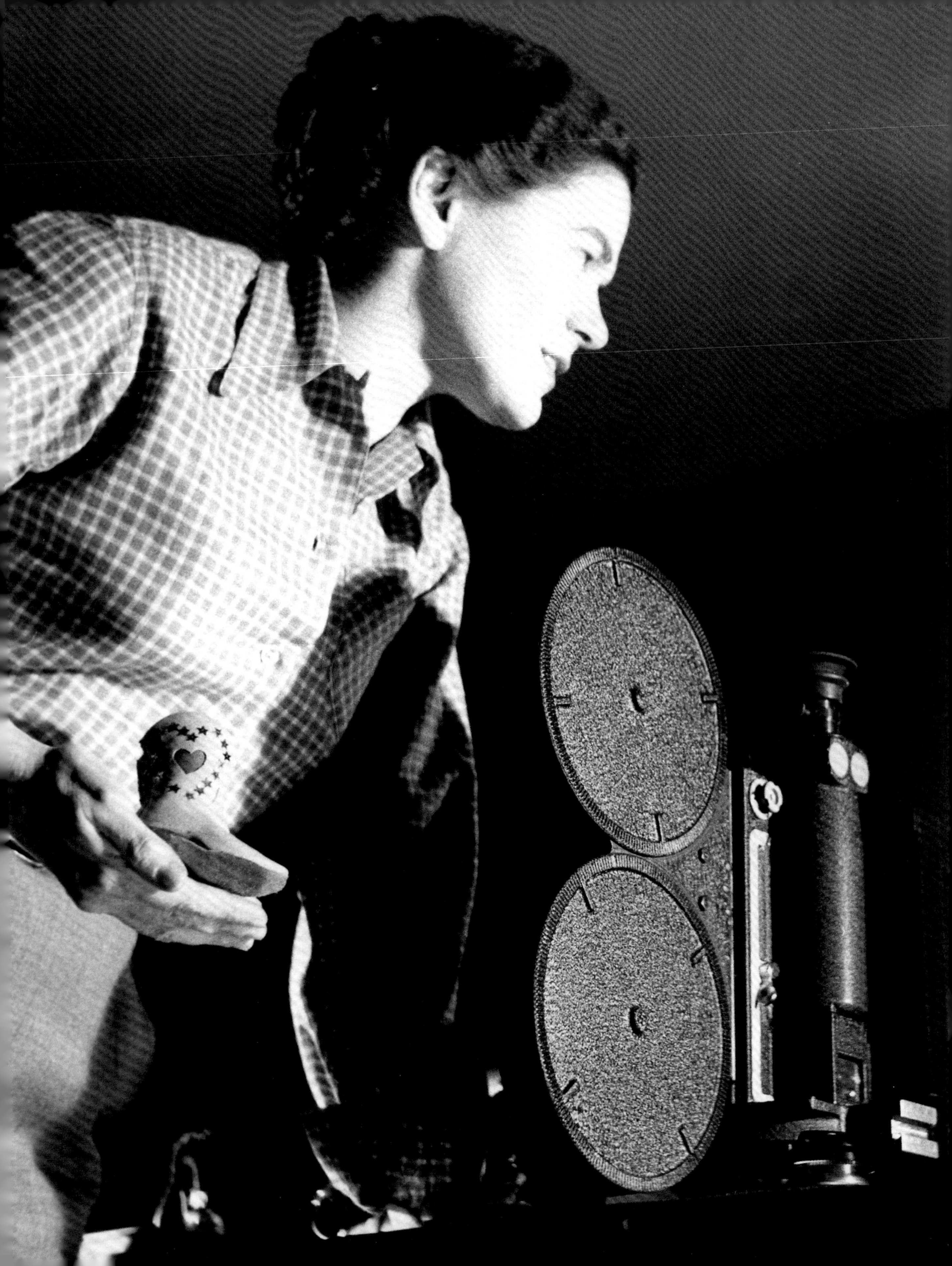

Contents

Alma Duncan working on the making of the film *Hearts and Soles*, 1955
Alma Duncan travaillant à la réalisation du film *L'amour pas-à-pas*, 1955

Table des matières

Self-Portrait with Blue Handkerchief | Autoportrait avec mouchoir bleu 1941 (cat. 8)
Art Gallery of Ontario | Musée des beaux-arts de l'Ontario

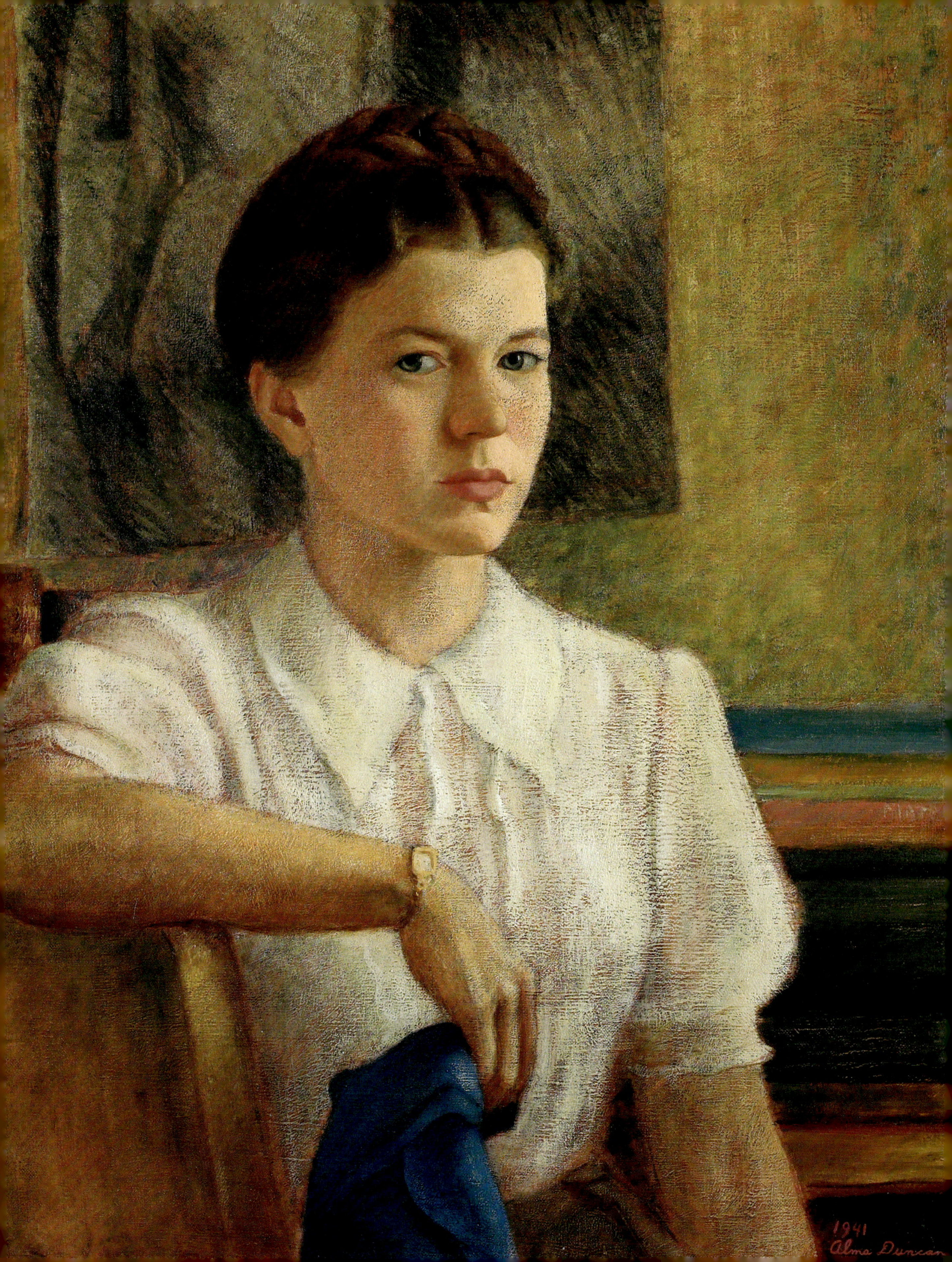
1941
Alma Duncan

To Babs, for being an incredible support to this project, and throughout the years to Alma.

À Babs, pour avoir été d'un incroyable appui, à la fois à ce projet et, au fil des ans, à Alma.

Foreword

Alma Duncan spent her entire life creating, interpreting, observing, and rendering. With pen in hand, she travelled the world recording the beauties of the land and the stories of her sitters, transcending the lines between modern interpreter and visual activist. Inherently interdisciplinary, her varied body of work spans numerous genres, including the machine æsthetic, puppetry, portraiture, and abstraction, and includes Dürer-quality drawings of the natural world around her. For the majority of her prolific career, Duncan resided with long-time friend and collaborator Audrey (Babs) McLaren in Ottawa's Centretown, New Edinburgh, and Cumberland's countryside until her passing in 2004. A familiar name in the regional art community, Duncan produced art that can be found in a variety of national collections, including the National Gallery of Canada, the Ottawa Art Gallery, the Canadian War Museum, the Library and Archives Canada, the Art Gallery of Ontario, and The Robert McLaughlin Art Gallery, in Oshawa, Ontario. The latter institution takes credit, along with its former director Joan Murray, as being the organizer of the first major touring exhibition of Duncan's work in 1987, *Alma Duncan: Men at Work*. Twenty-seven years later, the Ottawa Art Gallery (OAG) is proud to present this comprehensive retrospective exhibition, and, along with our publication partner, the Judith & Norman Alix Art Gallery (JNAAG) in Sarnia, Ontario, exhibition catalogue of Duncan's lifework.

This publication is a historical and critical interpretation of Duncan's contributions to Canadian visual culture. Co-curators Catherine Sinclair and Jaclyn Meloche consider Duncan's abstract works, portraits, and animated film within a socio-feminist discourse. Rosemarie Tovell, former Curator of Canadian Prints and Drawings at the National Gallery of Canada, tells the story of Duncan as an exquisite draughtswoman. Tom McSorley, director of the Canadian Film Institute, sketches a political and social history of Canadian film that highlights Duncan's contributions, coupled with an inside view of the National Film Board of Canada's mandate to promote and support national narratives locally and abroad. Finally, in a personal dedication to Alma and Babs, Anne Maheux, conservator at Library and Archives Canada, pens a touching account of her long-time friendship with both women. In its entirety, this retrospective brings together curators, collectors, friends, and scholars to celebrate Alma Duncan the woman, the colleague, and of course, the artist.

First and foremost, on behalf of the OAG, we would like to extend our sincere thanks to the late Ms. Audrey McLaren for her dedicated support of this exhibition and catalogue. Her recent passing this year caused us all to pause, and reflect on the importance of capturing such histories through exhibition and publication projects such as this. We are also grateful to Anne Maheux for her assistance in all matters of the research process. Special thanks to the OAG's Senior Curator, Catherine Sinclair, for her extensive coordination of this project, approached with her usual organizational wizardry and infectious enthusiasm. Gratitude is further extended to Co-curator Jaclyn Meloche, visual artist and independent scholar of fine arts and performance studies, for bringing her research on Alma Duncan forward; we appreciate them both for their in-depth research and unfailing vision. Jennifer Gilliland and Stephanie Germano, OAG's Collections Manager and Interim Collections Manager, must also be acknowledged for facilitating all the logistics of the loans and tour, and OAG interns Hannah van der Est and Teodora Dimitrova for their logistical assistance. We would also like to thank Marie-Camille Lalande for her sensitive translation of this catalogue, Mark Timmings for his thoughtful design, and Malcolm Sutton and Geneviève Letarte for their careful editing. This exhibition and catalogue could not have been realized without the assistance of OAG's talented staff, interns, volunteers, and technicians. We thank them all for their hard work and dedication.

We also extend thanks to all our lenders, with special mention of the Library and Archives Canada, who provided almost half of the objects included. Further, thanks to our touring partners for their support of the creation of this exhibition and catalogue. The OAG and JNAAG, of course, also gratefully acknowledge the ongoing support of their members, donors and sponsors, as well as the City of Ottawa, the Corporation of the County of Lambton, the Ontario Arts Council, and the Canada Council for the Arts. Finally, this exhibition, publication, and tour could not have existed in their current form without the assistance of the Canadian Heritage's Museum Assistance Program.

Alexandra Badzak, Director and CEO, Ottawa Art Gallery
Lisa Daniels, Director and Curator, Judith & Norman Alix Art Gallery

Avant-propos

Alma Duncan a passé sa vie à créer, interpréter, observer, représenter. Elle a parcouru le monde la plume à la main pour capter la beauté des paysages et les histoires de ses modèles, se faisant tour à tour interprète de la modernité et activiste du visuel. Son œuvre est essentiellement interdisciplinaire et touche à plusieurs genres : l'esthétique de la machine, les marionnettes, le portrait et l'abstraction, sans oublier les dessins délicats à la Dürer qu'elle faisait de la nature environnante. Durant la majeure partie de sa prolifique carrière et jusqu'à son décès en 2004, Duncan a vécu à dans le centre-ville d'Ottawa, New Edinburgh, ou dans la campagne de Cumberland avec Audrey « Babs » McLaren, sa collaboratrice et amie de longue date. Elle était bien connue dans la communauté artistique de la région, et ses œuvres se retrouvent aujourd'hui dans une grande variété de collections, dont le Musée des beaux-arts du Canada, la Galerie d'art d'Ottawa, le Musée canadien de la guerre, Bibliothèque et Archives Canada, le Musée des beaux-arts de l'Ontario, et la Robert McLaughlin Art Gallery à Oshawa, en Ontario. C'est à cette dernière, et à sa directrice Joan Murray, que revient le mérite d'avoir organisé la première exposition itinérante majeure du travail de Duncan, *Alma Duncan: Men at Work* (Hommes au travail) en 1987. Vingt-sept ans plus tard, la Galerie d'art d'Ottawa (GAO) est fière de présenter cette exposition rétrospective exhaustive de l'œuvre de Duncan, et, avec notre partenaire la Judith & Norman Alix Art Gallery (JNAAG) de Sarnia en Ontario, ce catalogue d'exposition.

Cette publication propose une interprétation historique et critique de l'apport artistique de Duncan à la culture visuelle du Canada. Les cocommissaires Catherine Sinclair et Jaclyn Meloche examinent les œuvres abstraites, les portraits et les films d'animation de Duncan à la lumière d'un discours socioféministe. Rosemarie Tovell, ancienne conservatrice des dessins et estampes canadiens au Musée des beaux-arts du Canada, dévoile le talent exquis de dessinatrice de Duncan. Tom McSorley, directeur de l'Institut canadien du film, raconte l'histoire politique et sociale du cinéma canadien de manière à faire ressortir les contributions de Duncan, tout en exposant le rôle qu'a joué l'Office national du film du Canada dans la promotion et le développement des récits nationaux au pays et à l'étranger. Enfin, Anne Maheux, conservatrice à Bibliothèque et

Archives Canada, signe un hommage personnel et touchant qui témoigne de la longue amitié qui l'a unie à Alma et Babs. Dans son ensemble, cette rétrospective rassemble des commissaires, des collectionneurs, des amis et des universitaires afin de célébrer Alma Duncan la femme, la collègue et, bien sûr, l'artiste.

La GAO aimerait tout d'abord remercier chaleureusement la regrettée Mme Audrey McLaren pour son appui résolu à la tenue de cette exposition et à la publication de ce catalogue. Son décès, survenu récemment, nous a amenés à réfléchir à l'importance de capter ces histoires, si rapidement disparues, par l'entremise de tels projets d'exposition et de publication. Nous sommes de plus reconnaissants envers Anne Maheux pour son aide lors du processus de recherche. Un merci particulier à Catherine Sinclair, la commissaire principale de la GAO, qui a coordonné l'ensemble du projet avec son sens magique de l'organisation et son enthousiasme contagieux. Nous exprimons aussi notre reconnaissance à la cocommissaire Jaclyn Meloche, artiste et chercheuse indépendante spécialisée en beaux-arts et en performance, de nous avoir fait part de ses travaux sur Alma Duncan; merci à toutes les deux pour vos recherches approfondies et votre vision inébranlable. Nous nous devons de reconnaître le travail de Jennifer Gilliland et de Stephanie Germano, respectivement gestionnaire des collections et gestionnaire intérimaire des collections de la GAO, qui ont coordonné la logistique des emprunts et de la tournée, ainsi que les stagiaires de la GAO Hannah van der Est et Teodora Dimitrova, qui ont contribué à l'organisation. Nous aimerions aussi remercier Marie-Camille Lalande pour sa traduction sensible de ce catalogue, Mark Timmings pour le design attentionné, ainsi que Malcolm Sutton et Geneviève Letarte pour leur révision soignée. Cette exposition et ce catalogue n'auraient pu être réalisés sans l'aide du personnel, des stagiaires, des bénévoles et des techniciens de la GAO. Nous les remercions tous pour leur travail et leur dévouement.

Nous remercions aussi tous les prêteurs, spécialement Bibliothèque et Archives Canada qui a fourni presque la moitié des objets compris dans l'exposition. Merci de plus aux partenaires de tournée, qui ont appuyé la création de cette exposition et de ce catalogue. La GAO et la JNAAG sont bien sûr très reconnaissantes envers leurs membres, donateurs et commanditaires, ainsi que la Ville d'Ottawa, le comté de Lambton, le Conseil des arts de l'Ontario et le Conseil des arts du Canada pour leur appui soutenu. Enfin, cette exposition, cette publication et cette tournée n'auraient pu exister dans leur forme actuelle sans le Programme d'aide aux musées de Patrimoine canadien.

Alexandra Badzak, Directrice et chef de la direction, Galerie d'art d'Ottawa
Lisa Daniels, Directrice et commissaire, Judith & Norman Alix Art Gallery

Alma Duncan, Montreal, c. 1943
Alma Duncan, Montréal, v. 1943

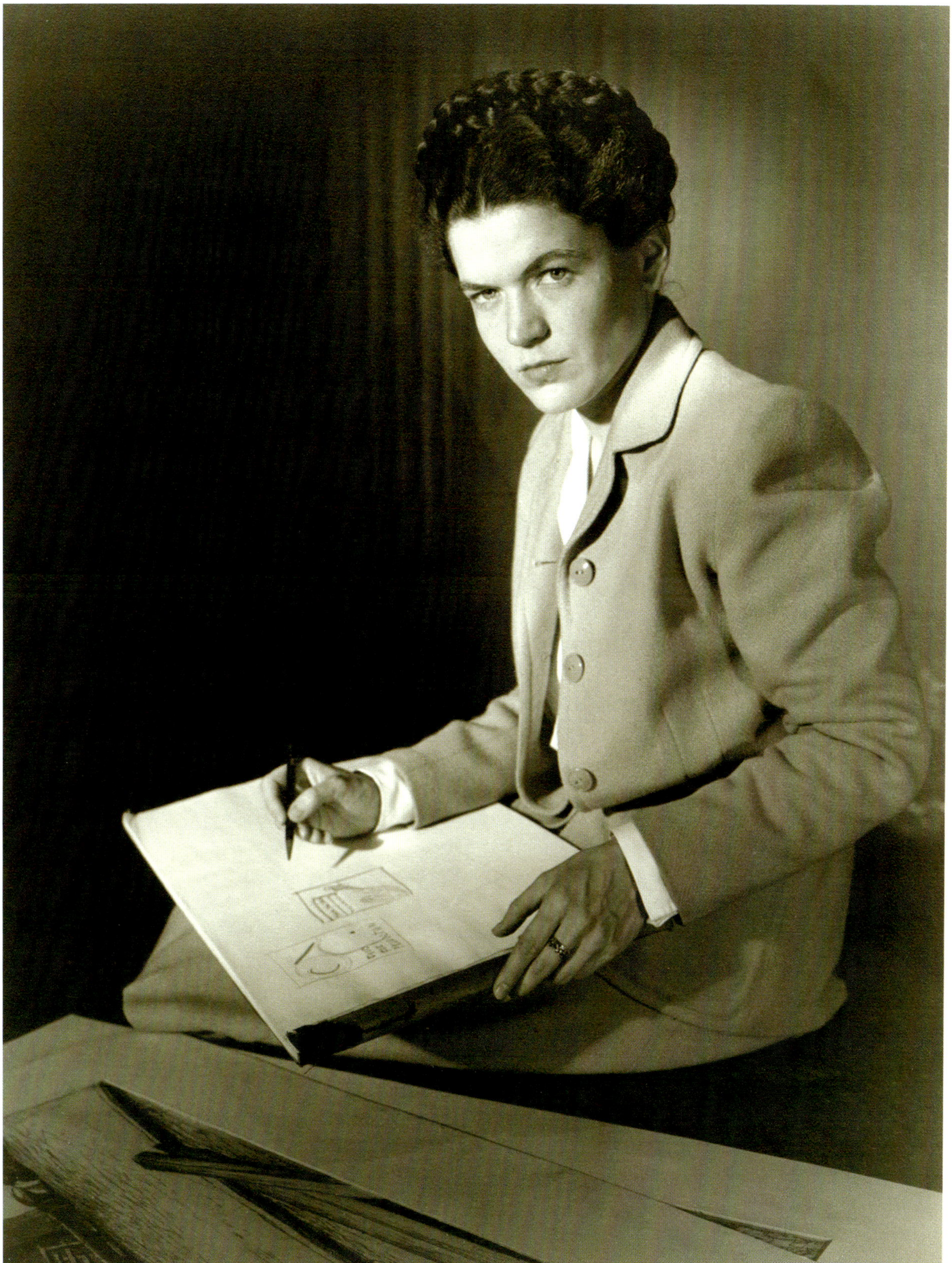

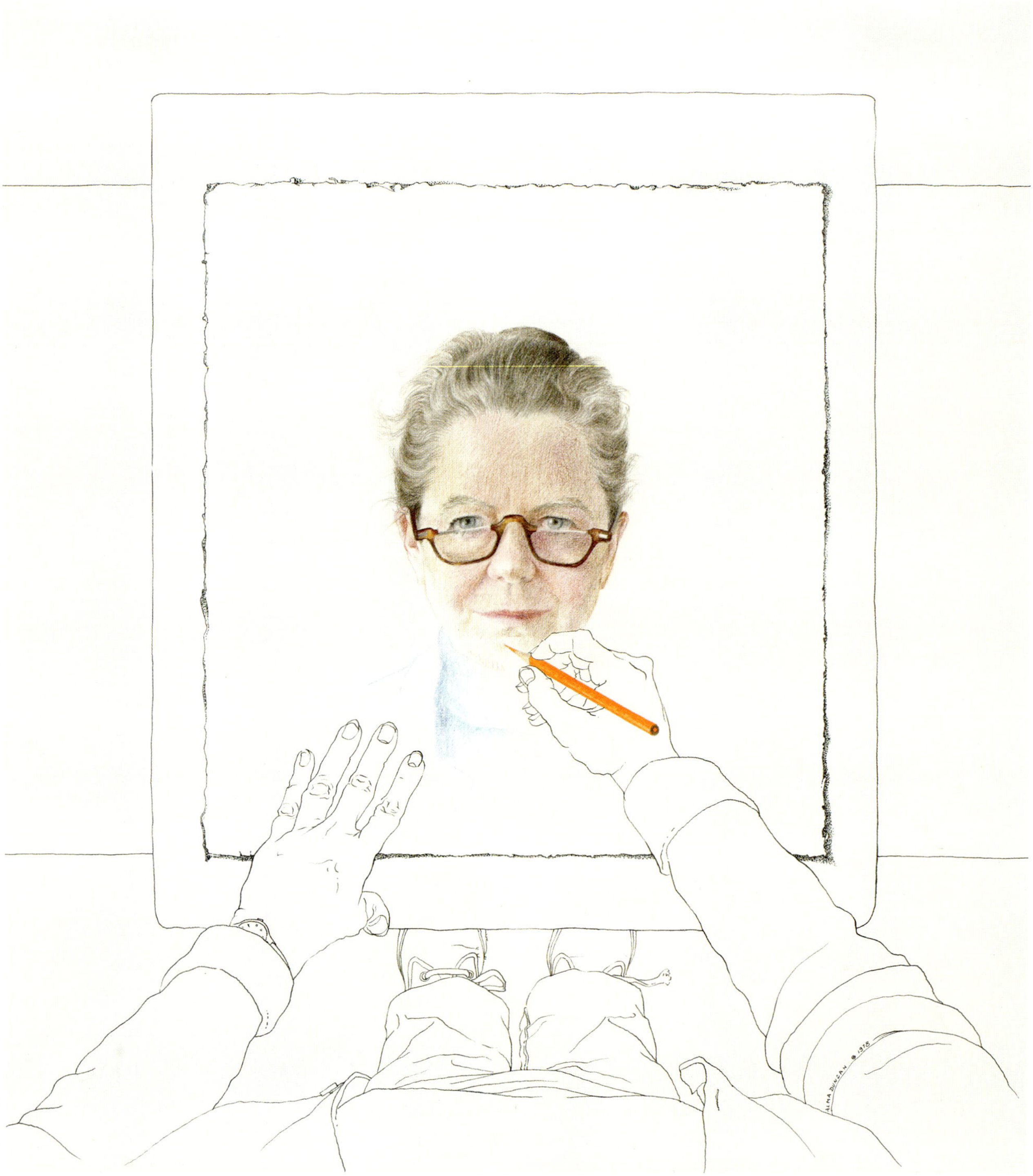

Self-Portrait | Autoportrait 1978 (cat. 80)
Library and Archives Canada | Bibliothèque et Archives Canada

“Now here’s something that just came off the end of my pen”

Alma Duncan’s Drawings

Rosemarie L. Tovell

The self-portrait from 1978 (cat. 80, opposite) tells it all. Upon meeting Alma Duncan one’s attention is caught by her piercing blue eyes and her quiet, self-contained demeanour, both deferential and assured. These are the characteristics that made her the perfect observer. It was these attributes that made her art what it is. Her art does not deal with overt narratives or polemics. If such elements do exist, they are subtle. Her preference was to examine, and then present her observations as factual. Yet despite their fidelity to observance, they are highly charged compositions that are arresting with inventive details that are elusive and surprising.

Alma Duncan divided her drawing subjects into series, which could be explored on and off over many years: the formally titled *Industrial Drawings*, *Forest Floor*, *Woman*, *Lady*, *Leaves*, *Grass* and *Forest’s Edge*. There were also the informally described subject series: portraits, the abstract dot drawings and the many closely observed objects within her world, be it her mother’s room on Christmas Day (cat. 30, p. 40) or the panorama outside the windows of her home (cat. 68, p. 34). During the later years — that is the Sixties and onwards — these subjects would work back and forth upon each other, intertwining their imagery and compositions. For example, the 1977 panorama *Small World* (1977) (cat. 69, p. 38) is closely related in composition and sensibility to the abstract dot drawing *A Round, II* (1966) (cat. 53, p. 28).

Alma Duncan was a young teenager when she attended Adam Sherriff Scott's life-drawing classes in Montreal. There she would have received standard academic instruction.[1] Perhaps it was her age, but she did not feel that it was time well spent. From 1936 to 1943, she worked at a commercial art studio whose principal clients published mail-order catalogues. Alma's talent for drawing was employed to provide accurate renderings of the products for sale. And while she later claimed this work did not affect her art, this early period showed her predilection for precise-detail drawing, underscored by her choice to draw specimens in the anatomy department at McGill University. The character of these commercial and anatomical drawings presages the detailed nature drawings that would come thirty years later.

As the commercial work was seasonal, it did leave Alma with some five months of the year to pursue her own interests. Not having abandoned the idea of a more serious application of her talents, she renewed her studies in life drawing when the opportunity arose. The Roberts-Neumann School of Art, run by Goodridge Roberts and Ernst Neumann from 1936 to 1939, was located in the same building at 1215 Green Avenue as the commercial studio in which she worked.[2] Apparently by the time Alma decided to enroll, the school had been disbanded, but Neumann continued to teach. For two years she attended Neumann's weekly night classes where instruction included life drawing and portraiture. Again, Alma would have received rather academic training. She noted Neumann's aversion for "polish or superficiality."[3] She found him very caustic and critical, but also very approving of her own work. At this time, Alma was also taking life-drawing classes with Goodridge Roberts at the Art Association of Montreal, whose work she admired for its honesty and lack of superficiality.

The 1938 portrait of her mother (cat. 3, opposite), and the 1942 portrait of Neumann (cat. 10, p. 20) demonstrate the progress Alma made under Neumann's tutelage as well as his influence on her drawing style. The 1938 portrait is crisply outlined and delicately modeled by smooth strokes of charcoal, shaping the face and hat in gradual shades. However, the subject lacks energy or personality. By comparison, the 1942 portrait of Neumann, very much in the sitter's style of drawing, is executed in a variety of boldly drawn lines and deeply contrasting shades of light and dark. It is a portrait of a man she described as "tough, big shoulders, outspoken."[4]

Through Neumann, Alma would have come in contact with Montreal's politically and socially conscious community of artists that included Fritz Brandtner, Fred Taylor, and Louis Muhlstock, to name just a few.[5] In 1941 Alma joined these artists on the executive of the Quebec branch of the Federation of Canadian Artists (FCA). With World War II

Mother in Ribbon Hat (Eleanor Duncan) |
Mère coiffée d'un chapeau à ruban (Eleanor Duncan) 1938 (cat. 3)
Library and Archives Canada | Bibliothèque et Archives Canada

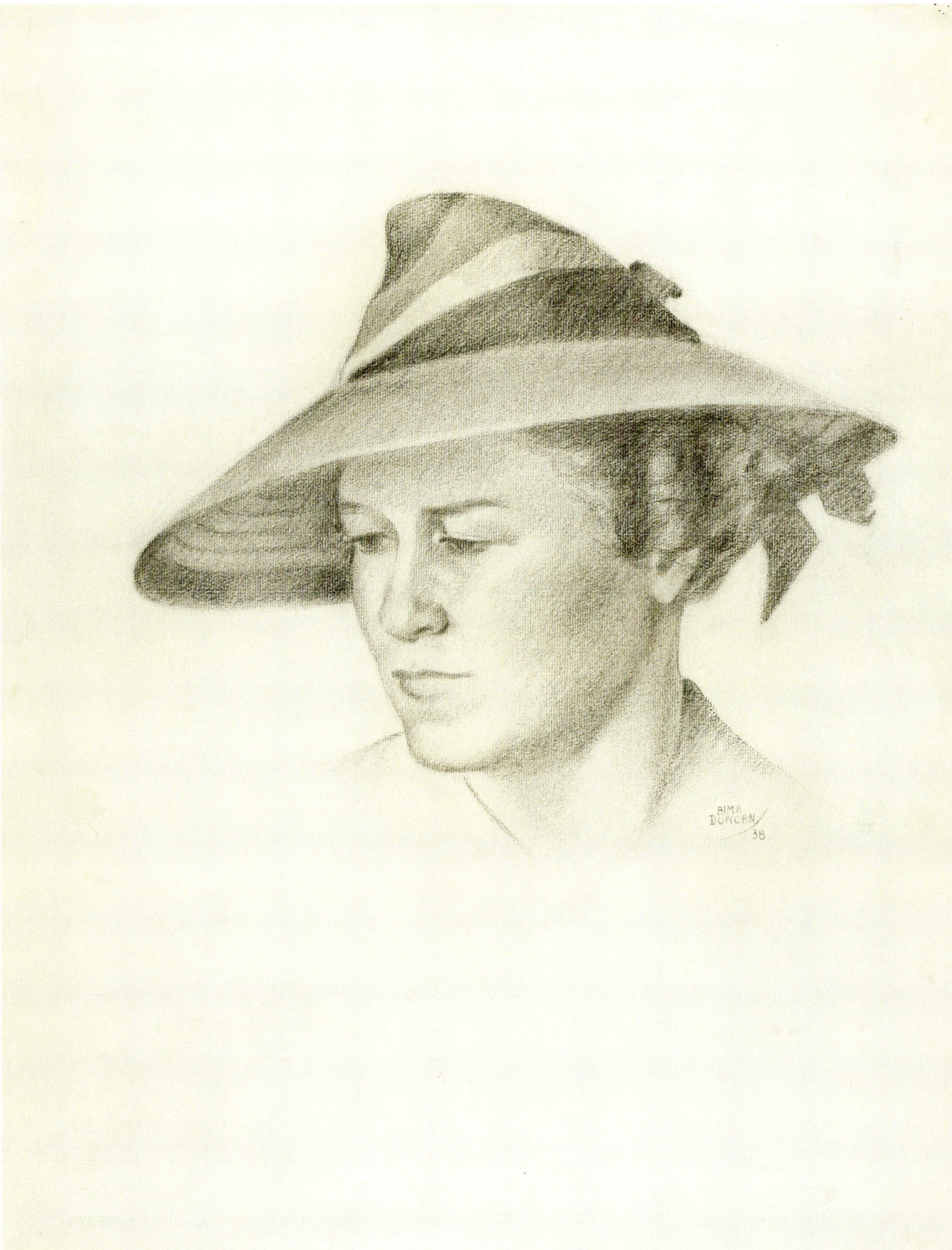
ALMA
DUNCAN
38

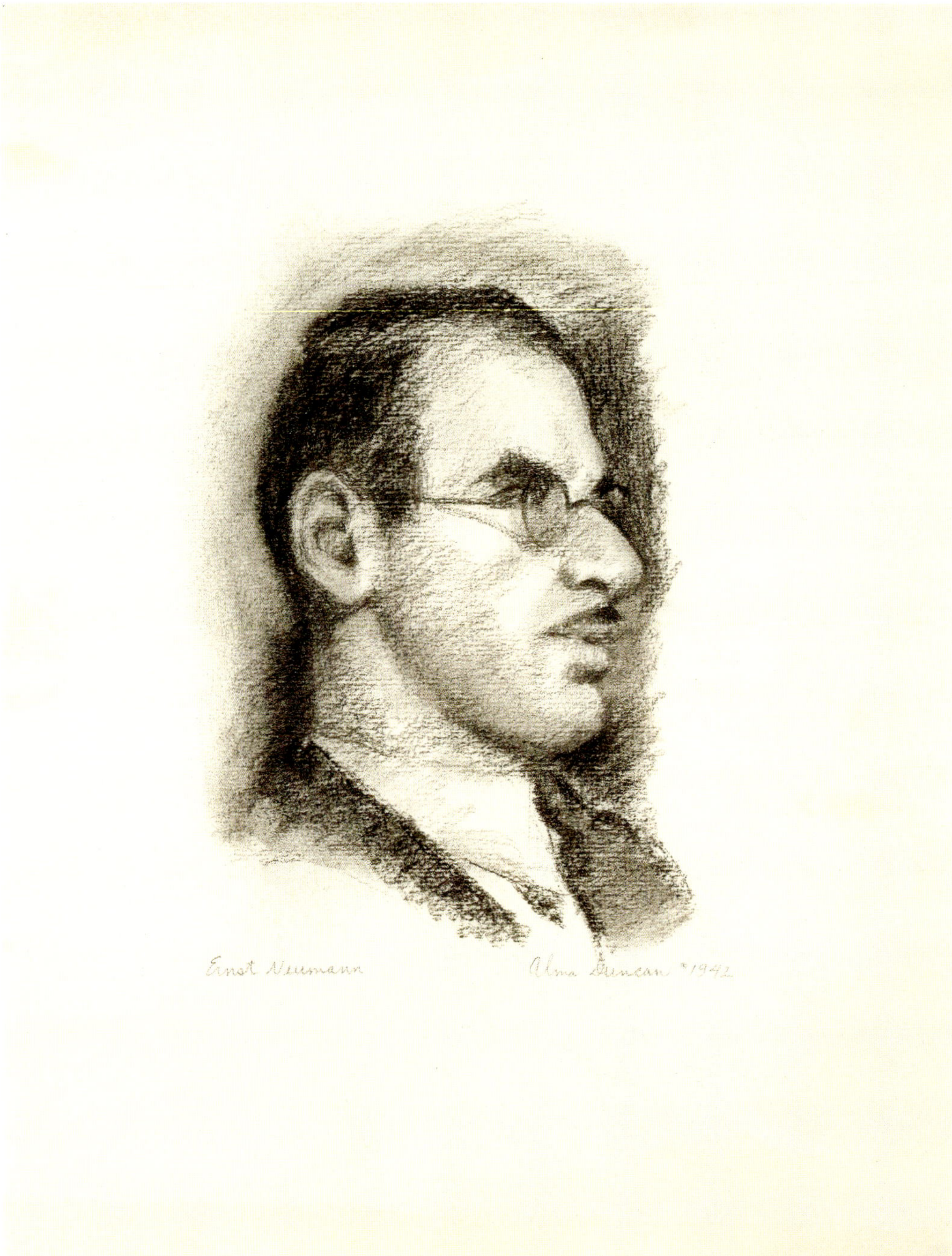

Ernst Neumann 1942 (cat. 10)

well underway, no official program for war artists was in place. Led by Brandtner, artists wishing to do their part applied to the Department of Munitions and Supply for permission to go into the factories and shipyards in order to create visual records of the war effort on the home front. In 1943, along with her FCA colleagues, Alma received a permit to draw in the Canadian Vickers Limited shipyards and Canadian Industries Limited munitions plant, both located in Montreal.

These "war" drawings, her first set of *Industrial Drawings*, were done in 1943 and executed in the aggressive and dense charcoal drawing style learned from Neumann. They are dynamic representations of the purposeful and patriotic work of Canada's industries. The labourers lean into their work amid the maze of machinery and the gloom of the factory floor. These drawings (cat. 13 and cat. 16, p. 42) would be the beginning of a continuing interest in industrial subjects. In 1947, by now working in Ottawa at the National Film Board's animation department, Alma took leave to travel around Ontario to make more drawings of industry. Her reasons for doing so were simple. She states in an interview: "I love the factories. I like the clutter [...] [S]o much was going on, the machines, the sounds [...] the activity."[6] Elsewhere in the interview: "I loved being there in the noise and activity, I enjoyed the images, the forms and textures and the abrasive music in the rhythmic sounds."[7] Closer to home, at the E.B. Eddy Plant in Hull, she made *Papermakers* (cat. 18, p. 43). It is almost lyrical. The harsh, dark charcoal drawing of the earlier work gave way to a lighter and more nuanced shading. The worker and the sheaf of paper he handles seem to be one, as if in a dance.

Nine years later, now working in pastel, Alma began a third set of industrial drawings, this time of the open-pit mines at the Steep Rock Iron Mines, near Atikokan, west of Lake Superior. With a dazzling burst of colour, *Open Pit and Skipway* (1956) (cat. 29, p. 44) expresses Alma's response to the rusty red soil of the mine and the varied hues of the disturbed landscape. Yet the achieved effect is not the terrible beauty that we see in contemporary work, such as that of Edward Burtynsky. Alma's work does not present a polemic on environmental destruction. Rather, the drawings are of their time — a celebration of the emergence of Canada's prosperous postwar industrial economy. In 1958 Alma returned to Steep Rock, this time entering the processing plant. *Giant Spiral, Processing Ore* (1958) (cat. 33, p. 46) continues the blazing use of colour, but displays a more complex, somewhat abstract composition, characterized by the intricate intertwining of angular elements such as the corkscrew separator, beams, and scaffolding. It is a precursor of the *Forest Floor* compositions that would follow in a few years.

Alma Duncan "retired" from animated filmmaking in 1960 in order to devote herself entirely to drawing and painting. As always, drawing was central to this endeavour.

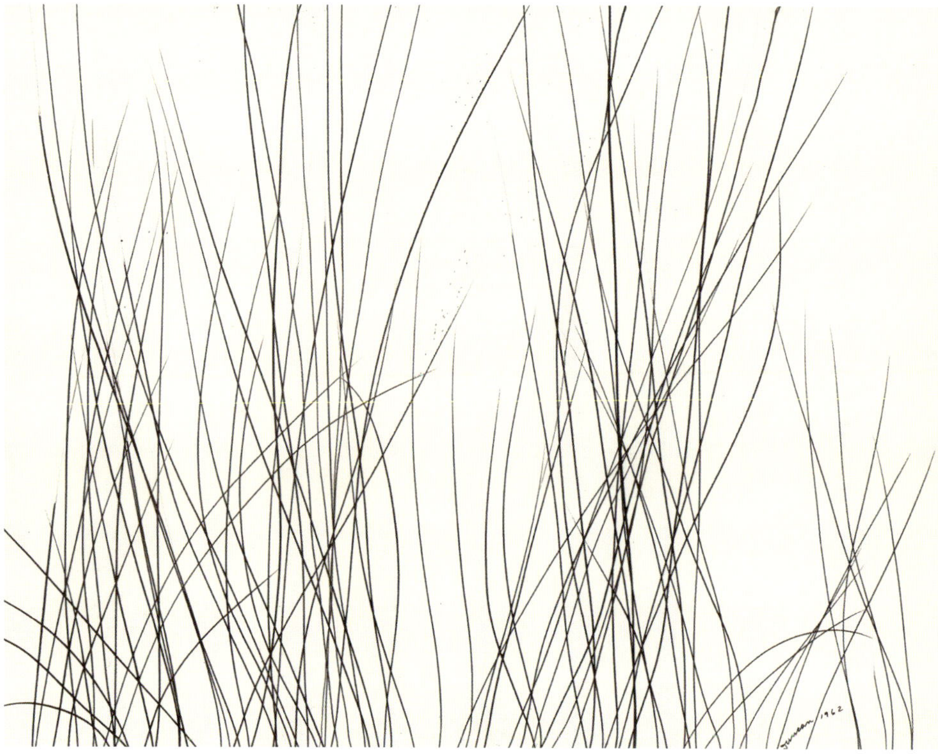

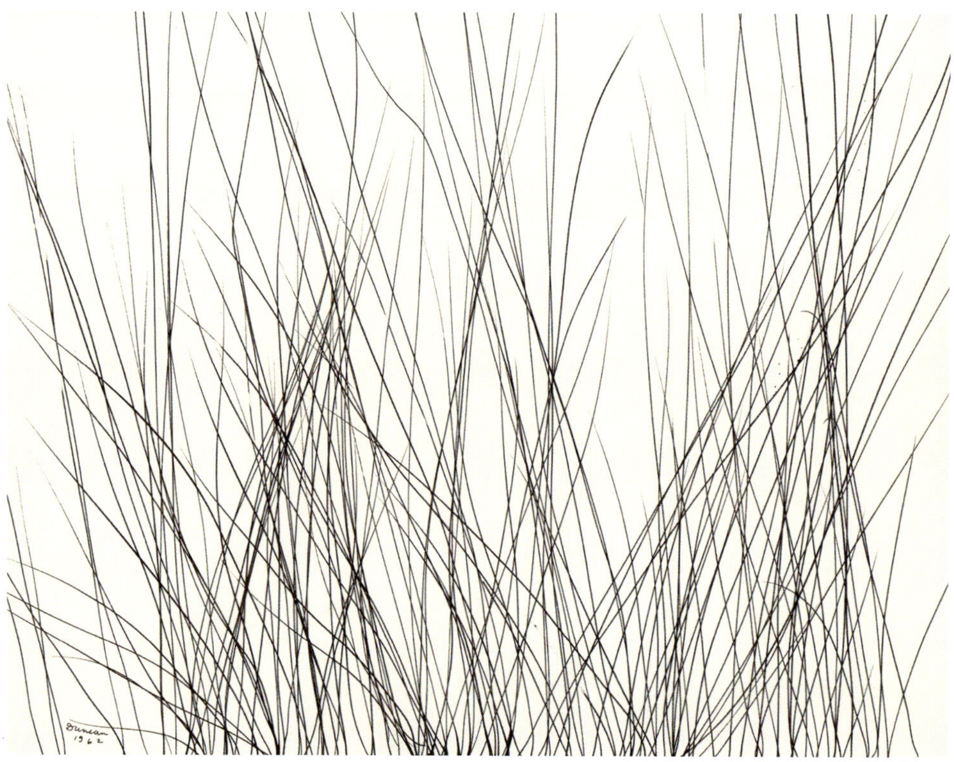

Grass, August 1 | Herbe, 1er août 1962 (cat. 35, top|haut); **Grass I | Herbe I** 1962 (cat. 37, bottom|bas)

Library and Archives Canada | Bibliothèque et Archives Canada

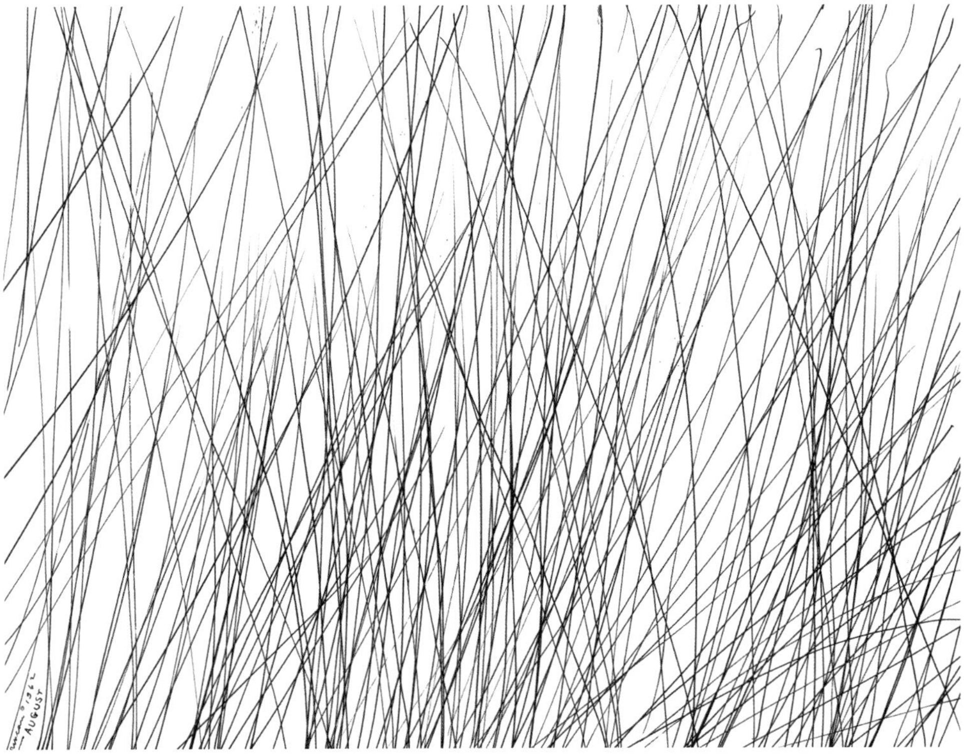

Grass, August 2 | Herbe, 2 août 1962 (cat. 36, top|haut); **Grass II | Herbe II** 1962 (cat. 38, bottom|bas)
Library and Archives Canada | Bibliothèque et Archives Canada

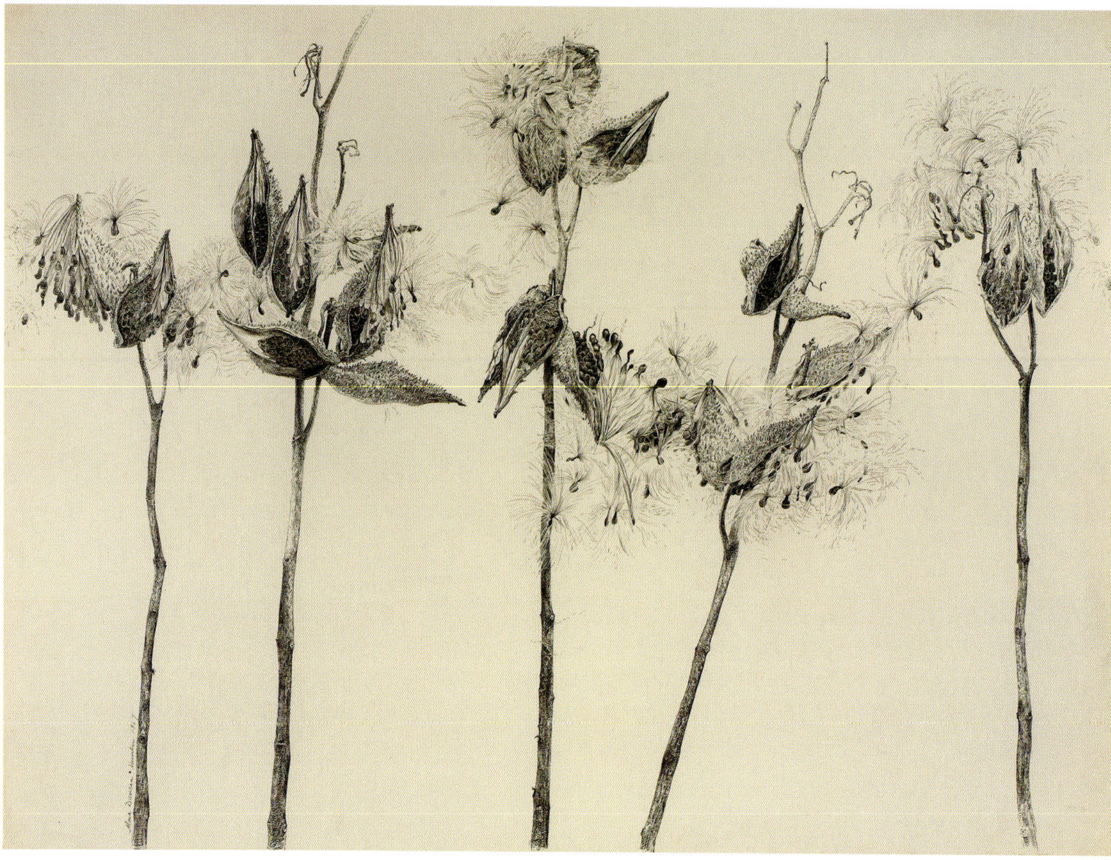

Milkweed | Laiteron 1967 (cat. 60)
National Gallery of Canada | Musée des beaux-arts du Canada

Abstraction was increasingly entering her art, and over the next decades non-figurative art would become a subject in itself. As she lived part-time in the country, the natural world entered her artistic vocabulary. The media she used for finished presentation drawings expanded to include pen and ink, watercolour, and conté crayon.

The first indication of these new trends appear in her first set of *Grass* drawings (1962) (cats. 35–38, pp. 22–23). Describing them as "just coming off the end of my pen," Alma reduced the leaves of grass, bending and swaying in the breeze, to single strokes.[8] They are like strings of a harp, vibrating to their own music. Indeed, music was important to Alma, and she would often make musical references particularly to her abstract and semi-abstract work.[9] In the pen-and-ink drawing *Milkweed* (1967) (cat. 60, above), she continues exploring the theme of grass, but now renders her subject in closely observed detail, capturing the shapes and textures of the stems and seed pods, as the fluffy seeds take flight in the wind.

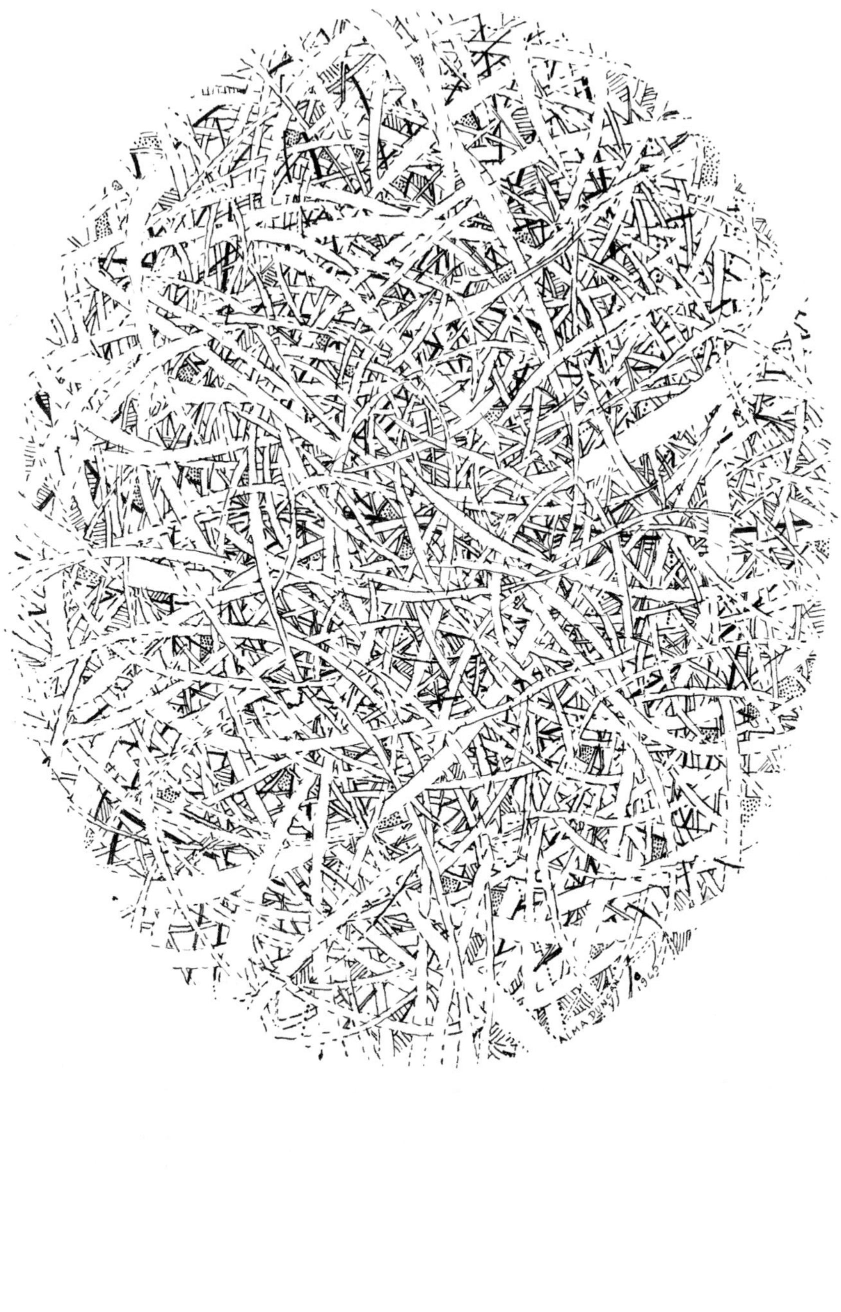

The Tangled Web | La toile enchevêtrée 1965 (cat. 41)
Library and Archives Canada | Bibliothèque et Archives Canada

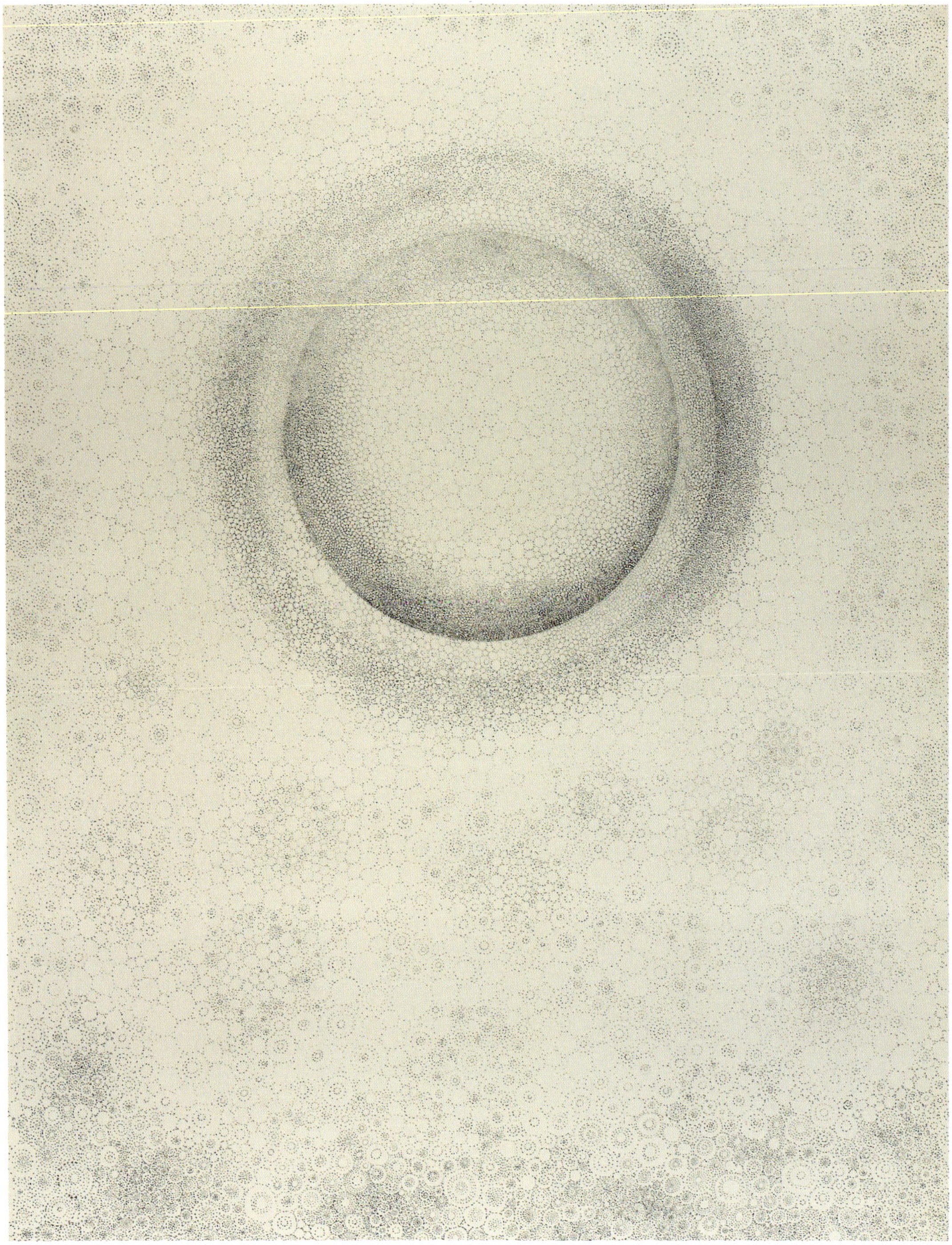

Untitled No. 1 | Sans titre n° 1 1964 (cat. 39)
National Gallery of Canada | Musée des beaux-arts du Canada

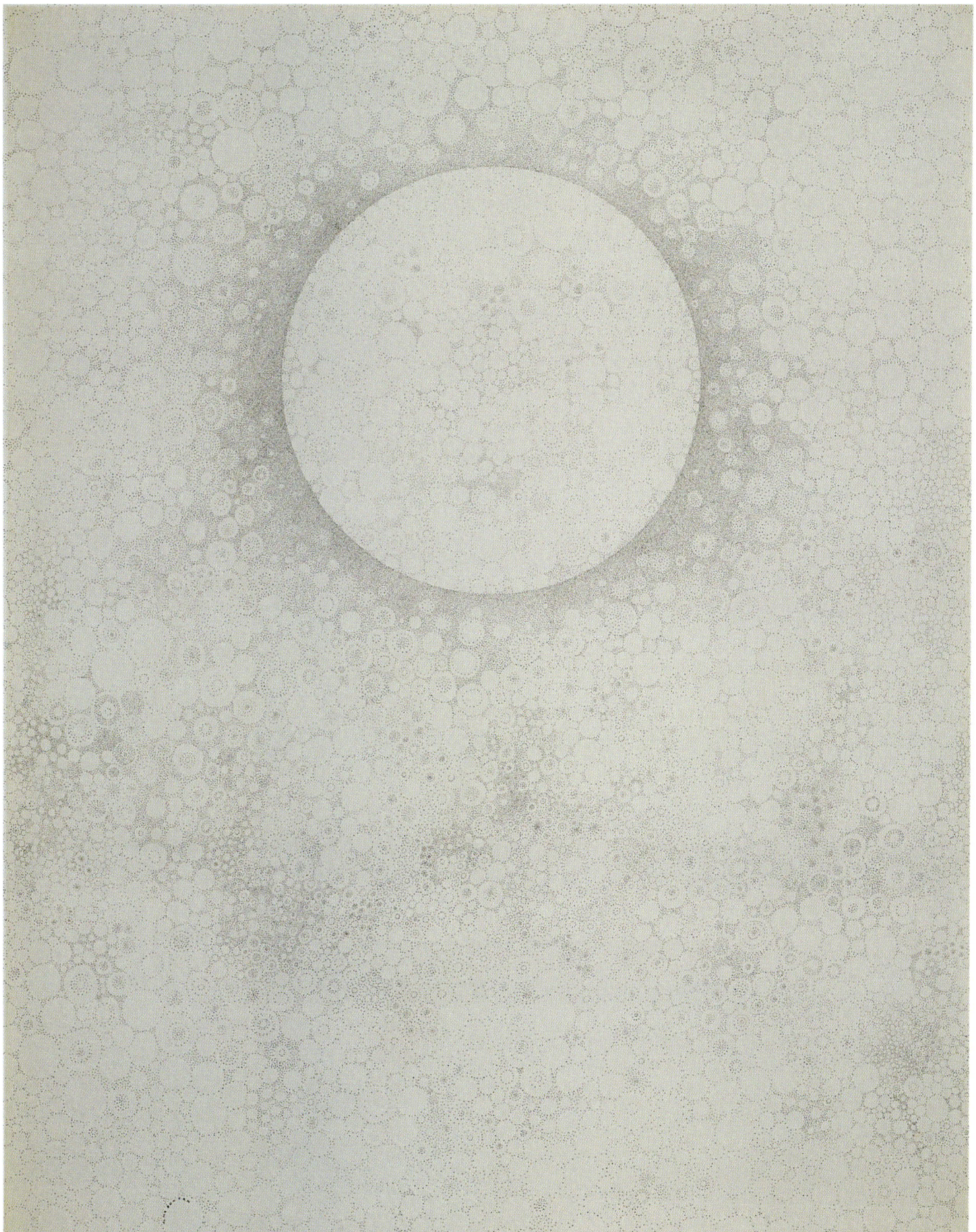

Untitled 3 | Sans titre 3 1965 (cat. 40)
Courtesy of Renato Albino | Gracieuseté de Renato Albino

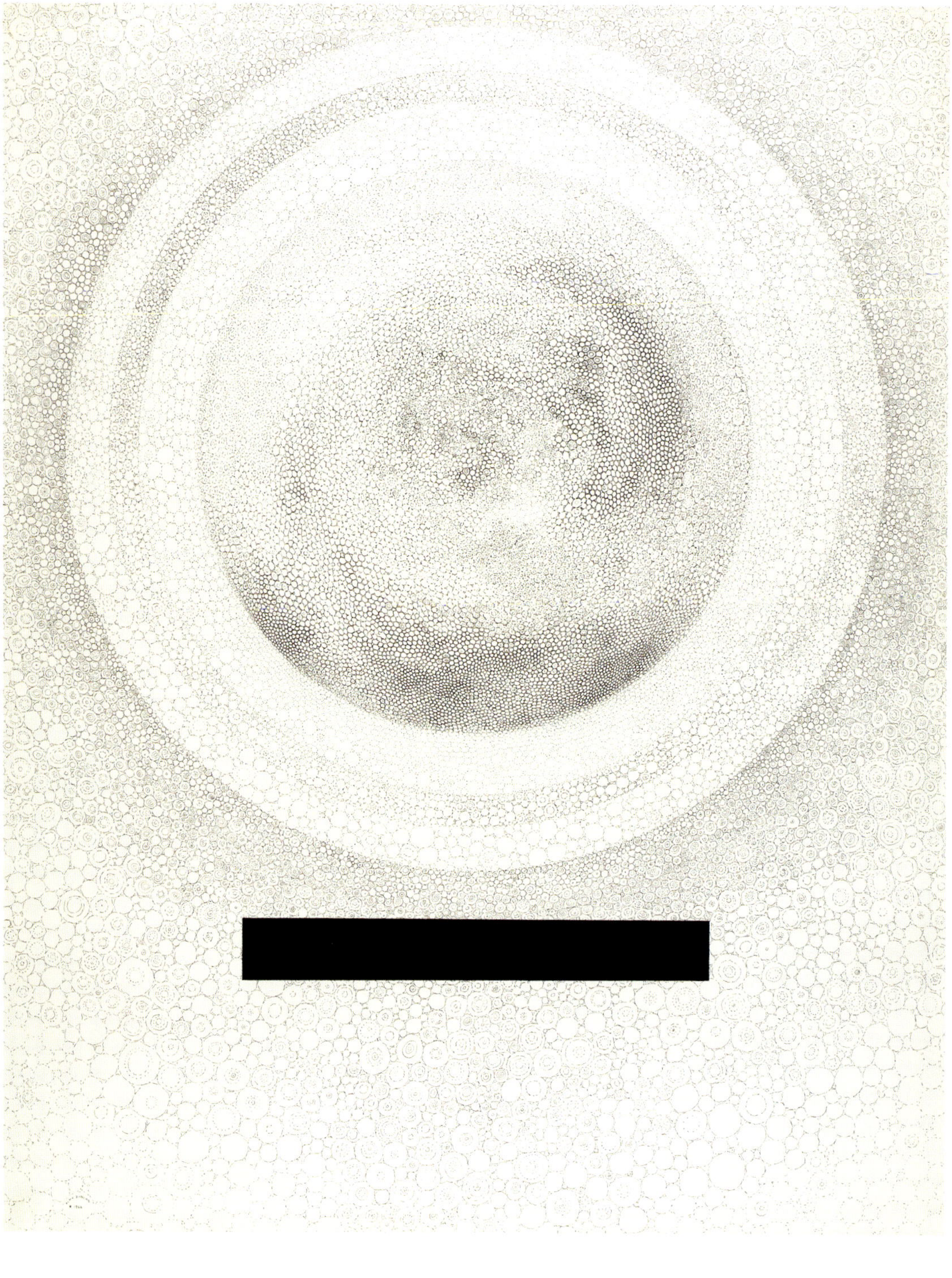

A Round, II | **Un cercle,** II 1966 (cat. 53)
Library and Archives Canada | Bibliothèque et Archives Canada

Tilt I | Inclinaison I 1967 (cat. 56)
Library and Archives Canada | Bibliothèque et Archives Canada

In the mid-sixties Alma began a series of non-figurative abstract drawings she called her "dot series." At first, these pen-and-ink drawings (represented by the 1964 *Untitled No. I* [cat. 39, p. 26]) were simple three-dimensional spheres created by a careful build-up of dots floating in an undefined space. The sphere is drawn in a manner that offers an optical illusion that can be read as either concave or convex. With the next drawing, made in 1965 the sphere is perfectly round and represents the moon as in *Untitled 3* (cat. 40, p. 27) where the moon floats in an undefined space. Other drawings in the series, though not included in the exhibition, depict the sphere above a softly drawn undulating landscape, establishing Alma's intent that it is indeed the moon. As she continued with the dot series in 1966 and 1967, the compositions became more complex. In *Tilt I* and *A Round, II* (cat. 56, p. 29 and cat. 53, p. 28) the simple spheres are now circles placed within solid, lopsided black frames. The nature of the frames destabilizes the circles which now seem to roll around on the sheet. In treating the background as an open patterning on one side and tighter patterning on the other, particularly in *A Round, II*, Alma adds to this optical illusion of movement and tension.

The introduction of the solid black frames of the later dot series is attributable to Alma's *Woman* and *Lady Series* made from 1965 to 1968, these images are perhaps Alma's most personal work, delving into her perception of female sexuality and psyche. As a series, they are unified by the stylized form of the female torso within which a variety of shapes and patterns are drawn. The *Woman Series* concentrates on female sexuality. Each work is rendered in black and white with an emphasis on circles and spheres embodying the portrayed woman's breasts and thighs. By contrast, the *Lady Series* is light-hearted. Its images have the same stylized format of the female torso as the *Woman Series*, but are now rendered in watercolour with different patterned textures to represent different activities: in *Lady in Bed* (1966 and 67) (cat. 50, p. 73 and cat. 52, p. 74) her torso is a patterned quilt, and in *Lady at a Picnic* (1967) (cat. 51) her torso is a picnic blanket crawling with bees and ants. With the use of the repeated image of the female torso, of all of Alma Duncan's drawings, the *Woman* and *Lady Series* come closest to reflecting her work with puppets for her animated films.

The most arresting drawings that came of this later period of Alma's career are those inspired by nature. Living in the country, surrounded by meadows and woods, she immersed herself in the seasonal cycle of life. Among the works she described as her *Forest Floor Series* are *Feathers and Grass* (1971) (cat. 64, opposite) and *Hepatica Leaves* (1974) (cat. 67, p. 32). Seated on the ground, drawing pad on her lap, Alma zeroed in on her subjects. Using pen and ink which can best capture the details of texture and form she stated: "I endeavor to make the subject instantly recognizable, and in the case of plant life, to suggest the feeling of organic growth. I also try to create interesting patterns. This is why

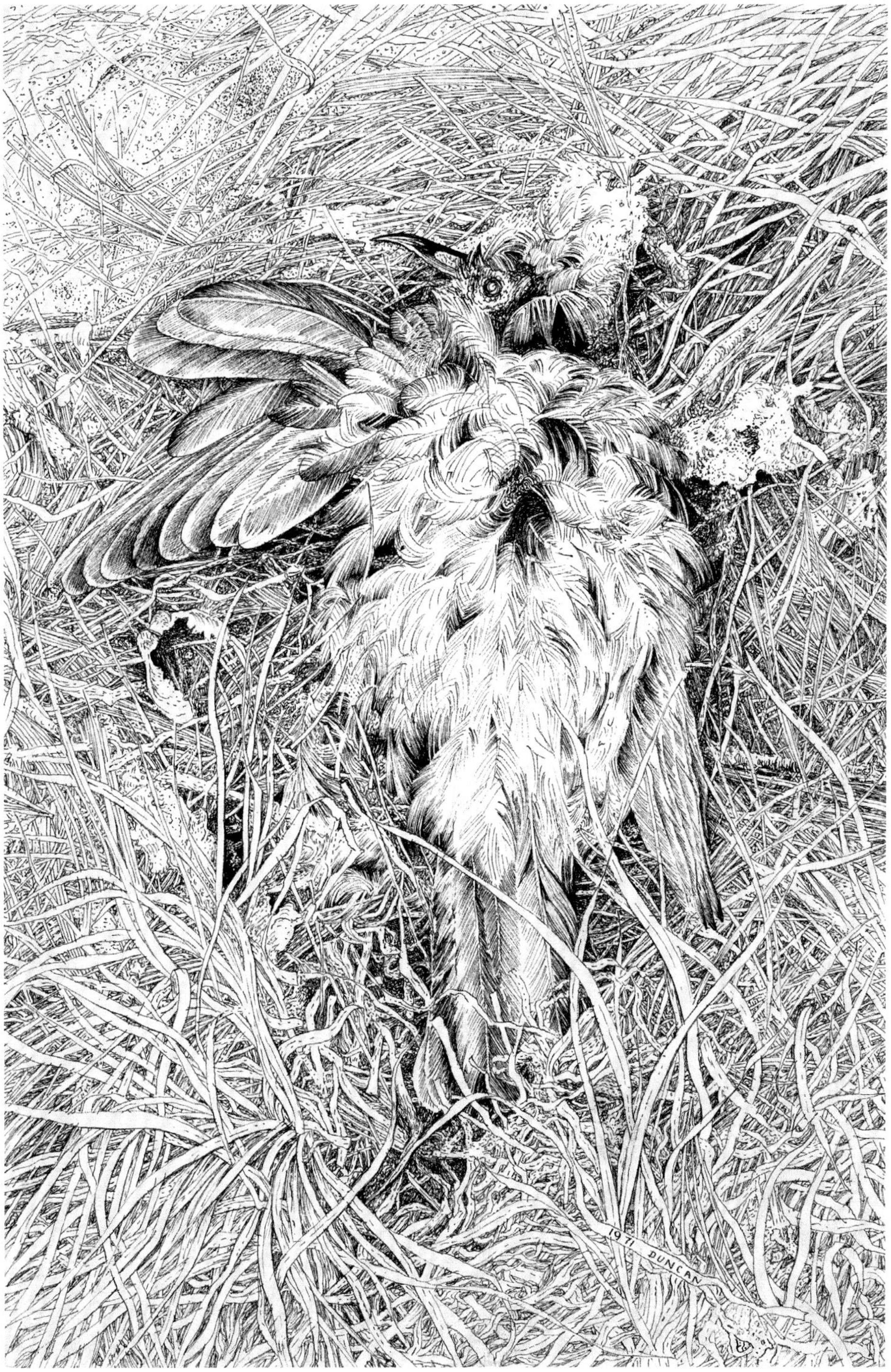

Feathers and Grass | Plumes et pelouse 1971 (cat. 64)
National Gallery of Canada | Musée des beaux-arts du Canada

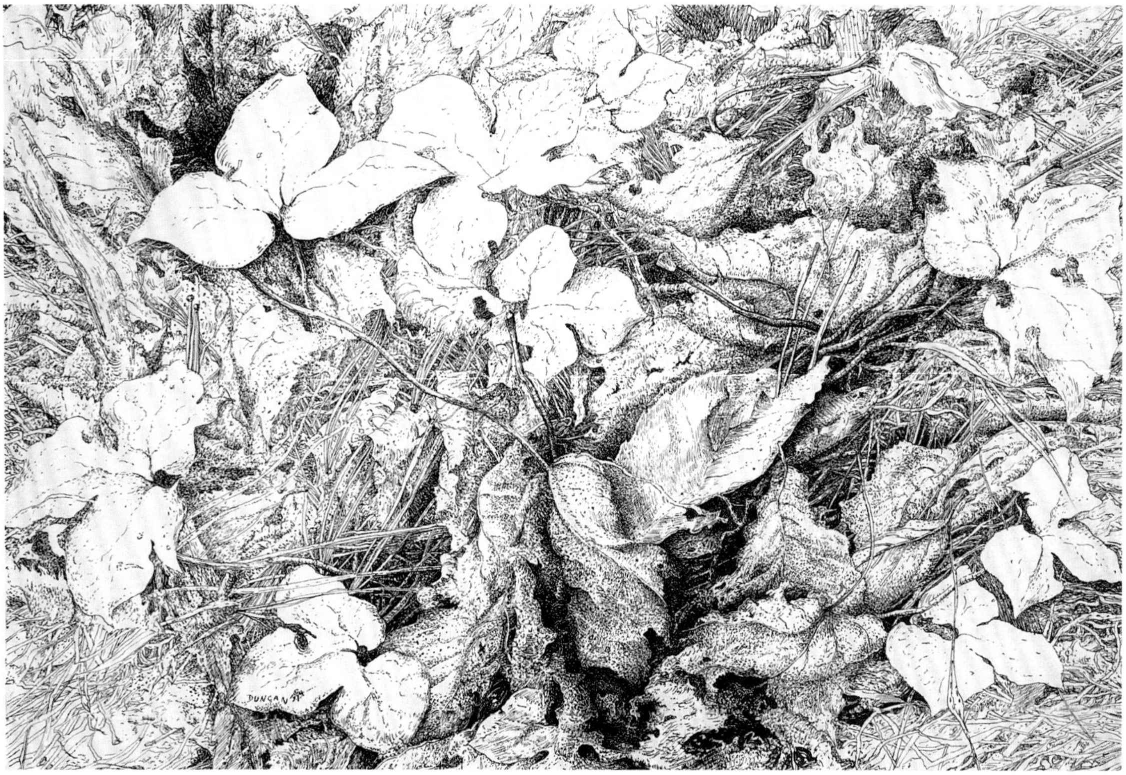

Hepatica Leaves | Feuilles d'hépatique 1974 (cat. 67)
Courtesy of Brian Oickle | Gracieuseté de Brian Oickle

my drawings are not truly realistic when compared with photographs."[10] She achieves an abstract, hyper-realistic effect by creating a moving point of view across the surface of the composition, as well as within the layers of the subject, so that everything is in an even, sharp focus. *Feathers and Grass* is not only an exploration of the contrasting weight and feel of the drawing's two subjects, it is also a dialogue between life and death. *Hepatica Leaves* repeats these themes. It is a tapestry-like rendering of flourishing and dying leaves growing among grasses and twigs. It is wrought in such rich, three-dimensional detail that one feels as though one could enter and explore the ground beneath the covering of hepatica leaves.

Edge of Woods (cat. 78) and *Winter Woods* (cat. 79, p. 36), both of 1979, belong to a series depicting the forest beside her home. "I lived in those woods," she stated. "I just became so much part of the woods."[11] Again the subjects are closely observed. In *Winter Woods*, the newly fallen snow hangs heavy in the trees. While apparently a hyper-realistic image, on close inspection we see that Alma has abstracted her subject by drawing each tree and bush in a different pattern.

From Dawn to Dusk (1977) (cat. 68, p. 34) and *Small World* (1977) (cat. 69, p. 38) stand between Alma's two artistic interests: realism and abstraction. They also present, in a very literal manner, her worldview. Each is the landscape around her home. *From Dawn to Dusk* is the east-to-west view looking towards the woods and fields. Composed horizontally, she tracks the passage of time, with a rain-laden dawn sky on one side transforming into the clear sky of dusk on the other. It belongs to the *Forest Edge Series*. *Small World* is the view all around her house. Moving from window to window and balcony to window, she started the drawing at six in the morning and finished it at six at night. Over that time the shadows changed position, a rain shower came and went, and her vegetable garden enjoyed full sunshine. But the world is represented as a globe and harks back to the spheres and moons of the dot drawings from the mid-sixties. The composition has no top or bottom, but can be rotated to take in the full view. There is a peace about both these drawings, a peace that reflects the artist's comfort with her world and her art.

Alma Duncan best summed up her modus operandi: "There is agony as well as joy in what you discover when you pursue the dialogue with the work that follows your first rather terrifying mark on paper or canvas. Even when working from nature or in a factory, I only know I am fascinated by the image. I don't know what the final result will be. That's part of what makes an artist's work an adventure."[12]

1 Alma Duncan, "The Artist at Work," in *Alma Duncan and Men at Work, 1943 to 1986*, ed. Joan Murray (Oshawa, ON: Robert McLaughlin Art Gallery, 1987), 6. **2** The Roberts-Neumann School of Art ran out of Neumann's studio and lasted for only three years, from September 1936 to 1939. Roberts left to teach at the Art Association of Montreal, but Neumann remained in the studio and took in students privately through the 1940s. **3** Alma Duncan, interview with Joan Murray, February 13, 1986, artist's documentation file, National Gallery of Canada, Ottawa. **4** Ibid. **5** Ibid. It should come as no surprise that when Alma Duncan made her first trip to New York in 1939 the only artist she arranged to meet was John Sloan, former teacher at the Art Students League and founder of The Ash Can School. **6** Ibid. **7** Duncan, "The Artist at Work," 8. **8** Duncan, interview. **9** Conversation with Audrey McLaren, March 25, 2014. **10** Alma Duncan quoted in Valerie Knowles, "Ottawa Artists (24) Remarkable drawing skill," *Ottawa Journal*, March 27, 1971. **11** Duncan, interview. **12** Duncan, "The Artist at Work," 13.

Rosemarie L. Tovell is former Curator of Canadian Prints and Drawings at the National Gallery of Canada. From 1971 until her retirement in 2005, she was responsible for developing the collection and promoting the subject of Canadian prints and drawings. She has curated many exhibitions and authored catalogues, articles and given many lectures. Principal publications include *A New Class of Art: The Artist's Print in Canadian Art 1877–1920* (1996) and catalogue raisonnés *Reflections in a Quiet Pool: The Prints of David Milne* (1980), and *The Prints of Betty Goodwin* (2002). Since her retirement, she has authored catalogue essays for the Art Gallery of Ontario, the Musée national des beaux-arts du Québec, The Montreal Museum of Fine Art, the Burnaby Art Gallery, the Winnipeg Art Gallery and Carleton University Art Gallery. She lectures regularly and writes articles for publications in Canada and the United States. She is a member of Print Council of America and is currently on the Board of Directors of the American Historical Print Collectors Society, and book review editor for *Imprint, Journal of the AHPCS*.

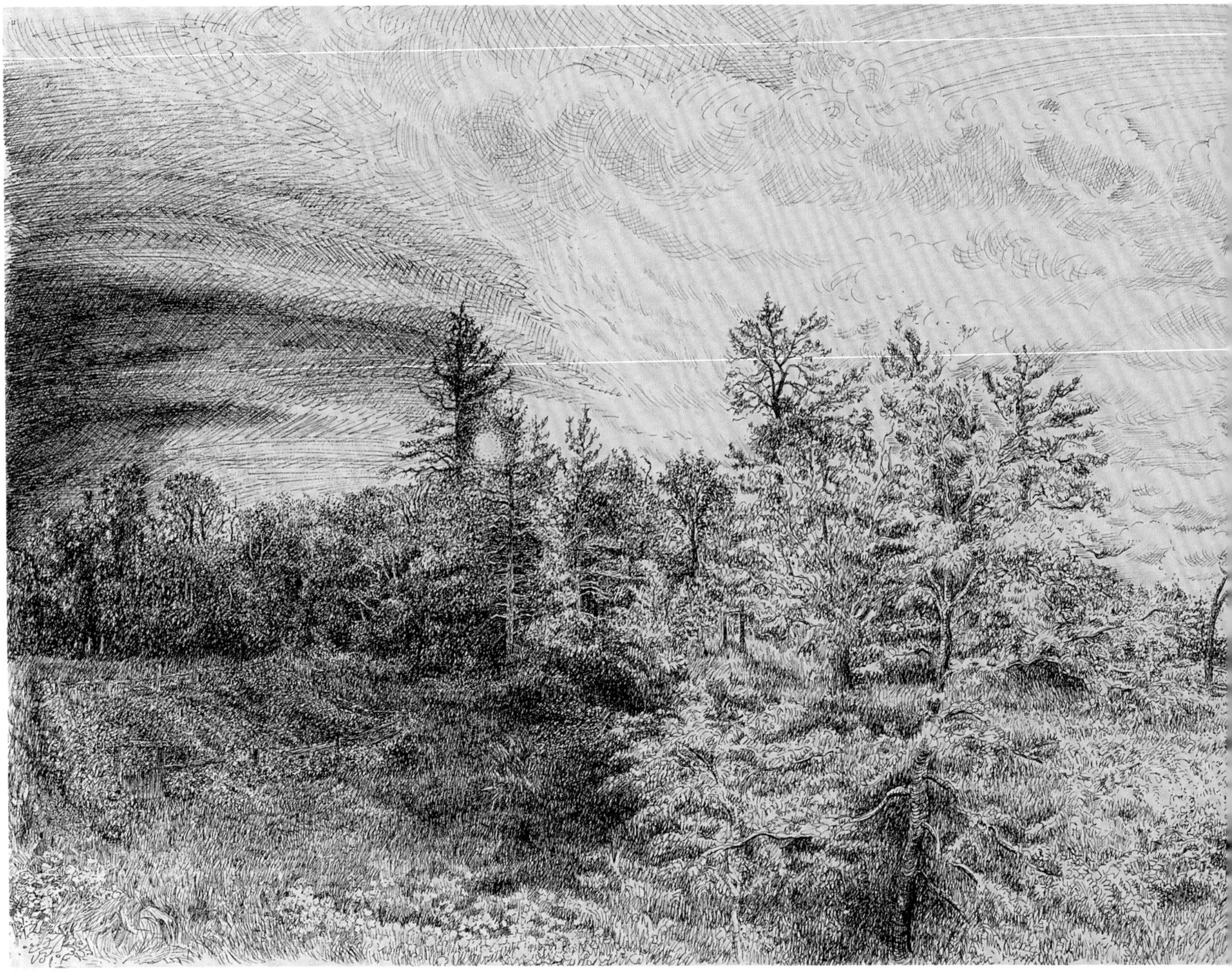

From Dawn to Dusk | De l'aube au crépuscule 1977 (cat. 68)
Art Gallery of Ontario | Musée des beaux-arts de l'Ontario

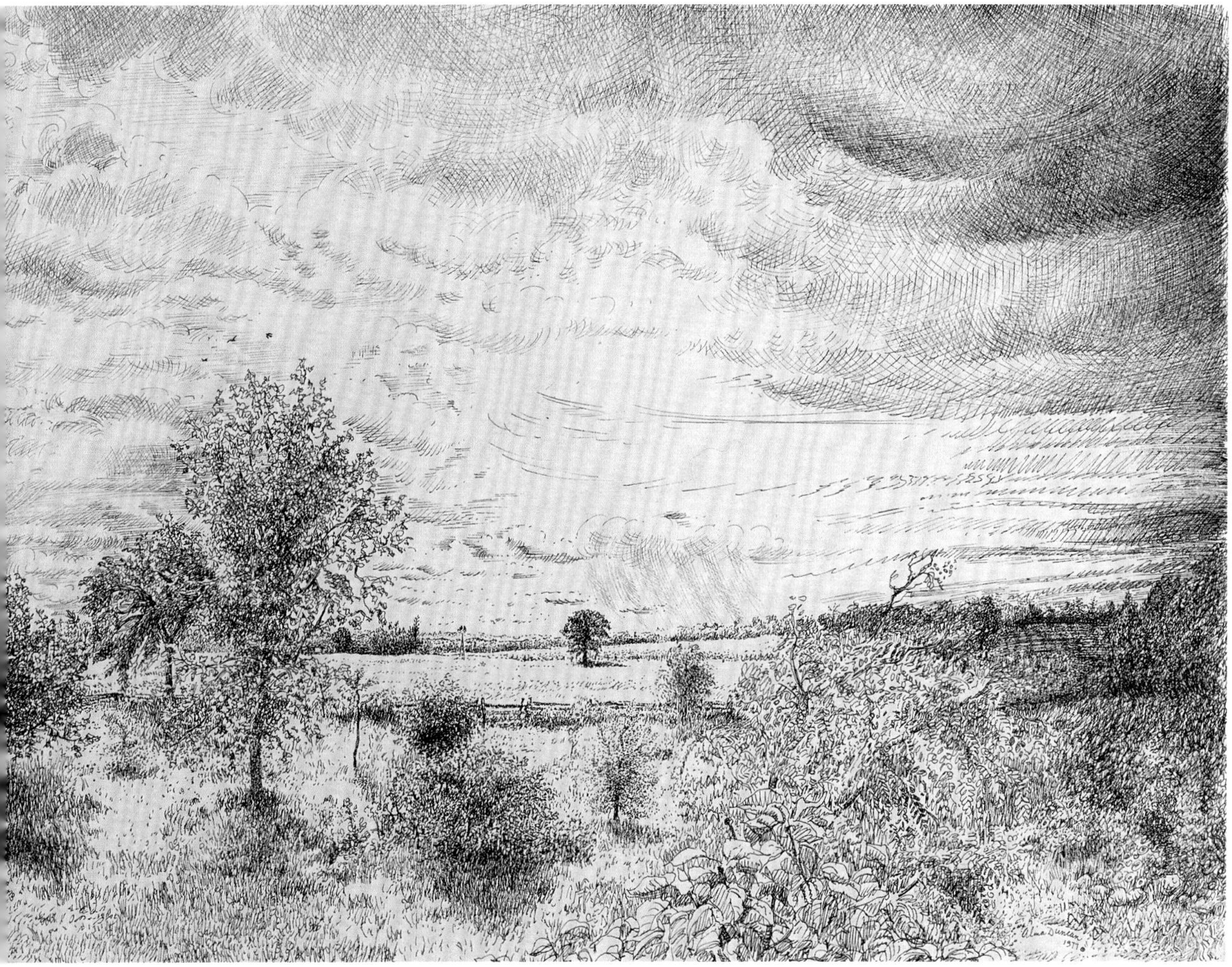

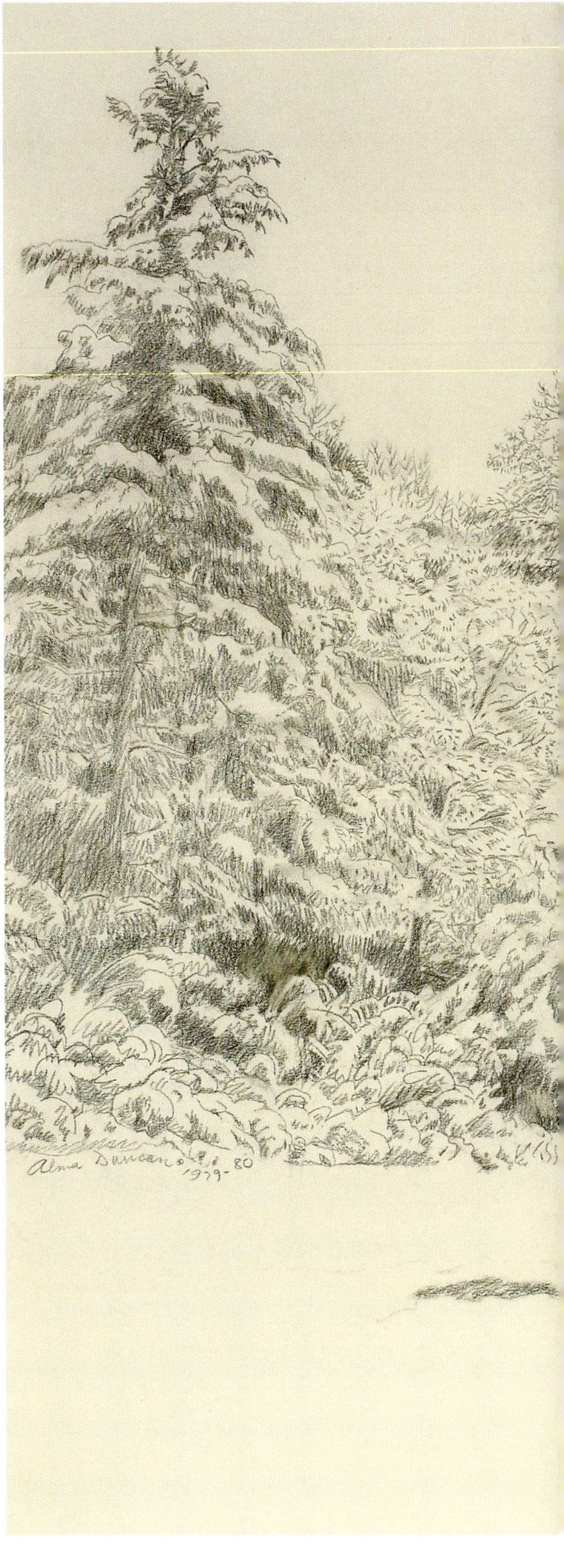

Winter Woods | Forêt d'hiver 1979–80 (cat. 79)
National Gallery of Canada | Musée des beaux-arts du Canada

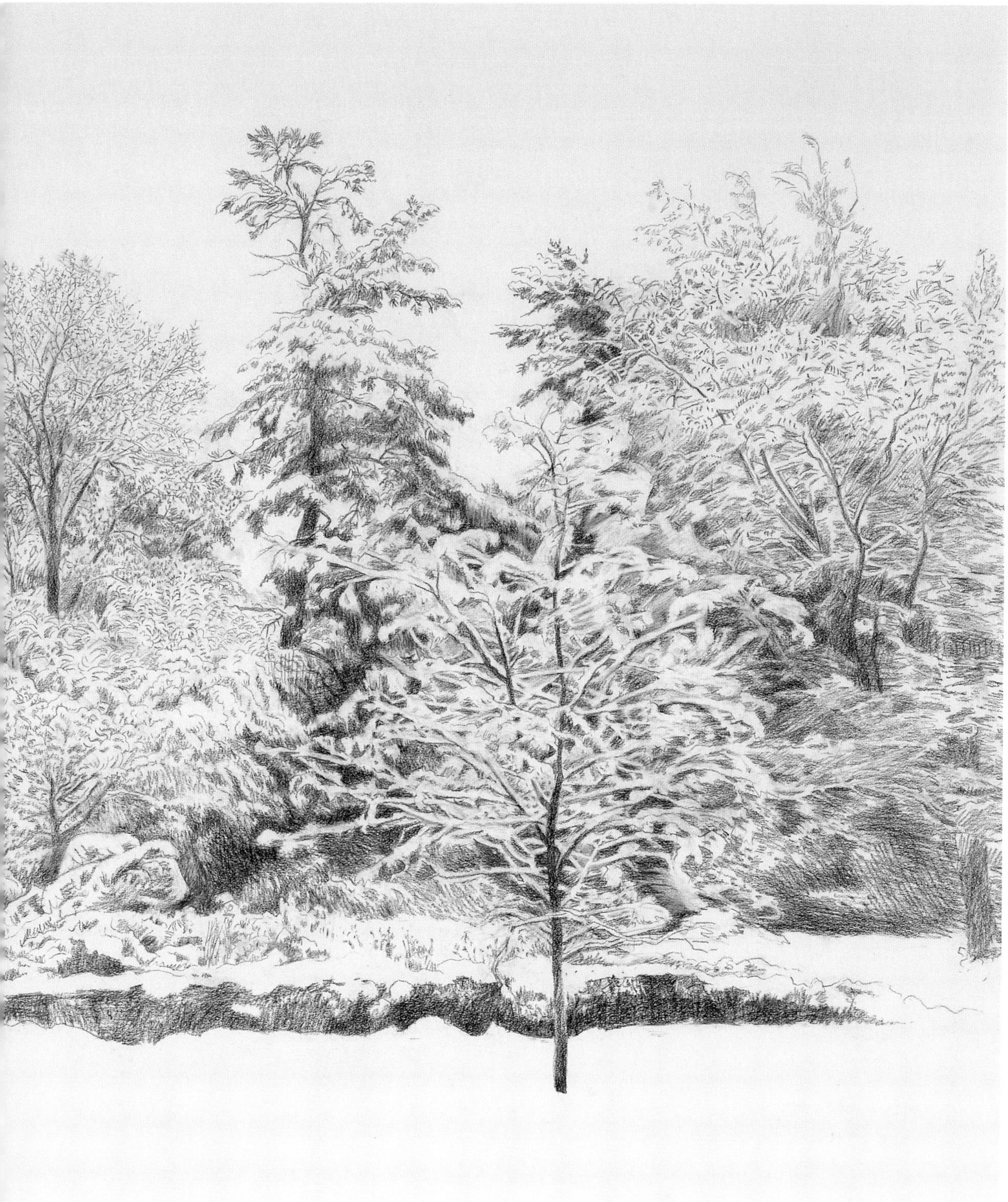

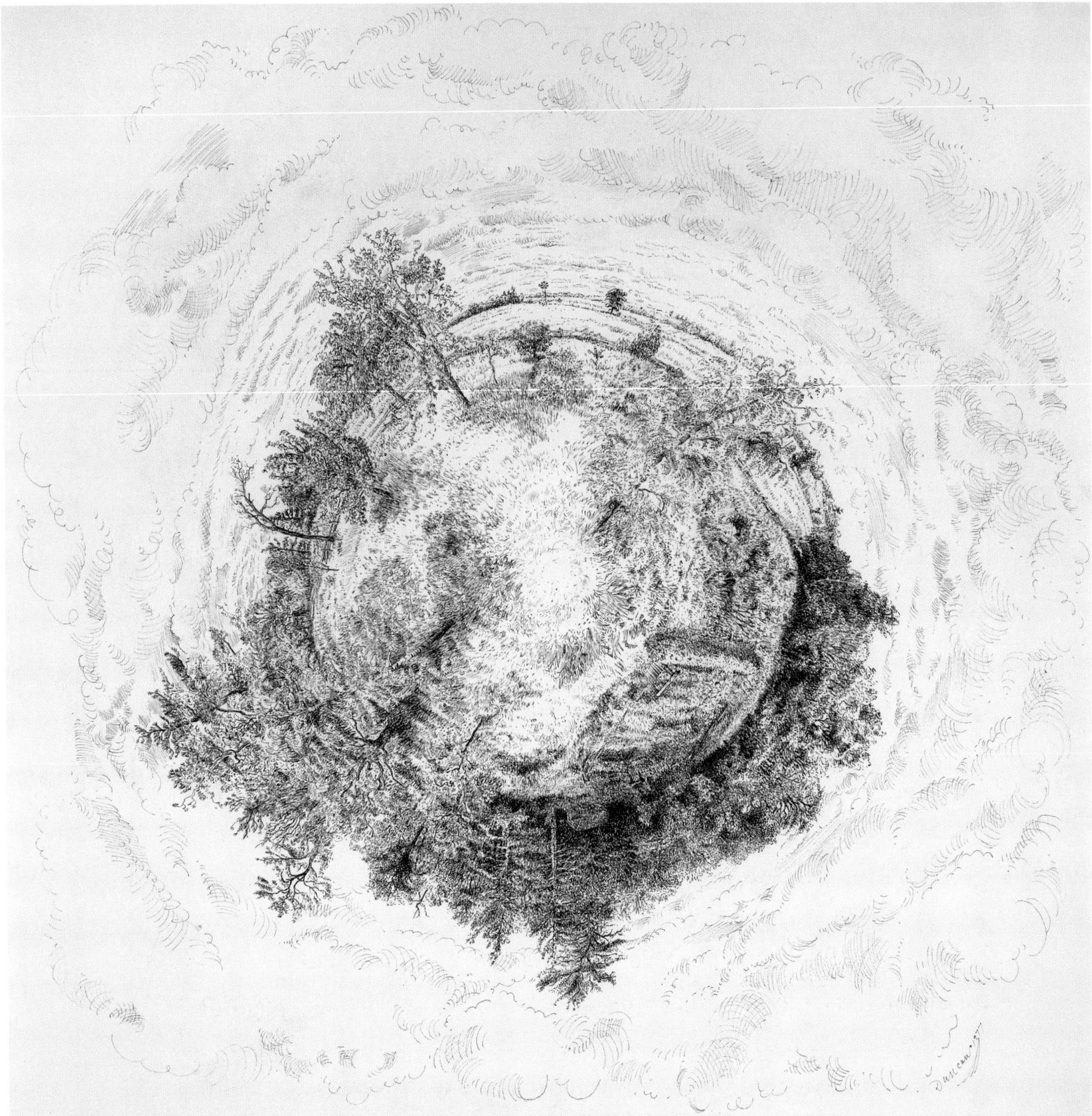

Small World | Le monde est petit 1977 (cat. 69)
National Gallery of Canada | Musée des beaux-arts du Canada

« Voici quelque chose qui vient de sortir de ma plume »

Les dessins d'Alma Duncan

Rosemarie L. Tovell

L'autoportrait de 1978 (cat. 80, p. 16) en dit beaucoup. Lorsqu'on rencontre Alma Duncan, on remarque immédiatement ses yeux bleus perçants ainsi que son comportement discret et indépendant, tant courtois qu'assuré. Ce sont ces caractéristiques qui ont fait d'elle une excellente observatrice, et ce sont ces qualités qui ont déterminé la nature de son art. Les œuvres d'Alma ne penchaient pas ouvertement vers la narration ou la polémique – si ces éléments existent parfois, ils sont subtils. Au contraire, elle préférait analyser pour ensuite présenter les faits dûment constatés. Cependant, malgré cette fidélité à l'observation pure, ses œuvres étaient très chargées et saisissantes, pleines de détails imaginatifs, mystérieux et surprenants.

Alma Duncan divisait ses sujets de dessins en séries et y travaillait par intermittence sur plusieurs années; leurs titres officiels sont *Dessins industriels*, *Sol de la forêt*, *Femme*, *Dame*, *Feuilles*, *Herbe* et *Lisière d'une forêt*. Il existe aussi des séries informelles de sujets : des portraits, des dessins abstraits composés de points, et des dessins minutieux d'objets de son environnement immédiat, que ce soit la chambre de sa mère le jour de Noël (cat. 30, p. 40) ou un croquis du panorama vu des fenêtres de sa maison (cat. 68, p. 34). Plus tard dans sa vie – à partir des années 1960 – ces sujets vont

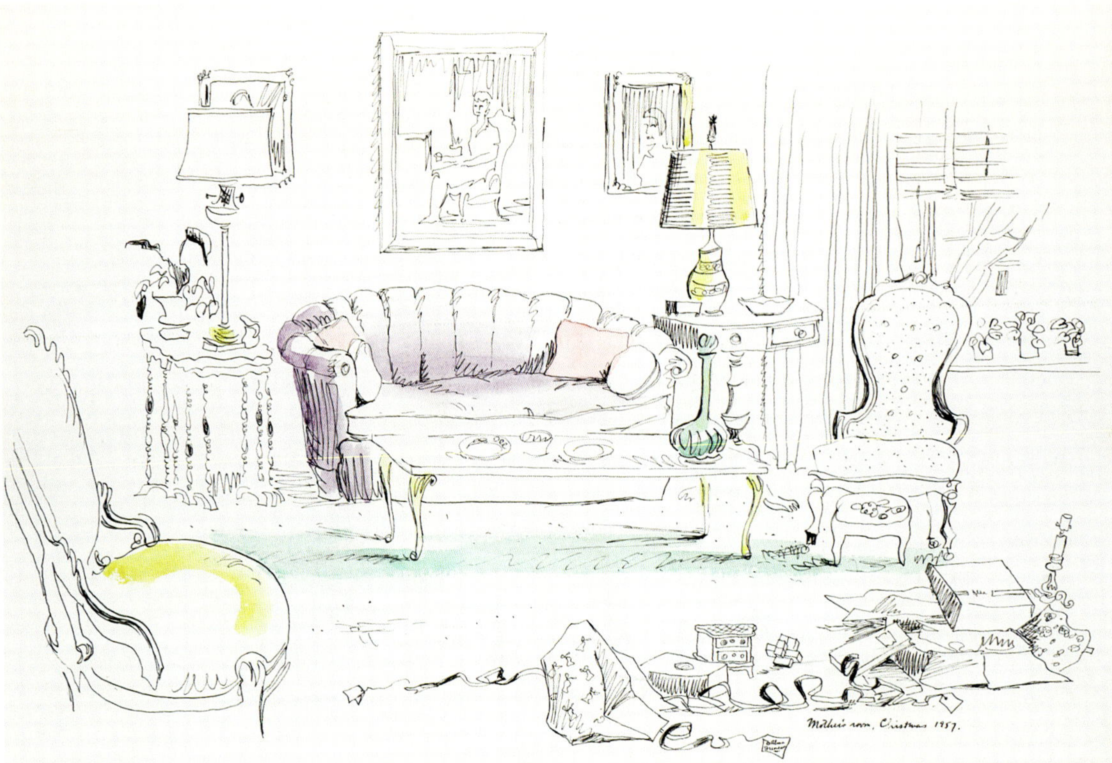

Mother's Room, Christmas | La chambre de ma mère, Noël 1957 (cat. 30)
Courtesy of D & E Lake Ltd. Fine Arts | Gracieuseté de D & E Lake Ltd. Fine Arts

se croiser, les compositions et les thématiques s'entrelacer. Par exemple, le panorama *Le monde est petit* (cat. 69, p. 38) de 1977 peut être assimilé, du point de vue de la composition et de la sensibilité, au dessin abstrait *Un cercle, II* (cat. 53, p. 29), qui date de 1966.

Alma assiste aux cours de dessins d'après modèles donnés par Adam Sherriff Scott à Montréal, alors qu'elle est une jeune adolescente; c'est là qu'elle reçoit une formation artistique de base[1]. Elle estime, peut-être en raison de son âge, que ce n'est pas un bon usage de son temps. De 1936 à 1943, elle travaille dans un bureau de graphisme publicitaire dont les clients principaux publient des catalogues de vente par correspondance. Grâce à son talent pour le dessin, Alma savait représenter exactement les produits à vendre. Elle prétendra plus tard que cet emploi n'aura exercé aucune influence sur son art, mais on constate sa prédilection pour le dessin aux détails très précis, comme en témoigne également sa décision de dessiner des spécimens au département d'anatomie de l'Université McGill. Les traits de ces dessins commerciaux et anatomiques présagent les dessins détaillés de la nature qui viendront trente ans plus tard.

Ce travail commercial étant saisonnier, Alma peut donc explorer ses propres champs d'intérêts pendant les cinq autres mois de l'année. Elle n'a pas abandonné l'idée de faire un usage plus sérieux de ses talents et reprend donc les cours de dessin d'après modèle dès que l'occasion se présente : la Roberts-Neumann School of Art, dirigée par Goodridge Roberts et Ernst Neumann de 1936 à 1939, est située dans le même immeuble que le bureau de graphisme où elle travaille[2]. L'école semble être dissoute à l'époque où Alma s'inscrit, mais Neumann enseigne toujours. Pendant deux ans elle étudie, entre autres, le dessin d'après modèle et le portrait lors de cours du soir hebdomadaires. Là encore, Alma reçoit une formation plutôt académique. Elle remarque d'ailleurs l'aversion de Neumann pour « l'éclat ou le superficiel »[3]. Elle le trouve très acerbe et critique, bien qu'il approuve son travail. Alma suit à la même époque des cours de dessin d'après modèle auprès de Goodridge Roberts à la Art Association of Montreal (prédécesseur du Musée des beaux-arts de Montréal); elle admire l'honnêteté et l'absence de superficialité dans le travail de ce dernier.

Le portrait de sa mère (cat. 3, p. 19), exécuté en 1938, et celui de Neumann (cat. 10, p. 20), réalisé en 1942, démontrent le progrès qu'Alma fait sous la tutelle de Neumann et l'influence de son professeur sur sa façon de dessiner. Dans le portrait de 1938, les lignes de contour sont très vives, le visage et le chapeau sont délicatement modelés avec des traits de fusain doux et graduels. Cependant, le sujet manque d'énergie et de personnalité. En revanche, le portrait de Neumann de 1942, exécuté dans un style de dessin rappelant celui de son modèle, est rendu avec une variété de traits puissants et de dégradés entre ombre et lumière fort contrastants. Voilà le portrait d'un homme qu'elle décrivait comme étant « rude, aux larges épaules, au franc-parler »[4].

C'est sûrement par l'entremise de Neumann qu'Alma rencontre la communauté d'artistes montréalais dotés d'une conscience politique et sociale, notamment Fritz Brandtner, Fred Taylor et Louis Muhlstock[5]. En 1941, Alma se joint à ces artistes pour former l'exécutif de la section québécoise de la Fédération des artistes canadiens (FAC). La Seconde Guerre mondiale a beau être déjà bien avancée, aucun programme pour les artistes de guerre n'est toutefois en place. Avec Brandtner en tête, les artistes souhaitant participer demandent au ministère des Munitions et des Approvisionnements l'autorisation de se rendre dans les usines et les chantiers navals afin de documenter l'effort de guerre sur le front intérieur. En 1943, avec ses collègues de la FAC, Alma obtient la permission de dessiner au chantier naval de la Canadian Vickers Limited et à l'usine de munitions Canadian Industries Limited, tous deux situés à Montréal.

Ces dessins « de guerre », les premiers de la série *Dessins industriels*, sont créés en 1943, dans le style agressif et dense qu'elle avait appris de Neumann. Ils représentent de

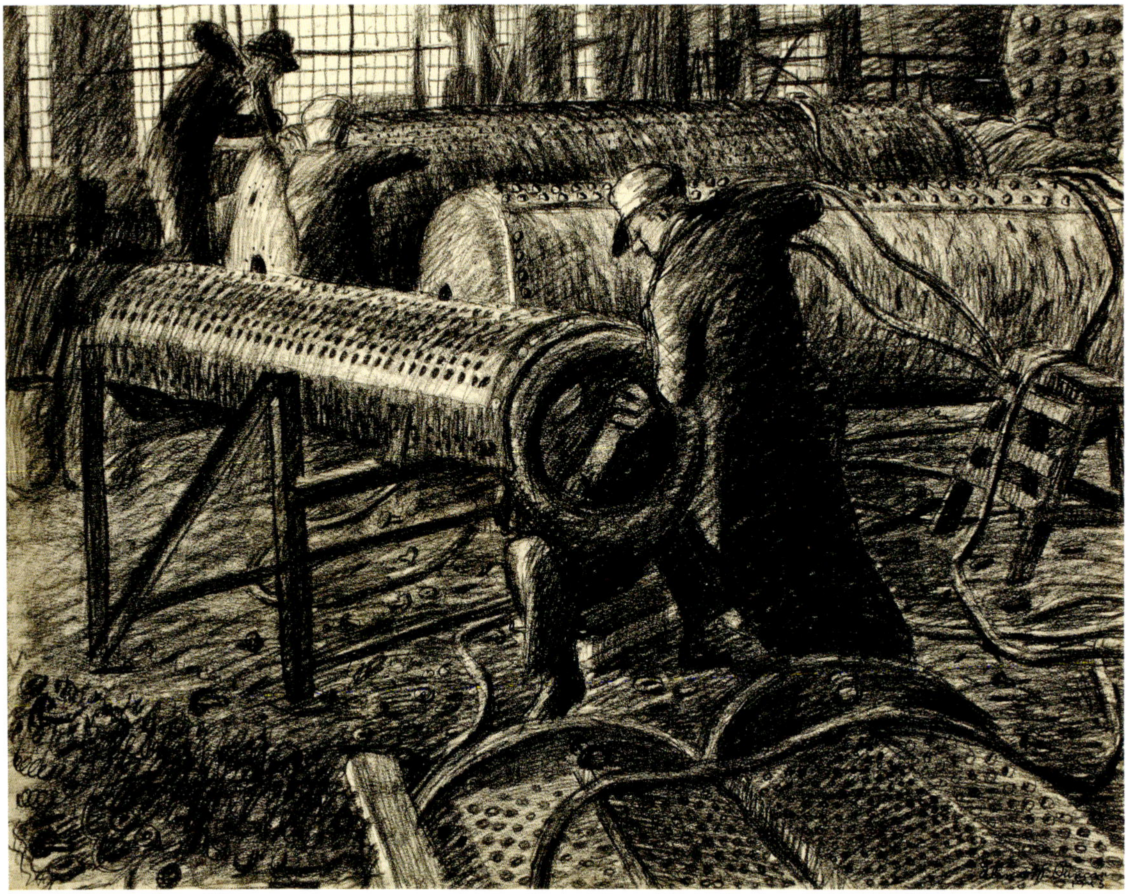

Riveters in Boiler Shop | Riveurs dans un atelier de montage de chaudières 1943 (cat. 16)
The Robert McLaughlin Gallery

façon dynamique la contribution à la guerre, déterminée et patriotique, des industries du Canada; les ouvriers sont penchés sur leur ouvrage dans le labyrinthe des machines et l'atmosphère glauque qui règne dans l'usine. Ces dessins (cat. 13 et 16, ci-dessus) marquent le début d'un intérêt pour les sujets industriels qui durera longtemps. En 1947, Alma prend un congé du département d'animation de l'Office national du film à Ottawa pour voyager en Ontario afin de faire d'autres dessins en milieu industriel. Sa motivation est simple : « J'adore les usines. J'aime le fouillis [...]. Il y avait tellement d'action, avec les machines, les sons [...], toute cette activité », déclare-t-elle dans une entrevue[6]. Plus loin : « J'aimais faire partie du bruit et de l'énergie, j'appréciais les images, les formes et les textures, et la musique rauque des sons rythmés »[7]. Plus près de chez elle, elle réalise *La papetière E.B. Eddy* (cat. 18, page suivante) à l'usine E.B. Eddy à Hull. L'œuvre est presque lyrique. Les dessins rudes

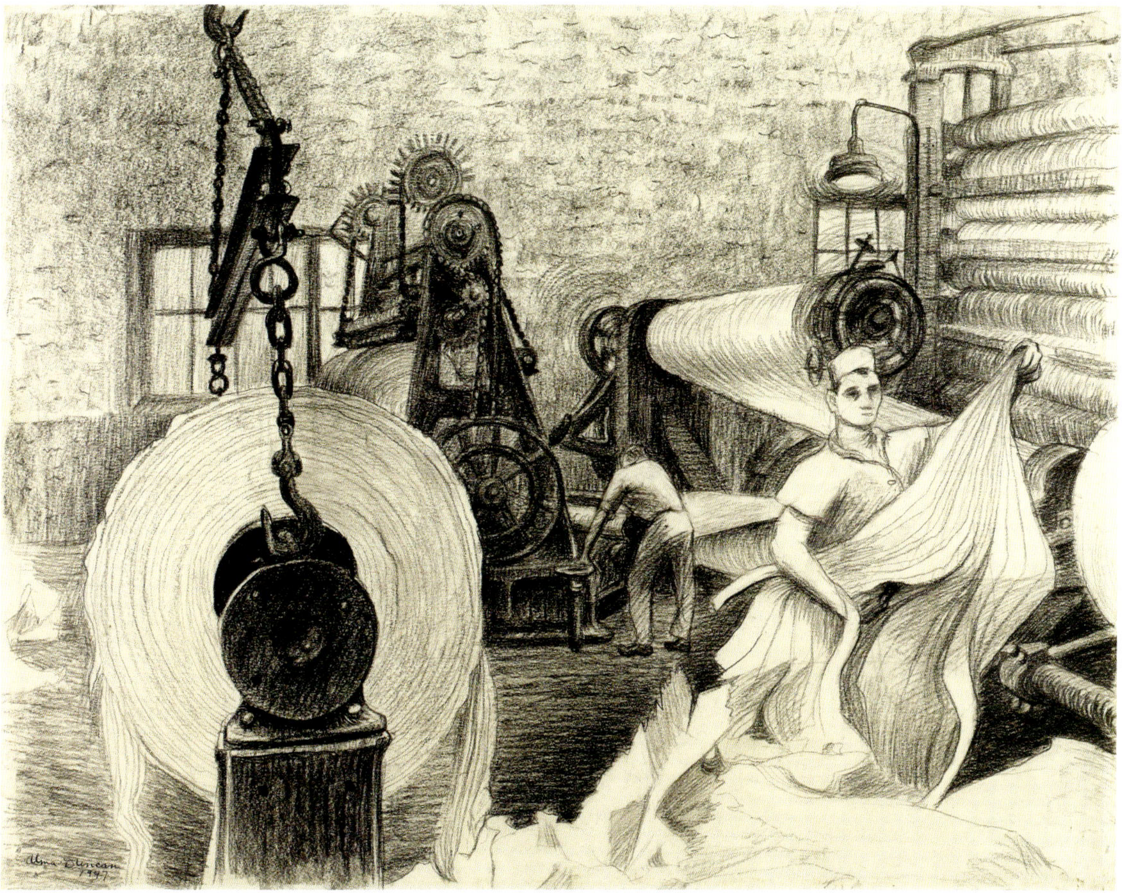

Papermakers, E.B. Eddy Company | La papetière E.B. Eddy 1947 (cat. 18)
Library and Archives Canada | Bibliothèque et Archives Canada

et sombres des premières années font place à un travail des ombres plus léger et nuancé. L'ouvrier et le papier qu'il fabrique ne font qu'un, s'enlaçant comme dans une danse.

Neuf ans plus tard, Alma amorce une nouvelle série de dessins, au pastel cette fois, de la mine à ciel ouvert de Steep Rock Iron Mines près d'Atikokan, à l'ouest du lac Supérieur. La charge de couleurs éclatantes de *Mine ouverte et passerelle* (1956) (cat. 29, p. 44) traduit bien l'impression qu'Alma aura eue face à la terre rouillée de la mine et aux teintes variées du paysage bouleversé. Le résultat, pourtant, ne présente pas la beauté terrifiante de certaines œuvres contemporaines, notamment celles d'Edward Burtynsky. Dans son travail, Alma ne fait pas de polémique sur la destruction de l'environnement. Au contraire, ces dessins sont de leur époque : ils célèbrent l'émergence de l'économie industrielle d'après-guerre prospère du Canada. Alma retourne à Steep Rock en 1958 et pénètre cette fois-ci dans l'usine

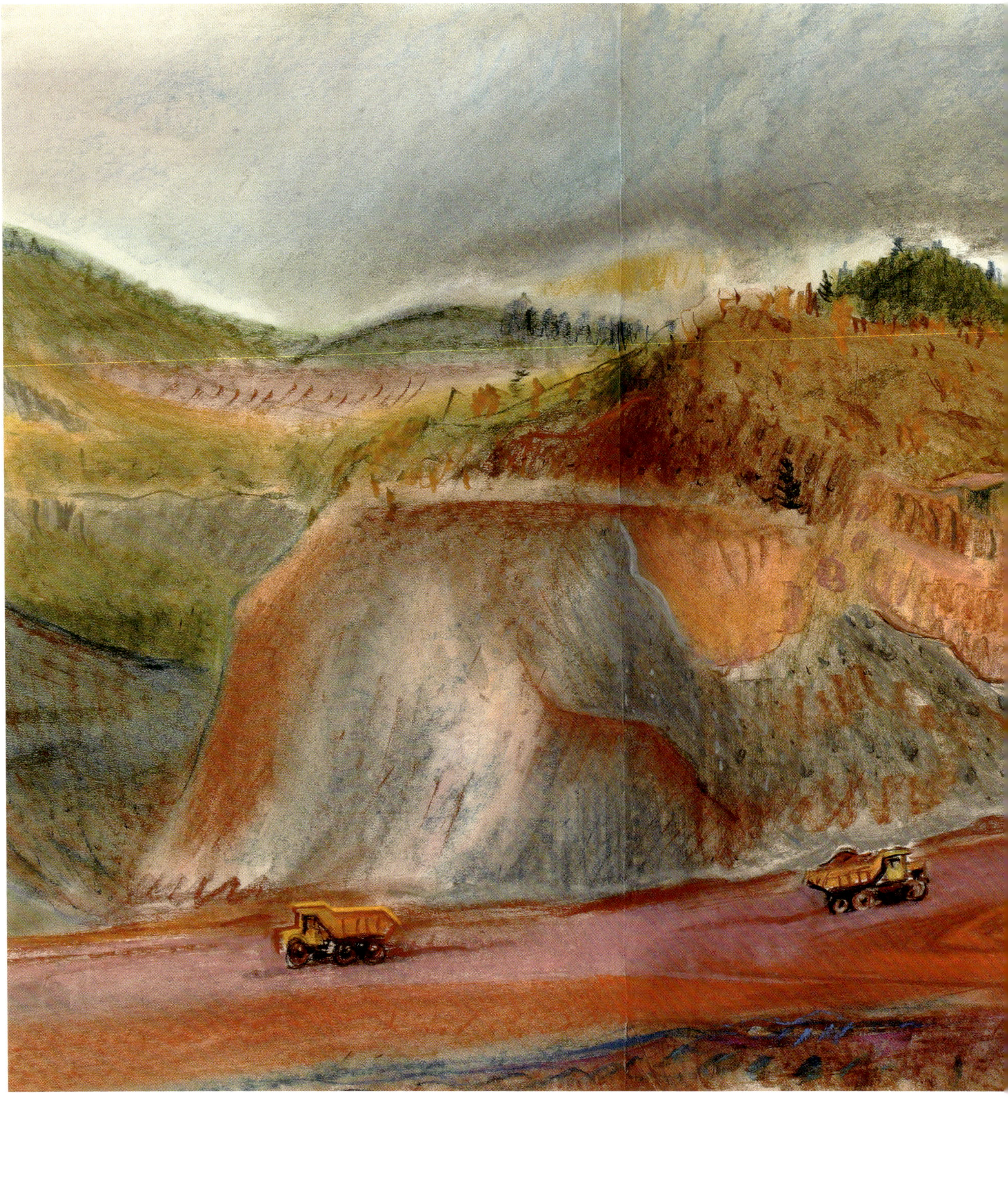

Open Pit and Skipway | Mine ouverte et passerelle 1956 (cat. 29)
The Robert McLaughlin Gallery

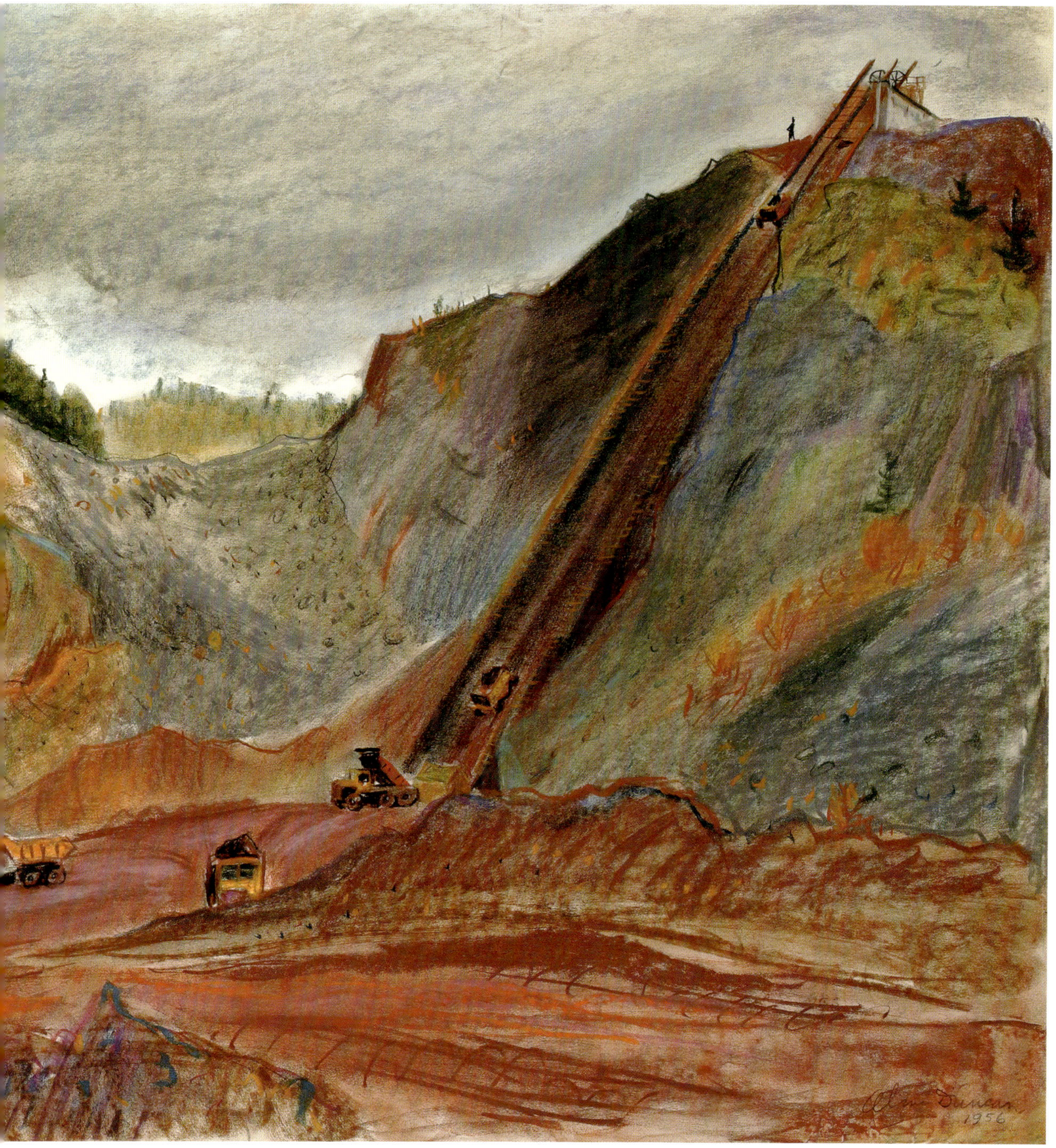

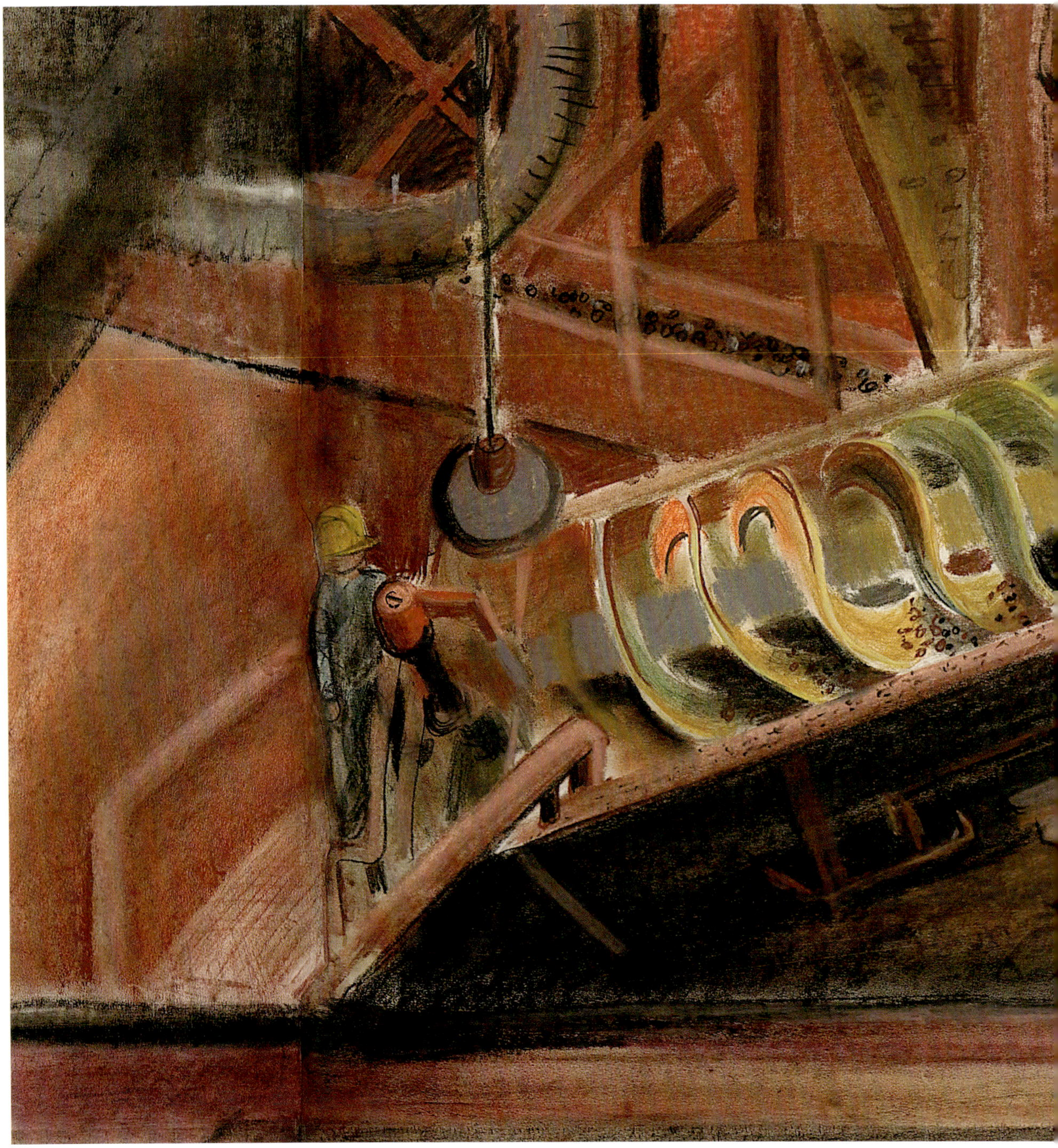

Giant Spiral, Processing Ore | Spirale géante, traitement du minerai 1958 (cat. 33)
Private Collection | Collection privée

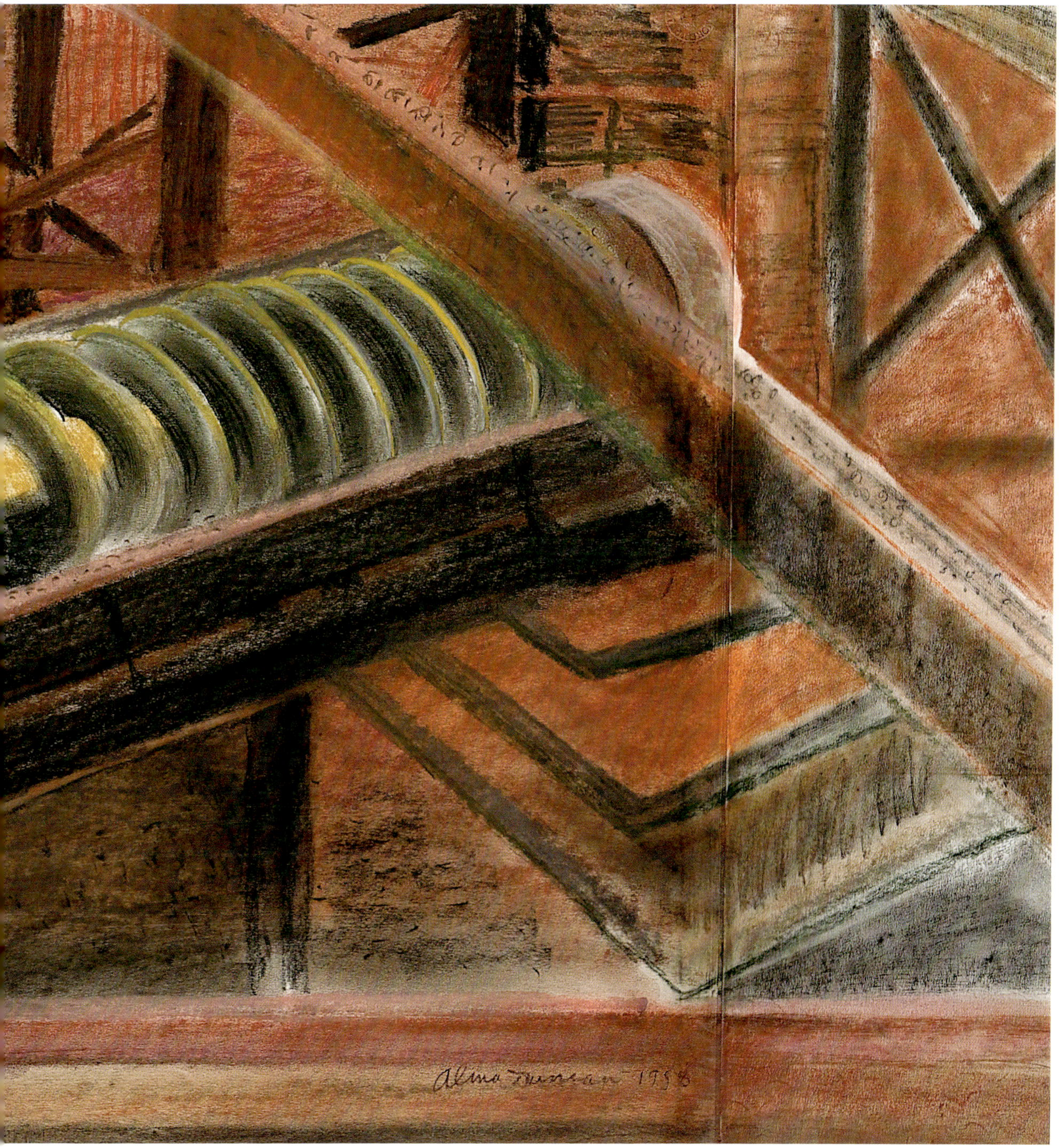

de traitement. *Spirale géante, traitement du minerai* (1958) (cat. 33, p. 46) reprend l'usage de couleurs éclatantes mais présente une composition plus complexe, presque abstraite : un entrelacement compliqué d'angles tels que le séparateur en spirale, les poutres et l'échafaudage. Cette œuvre présage la série *Sol de la forêt* qui viendra quelques années plus tard.

Alma Duncan prend sa « retraite » du cinéma d'animation en 1960 afin de se consacrer entièrement au dessin et à la peinture. Comme toujours, le dessin joue un rôle central dans ses efforts. Son travail devient de plus en plus abstrait, et l'art non figuratif deviendra même un sujet à part entière dans les années qui suivent. Comme elle habite à temps partiel à la campagne, le monde naturel s'introduit dans son vocabulaire artistique. Le répertoire des matériaux qu'elle utilise pour les dessins de présentation achevée comprend maintenant la plume et l'encre, l'aquarelle et le crayon conté.

La première démonstration de cette nouvelle tendance apparaît dans la série *Herbe* (1962) (cat. 35–38, p. 22–23). Alma décrit ces dessins comme étant tout simplement « sortis du bout de ma plume » : les brins d'herbe oscillant au vent sont réduits à de simples traits[8]. Ils sont comme les cordes d'une harpe qui résonnent au son de leur propre musique. En fait, la musique est très importante pour Alma, et elle use souvent de références musicales pour évoquer son travail abstrait et semi-abstrait[9]. Dans le dessin à la plume et à l'encre *Laiteron* (1967) (cat. 60, p. 24), elle continue d'explorer le thème de l'herbe, mais représente maintenant son sujet dans tous ses détails, observés de très près, captant les formes et les textures des tiges et des gousses, les graines duveteuses s'envolant dans la brise.

Au milieu des années 1960, Alma entreprend une série de dessins abstraits qu'elle nomme « série en pointillé ». Au début, ces dessins à la plume et à l'encre (tels que représentés par *Sans titre nº 1*, datant de 1964 [cat. 39, p. 26]) sont de simples sphères tridimensionnelles créées par l'accumulation minutieuse de points flottant dans un espace non défini. La sphère est une illusion d'optique : elle est dessinée de manière à être perçue comme concave ou convexe. Dans le dessin suivant, datant de 1965, la sphère est parfaitement ronde et représente la lune, comme dans *Sans titre 3* (cat. 40, p. 27) où elle flotte dans un espace non défini. Dans d'autres dessins de cette série, qui ne sont pas compris dans cette exposition, la sphère plane au-dessus des douces ondulations d'un paysage, confirmant l'intention d'Alma de représenter la lune. En 1966 et 1967, les compositions de la série en pointillé deviennent de plus en plus complexes. Dans *Inclinaison I* et *Un cercle, II* (cat. 56, p. 28 et 53, p. 29), les simples sphères sont devenues des cercles placés dans des cadres noirs unis et de guingois. L'asymétrie du cadre déstabilise le cercle, qui semble rouler sur la feuille. Alma accentue l'illusion de mouvement et de tension en couvrant l'arrière-plan d'un motif aéré d'un côté et d'un motif resserré de l'autre, particulièrement dans *Un cercle, II.*

L'introduction du cadre noir uni dans les œuvres tardives de la série en pointillé est attribuable aux séries *Femme* et *Dame*, réalisées entre 1965 et 1968. Peut-être les plus personnelles de l'artiste, ces images traduisent sa perception de la sexualité et de la psyché féminines. En tant que série, les œuvres sont unifiées par la forme stylisée du torse à l'intérieur duquel sont dessinés des formes et des motifs différents. La série *Femme* se penche sur la sexualité féminine : chaque œuvre est en noir et blanc, et l'accent est mis sur des cercles et des sphères qui incarnent les seins et les cuisses de la femme représentée. La série *Dame* quant à elle est plus gaie : les images reprennent les torsess stylisés vus dans la série *Femme*, mais ils sont maintenant représentés à l'aquarelle et les motifs qui les remplissent évoquent différentes activités. Dans *Dame au lit* (1966 et 67) (cat. 50, p. 73 et 52, p. 74) par exemple, le torse est une courtepointe aux multiples motifs, et dans *Dame en pique-nique* (1967) (cat. 51) le torse est une nappe de pique-nique pleine d'abeilles et de fourmis. En raison de cette répétition de l'image du torse féminin, ce sont les séries *Femme* et *Dame* qui, de tous les dessins d'Alma Duncan, s'apparentent le plus à son travail avec les marionnettes des films d'animation.

Les dessins les plus frappants produits durant cette époque tardive de la carrière d'Alma sont ceux qui ont été inspirés par la nature. Elle habite maintenant la campagne où, entourée de prés et de bois, elle se plonge dans le cycle des saisons. Parmi les œuvres de la *Sol de la forêt*, on retrouve *Plumes et pelouse* (1971) (cat. 64, p. 31) et *Feuilles d'hépatique* (1974) (cat. 67, p. 32). Assise sur le sol, carnet genoux, Alma porte toute son attention ses sujets. Elle utilise la plume et l'encre, car ils captent le mieux les menus détails des textures et des formes : « Je tente de rendre le sujet immédiatement reconnaissable et, dans le cas de la flore, d'offrir une impression de croissance organique. J'essaie aussi de créer des motifs intéressants. Voilà pourquoi mes dessins ne sont pas absolument réalistes lorsqu'on les compare à des photographies »[10]. Elle obtient un effet abstrait hyperréaliste en créant un point de vue qui se déplace la surface de la composition aussi bien que parmi les couches du sujet, de sorte que toutes les prises de vue soient nettes et unies. *Plumes et pelouse* est plus qu'une exploration des contrastes de pesanteurs et de sensations entre les deux sujets du dessin : c'est aussi un dialogue entre la vie et la mort. *Feuilles d'hépatique* reprend ces thèmes. Cette représentation, à effet de tapisserie, de feuilles florissantes et mourantes dans l'herbe et les brindilles est si riche de détails tridimensionnels qu'on croirait pouvoir y entrer et explorer le sol qui gît sous cette couverture de feuilles d'hépatique.

Lisière d'une forêt (cat. 78) et *Forêt d'hiver* (cat. 79, p. 36), tous deux de 1979, appartiennent à une série qui dépeint la forêt près de sa maison. « Je vivais dans ces bois »,[11]. Ici aussi, les sujets sont observés de très près. Dans *Forêt d'hiver*, la neige fraîchement tombée encombre lourdement les branches des arbres. Il s'agit en apparence d'une image hyperréaliste, mais en regardant de plus près on constate qu'Alma a rendu son sujet abstrait en dessinant un motif différent dans chaque arbre et arbuste.

De l'aube au crépuscule (1977) (cat. 68, p. 34) et *Le monde est petit* (1977) (cat. 69, p. 38) se situent entre les deux intérêts artistiques d'Alma : le réalisme et l'abstraction. Ils représentent aussi, au sens propre, sa vision du monde, car chacun dépeint le paysage autour de sa maison. *De l'aube au crépuscule* présente une vue panoramique d'est en ouest, en regardant vers les bois et les champs. L'œuvre est composée horizontalement, et Alma suit la journée qui défile, le ciel matinal orageux d'un côté se transformant en ciel clair de fin de journée de l'autre côté. Ce dessin s'inscrit dans la série *Lisière d'une forêt*. *Le monde est petit* quant à lui représente la vue qu'elle a autour de sa maison. Se déplaçant d'une fenêtre à l'autre et du balcon à la fenêtre, elle commence le dessin à six heures du matin et le termine à dix-huit heures. Pendant ce temps, les ombres se déplacent, un orage passe, son jardin potager profite du soleil. Mais ce monde est représenté comme un globe, qui rappelle les sphères et les lunes des dessins en pointillé du milieu des années 1960. La composition n'a ni haut ni bas; on peut la faire tourner sur elle-même pour profiter entiont quelque chose de paisible, qui reflète la sensation de confort qu'éprouve l'artiste dans son monde et dans son art.

Alma Duncan a bien résumé sa manière de faire : « Il y a autant de joie que de tourment dans les découvertes qu'on fait quand on pousse le dialogue avec une œuvre d'art, passé la première marque – d'ailleurs assez terrorisante – qu'on appose sur le papier ou la toile. Que je travaille à partir de la nature ou dans une usine, je sais seulement que je suis fascinée par l'image. Je ne sais pas quel sera le résultat final. C'est en partie ce qui fait que le travail de l'artiste est une aventure »[12].

1 Alma Duncan, « The Artist at Work » (L'artiste au travail), *Alma Duncan and Men at Work, 1943–1986* (Alma Duncan et Hommes au travail, 1943–1986), Joan Murray, éd., Oshawa, Robert McLaughlin Art Gallery, 1987, p. 6. **2** La Roberts-Neumann School of Art logeait dans le studio de Neumann et ne dura que trois ans, de 1936 à 1939. Roberts la quitta pour enseigner à la Art Association of Montreal (prédécesseur du Musée des beaux-arts de Montréal); Neumann demeura au studio et donna des cours privés dans les années 1940. **3** Alma Duncan, entrevue avec Joan Murray, le 13 février 1986, dossier documentaire de l'artiste, Musée des beaux-arts du Canada, Ottawa. **4** Ibid. **5** Ibid. Il n'est pas étonnant d'apprendre que, lors de son premier voyage à New York en 1939, le seul rendez-vous qu'Alma Duncan organise est une rencontre avec John Sloan, un ancien enseignant de la Art Students League et fondateur de la Ash Can School. **6** Ibid. **7** Duncan, « The Artist at Work » (L'artiste au travail), p. 8. **8** Duncan, entrevue. **9** Conversation avec Audrey McLaren, le 25 mars 2014. **10** Alma Duncan, citée dans Valerie Knowles, « Ottawa Artists (24) Remarkable Drawing Skill *Ottawa Journal*, 27 mars 1971. **11** Duncan, entrevue. **12** Duncan, « The Artist at Work » (L'artiste au travail), p. 13.

Rosemarie L. Tovell a longtemps été la conservatrice des dessins et estampes canadiens au Musée des beaux-arts du Canada. De 1971 jusqu'à sa retraite en 2005, elle a développé la collection et assuré la promotion des

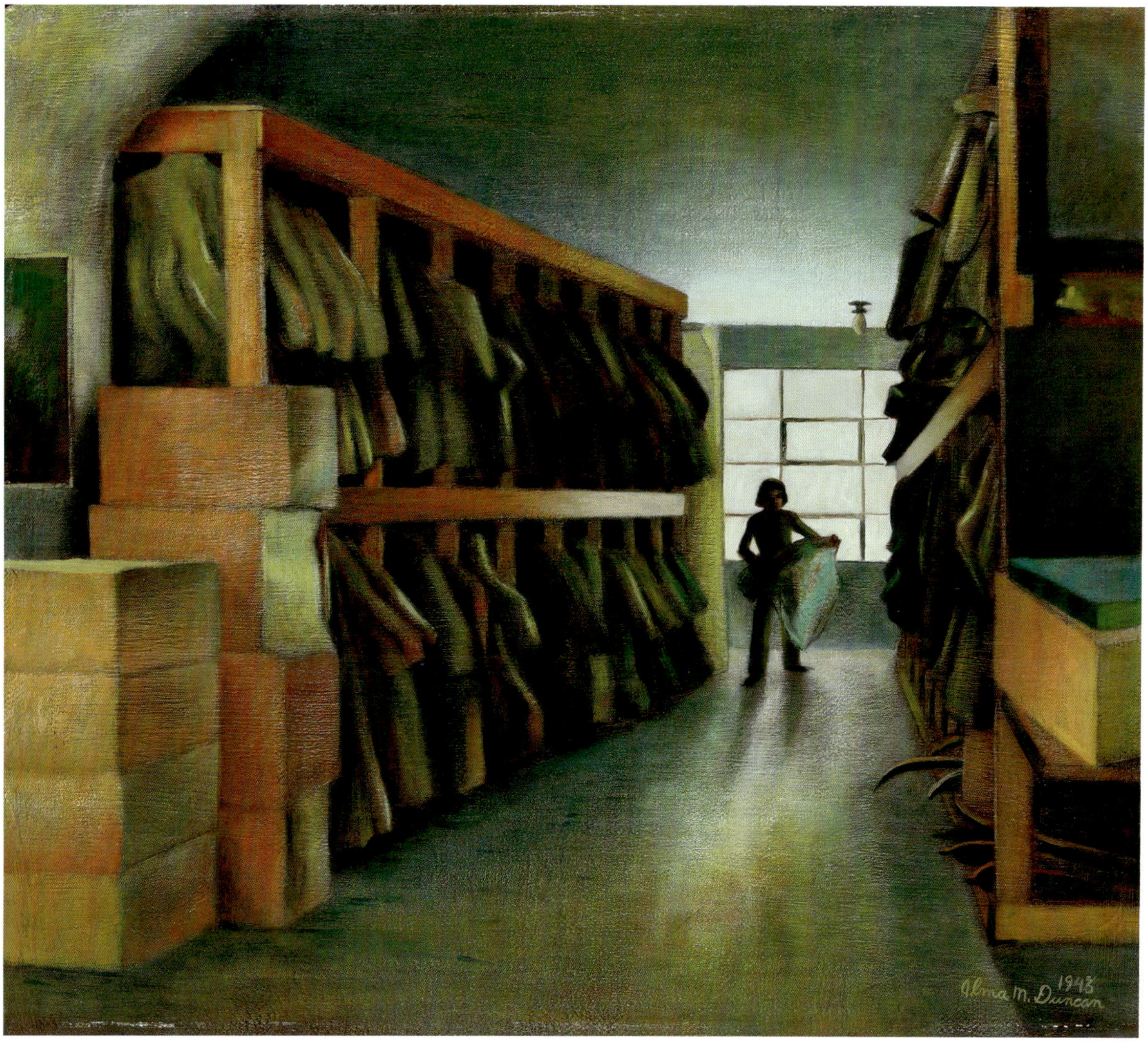

Army Girl in Warehouse | Jeune soldate dans un entrepôt 1943 (cat. 14)
Library and Archives Canada | Bibliothèque et Archives Canada

dessins et estampes canadiens. Elle a monté plusieurs expositions, rédigé des catalogues et des articles, et donné de nombreuses conférences. On compte parmi ses principales publications *Un nouvel art. L'estampe originale au Canada de 1877 à 1920* (1996) et les catalogues raisonnés *Reflets dans un miroir d'eau. Estampes de David Milne* (1981) et *Les estampes de Betty Goodwin* (2002). Depuis qu'elle a pris sa retraite, elle a signé des textes de catalogues pour le Musée des beaux-arts de l'Ontario, le Musée national des beaux-arts du Québec, le Musée des beaux-arts de Montréal, la Burnaby Art Gallery, le Musée des beaux-arts de Winnipeg et la Carleton University Art Gallery. Elle donne des conférences fréquemment et rédige des articles pour diverses publications au Canada et aux États-Unis. Elle est membre du Print Council of America, siège au conseil d'administration de la American Historical Print Collectors Society et dirige la section critique de livres du journal *Imprint* de la AHPCS.

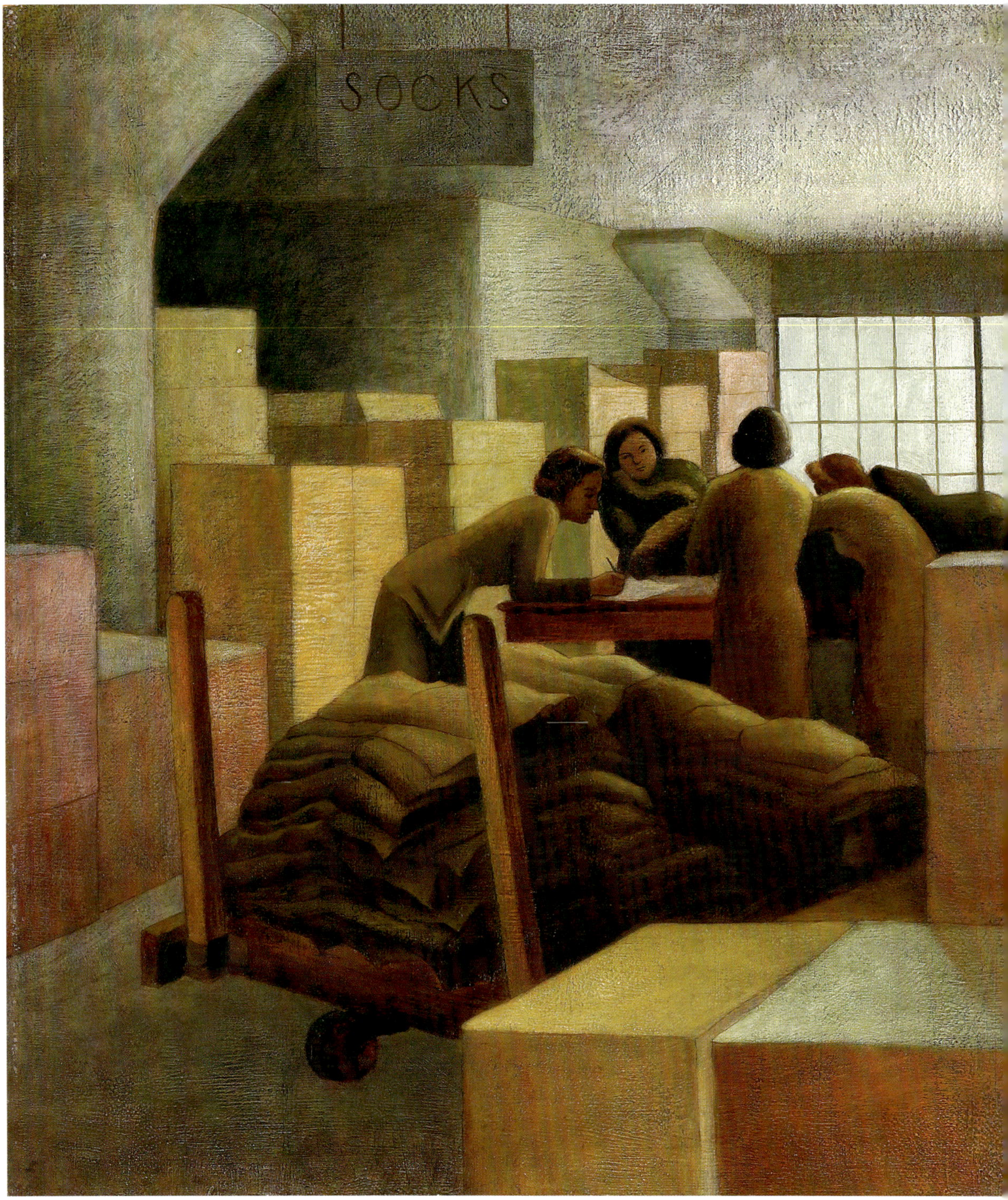
SOCKS

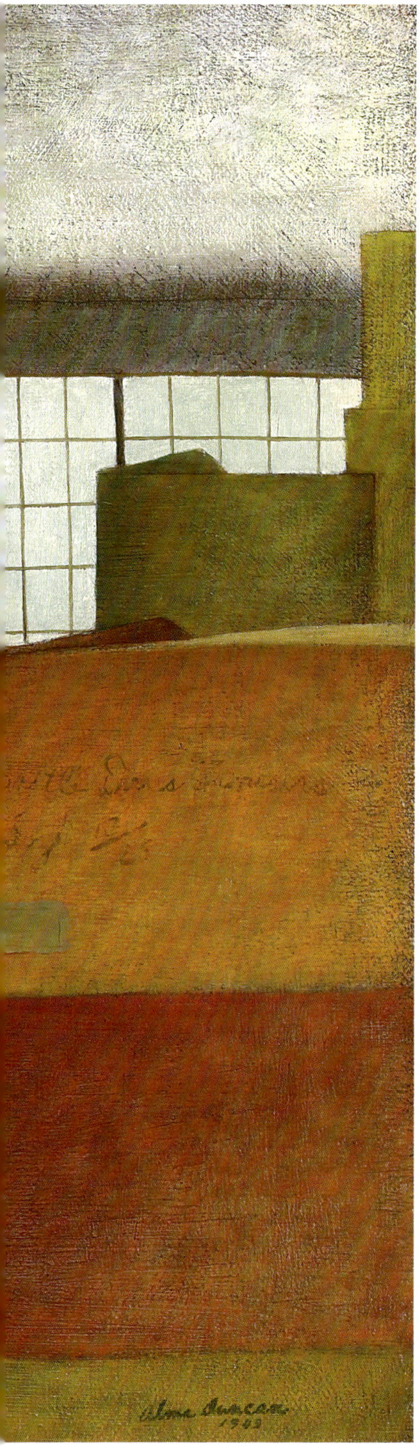

Army Women in Warehouse | Femmes de l'armée dans un entrepôt 1943 (cat. 15)
National Gallery of Canada | Musée des beaux-arts du Canada

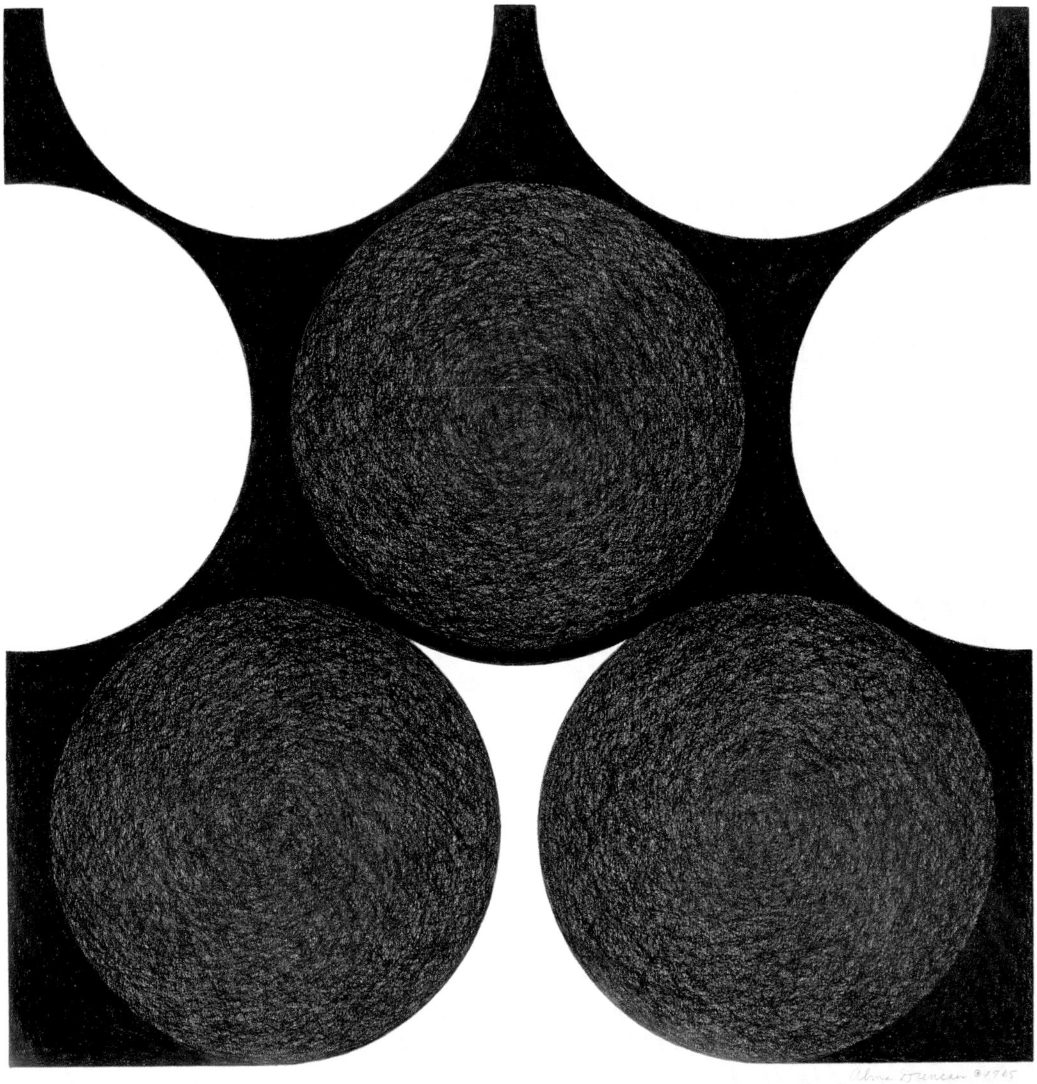

Woman Series – Torso | Série Femme – Torse 1965 (cat. 43)
Library and Archives Canada | Bibliothèque et Archives Canada

Circling the Essential

Alma Duncan, Abstraction, and a Quiet Feminism

Catherine Sinclair

I have a soft spot for women artists working in postwar Canada. There is something fascinating to me about the ways in which the exciting changes of the Canadian art milieu were entangled with the challenges these women faced while working in what was still a man's world. These challenges included negotiating family responsibilities, fighting to achieve recognition in art school, and maintaining relevancy in their practices. Working in a contemporary climate, I am myself all too aware that many of these struggles still influence women practitioners and professionals today. In the postwar era, Alma Duncan, like many women artists of her generation, defied many social and gender barriers, from sketching in munitions factories to working at the National Film Board of Canada. What is most curious to me is that despite not having identified as a feminist, she dared to deconstruct the feminine body in a collection of abstract drawings entitled *Woman Series*, which reflect larger concerns surrounding the domestic, sexual, and political roles that continue to stereotype women in the professional sphere.

The Ottawa Art Gallery's Permanent Collection contains four portraits by the Ottawa-based artist. In a personal favourite, *Self-Portrait* (1943) (cat. 11, p. 102), Duncan depicts herself as an attractive, self-assured young female artist. When Jaclyn Meloche and I embarked on the journey of reviewing work for this exhibition, I was introduced to the varied œuvre of this energetic and prolific artist. Beyond her well-executed portraits, her refined draughtswoman skills could rival the best artists in the country; she had the gusto required to wear a hard-hat in munitions plants and industrial factory sites, and the craftsman skills and creative will to create short stop-motion puppetry animation films from scratch.

Amid all the variety of her work, what struck me the most were the ways in which she blurs the lines between representation and abstraction. For this reason, when we came across the powerful large-format black-and-white drawings within this particular series at the Library and Archives Canada, I knew we had found something special. Potent in their simplicity, these drawings are executed with black conté on white paper. They exhibit geometrically anthropomorphic forms that hover between realism and abstraction and are ripe with conceptual meaning in their exploration of the physicality of the female body.

Duncan's *Woman Series* reflects the political stirrings of the second-wave feminist revolution, which began in the 1960s. In contrast to the first wave's focus on the suffragette movement and gender equality at the turn-of-the-century, the second wave was largely centred on sexual liberation and a politic of the body. Feminist artists were beginning to create work that challenged patriarchal societal norms. At the time, Duncan, however, did not cite any feminist influences in her research, writing, or art. Instead, she focused on the importance of plasticity, paying rapt attention to the colour theory of the Abstract Expressionists. Yet despite this lack of adherence to an explicit feminist goal, I see the *Woman Series* as Duncan's most overt feminist statement, situated directly within second-wave feminism, and representative of Duncan's quiet contribution to feminist visual culture in the mid-twentieth century.

Duncan began to experiment with the expressive qualities of form and line in the early forties in her first series of munitions drawings: expressionistic chalk renderings of men at work in munitions factories, such as *Riveters in a Boiler Shop* (1943) (cat. 16, p. 42). Aptly described by curator Joan Murray in her 1987 exhibition catalogue, many of these works presented an "intricate structure balancing on the borderline of abstraction and realism."[1] Yet it was not until the 1960s that Duncan really engaged with abstraction. In her own words, "The sixties were a wonderful time for experimenting and the beginning of many things."[2]

In 1964, the year she created the *Woman Series*, Duncan was 47 years old and living in Ottawa on Somerset Street, but spending summers at Windrush, a home near Galetta in the Upper Ottawa Valley. That year, she began to merge realism with abstraction in a series she called her "dot" drawings: delicate pen-and-ink renderings of celestial bodies in space or in muted landscapes. One drawing from this series, *Untitled No.I* (1964) (cat. 39, p. 26), was her first work to be purchased by the National Gallery of Canada. Duncan's experimentation with form during this time was particularly focused on the circle. Found in the "dot" drawings, the circle was also used by Duncan to represent the basic contours of a female body in the block-like geometric shapes of her *Woman Series*, as seen in *Woman Series – II* (1965) (cat. 42, p. 58). Like the "dot" drawings, the *Woman Series* also received national and international recognition.[3] Yet this latter series was vastly different from Duncan's prior work, both in its use of geometric abstraction and conceptual expression.

The human form was Duncan's first subject matter. Throughout the years, she often returned to it in the form of portraiture, self-portraiture and puppetry. In 1936, at age 19, she moved to Montreal to study political economy at McGill University. She remained there for seven years until 1943, and arranged to visit the Medical School anatomy labs during the summer months to practice her figurative sketching. By the time Duncan created the *Woman Series* in 1964, she had been drawing the human form in portraiture and life drawing for more than twenty-five years. Yet, this series represents her first attempt to conceptualize the body, and more specifically, the female body.

It is hard not to connect Duncan's work sketching in the anatomy lab in the late 1930s to her later abstracted bodies in *Woman Series*. For example, *Woman Series – Square Torso* (1965) and *Woman Series – Torso* (1965) (cat. 44, p. 59 and cat. 43, p. 54), by title and by subject, are eerily evocative of the truncated human cadaver one might find in such a lab. Quite literally, Duncan evokes the human female form, depicting breasts, waist, hips, pubic triangle and round thighs. In presenting a universalized feminine form, these drawings are linked to the history of the "essentialist" argument, deconstructed within second-wave feminism.

Duncan's drawings recall the dissections of the human body found elsewhere in Western art, especially those famously depicted in fifteenth- and sixteenth-century paintings by Michelangelo and Leonardo da Vinci. These "artist-anatomists" kept skeletons and skulls in their studios and often made wax models of various muscle poses. Though not viewed by the public due to societal taboos around cadavers, as well as to the preparatory nature of the work, these paintings demonstrate the Italian Renaissance's scientific interest in the body. Da Vinci, in particular, saw the human body as the "measure of all things."[4] However, by the eighteenth century, the scientific interest in human anatomy became synonymous with the representation of gender divisions. In the words of art historian Deanna Petherbridge, " The comparative anatomy of the sexes became very important in the eighteenth century, concurrently with new ideas about

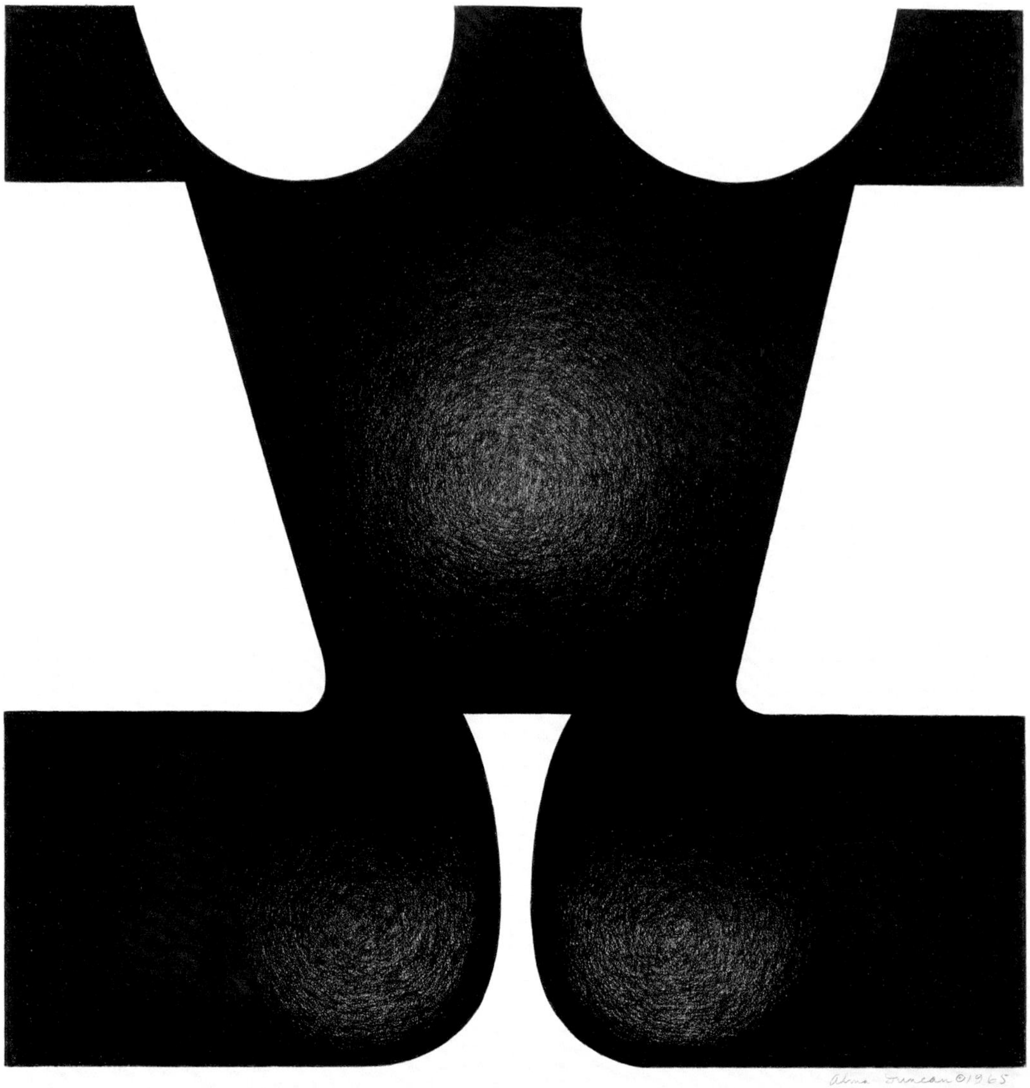

Woman Series – II | Série Femme – II 1965 (cat. 42)
Library and Archives Canada | Bibliothèque et Archives Canada

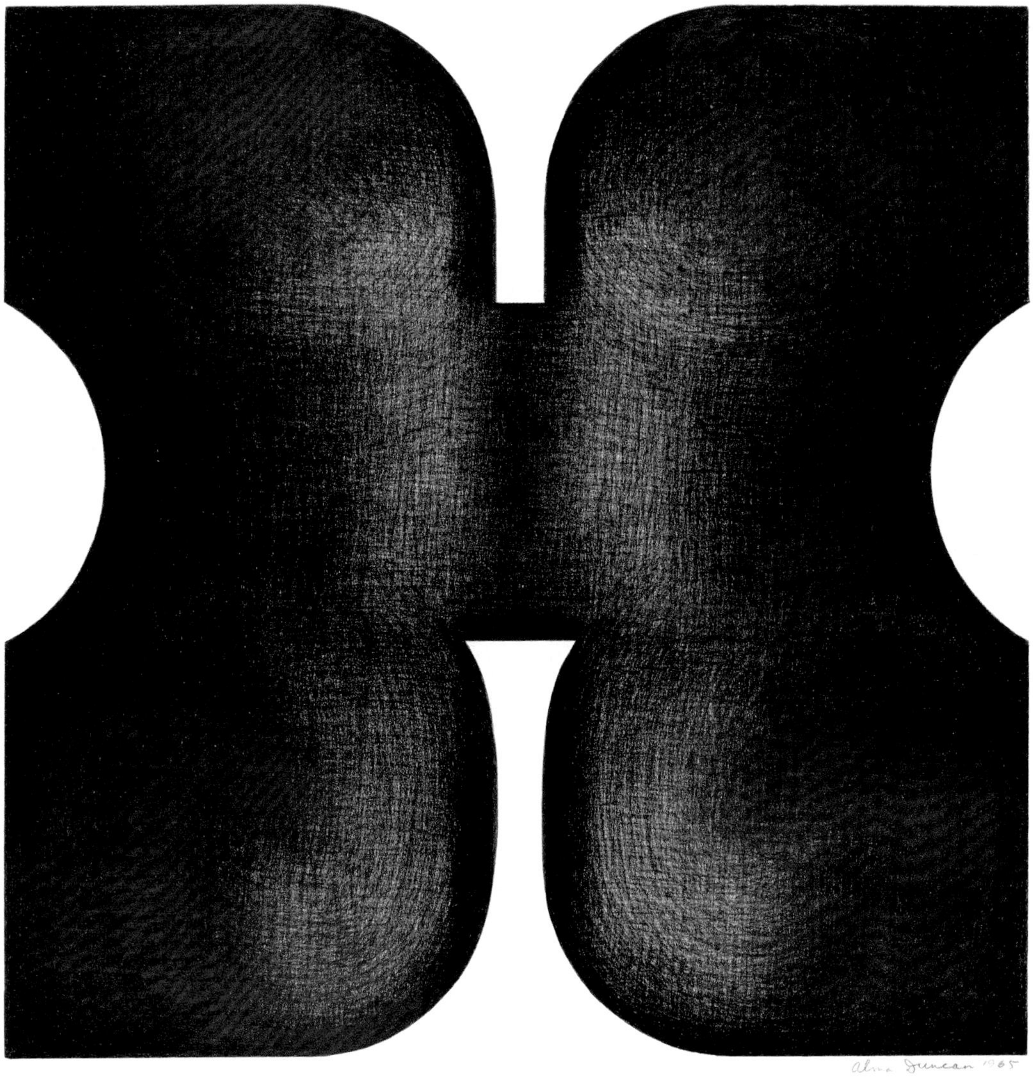

Woman Series – Square Torso | Série Femme – Torse carré 1965 (cat. 44)

Library and Archives Canada | Bibliothèque et Archives Canada

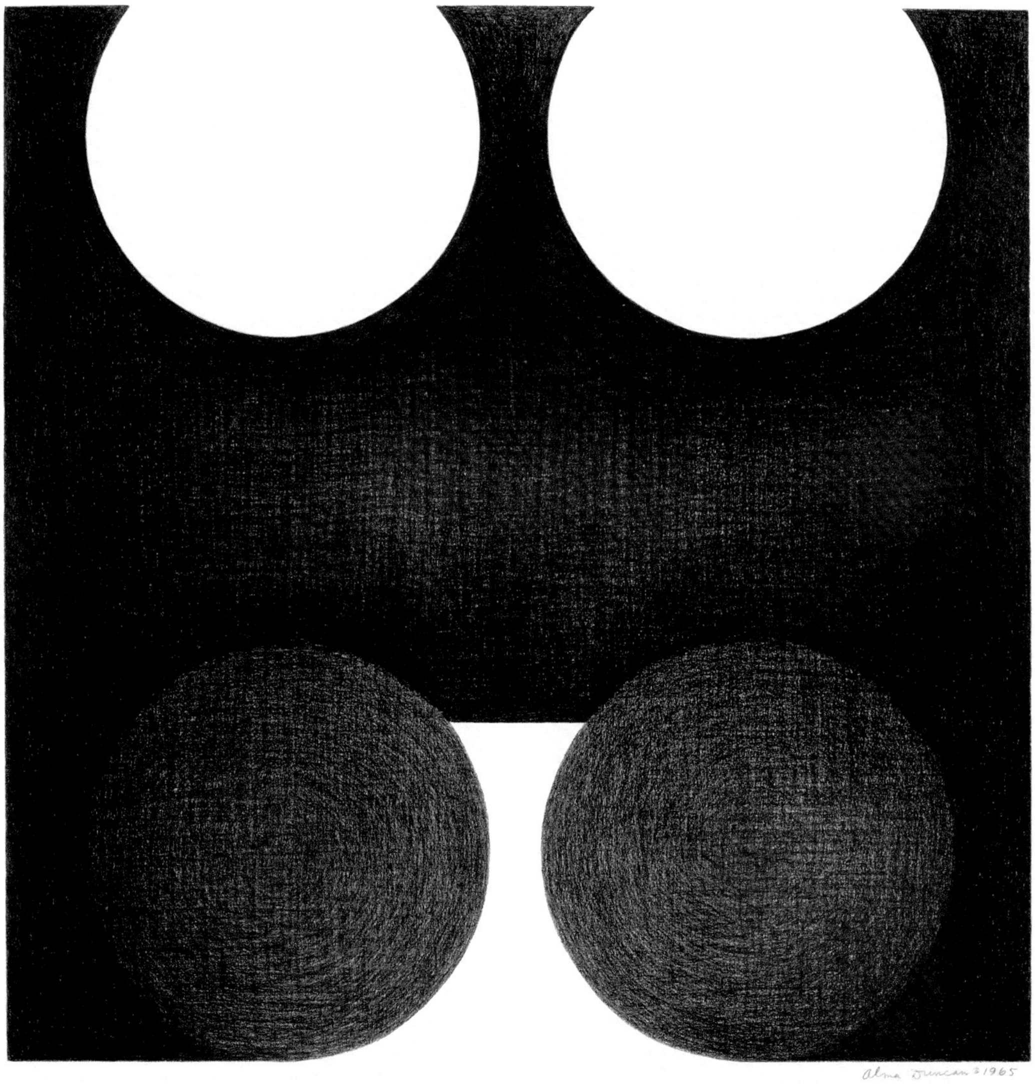

Woman Series – Matron | Série Femme – Madame 1965 (cat. 46)
Library and Archives Canada | Bibliothèque et Archives Canada

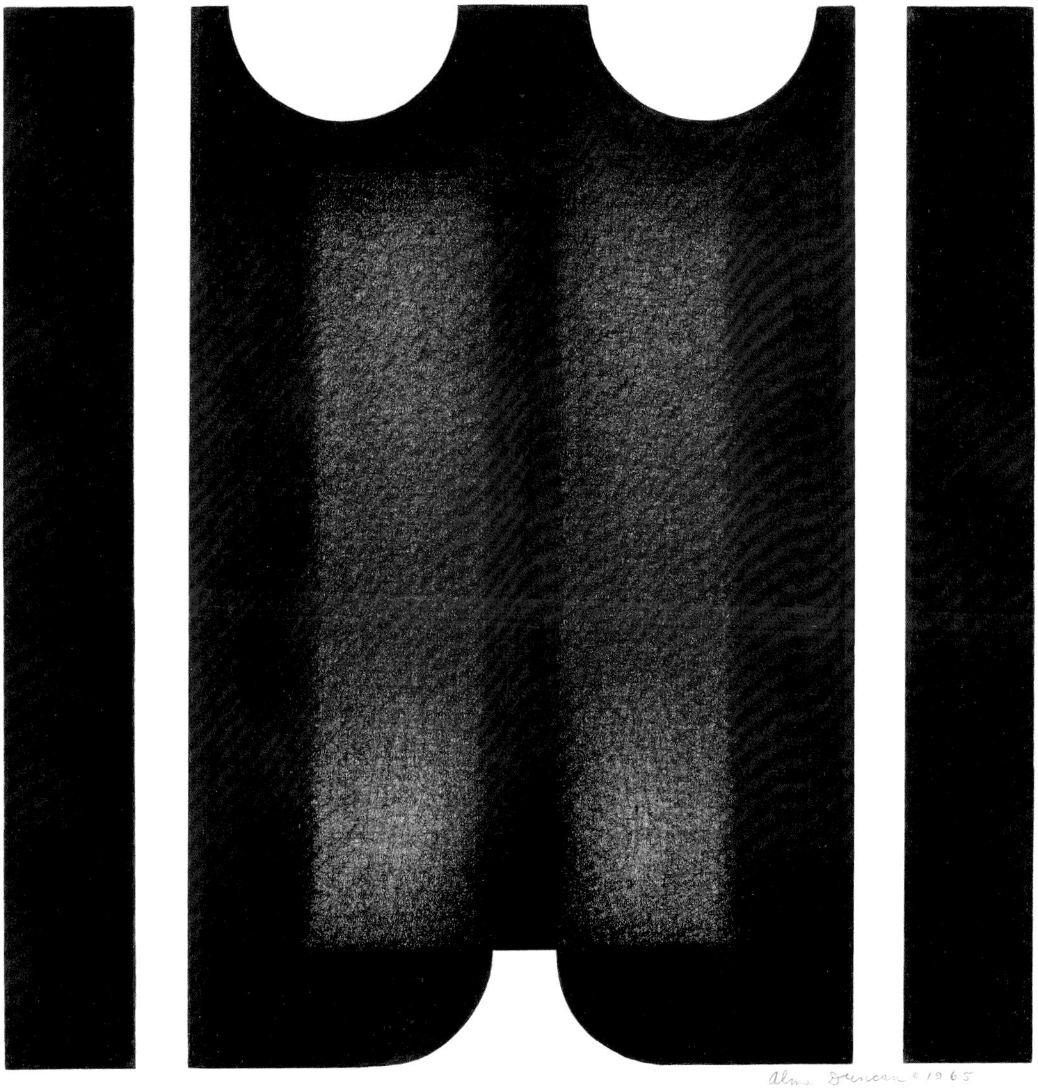

Woman Series – Maiden | Série Femme – Demoiselle 1965 (cat. 45)
Library and Archives Canada | Bibliothèque et Archives Canada

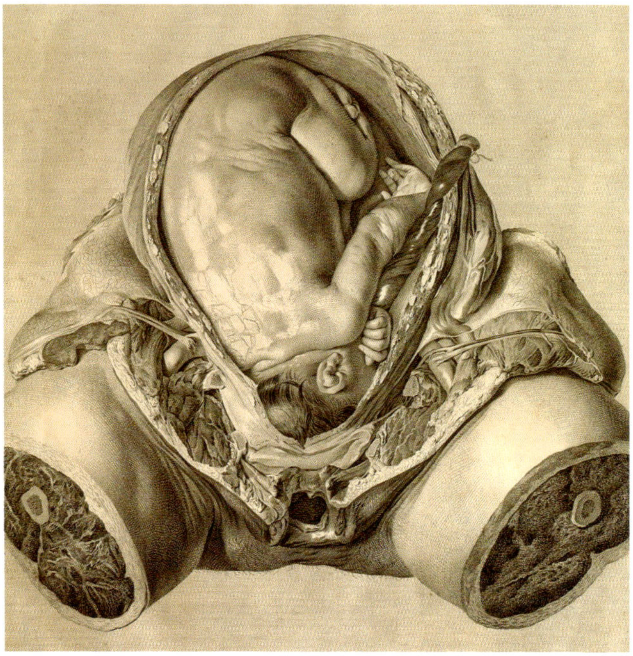

Jan van Riemsdyck, copperplate engraving, published in William Hunter, *The Anatomy of the Human Gravid Uterus*, Birmingham, 1774, courtesy of the US National Library of Medicine

Jan van Riemsdyck, gravure sur cuivre, publiée dans William Hunter, *Anatomie de l'utérus humain gravide*, Birmingham, 1774, gracieuseté de la US National Library of Medicine

ideals of motherhood, the breast, breast feeding, female responsibilities for healthy practices and the relegation of women to a domestic and nurturing role in the home."[5] Drawings of the mother's womb often referenced the deconstructed and sectional maternal body — a subject so famously depicted in Jan van Riemsdyck's drawing of a woman's truncated torso, with uterus, folded skin and suggested limbs, published in William Hunter's *Anatomy of the Human Gravid Uterus* (1774) (opposite).[6]

The female body is without doubt a loaded image. If we follow Janet Wolff's understanding of the second-wave feminist movement, and through it the politics of the domestic body, we recognize a stereotype connecting gender to the reproductive system. This stereotype is "largely a product of eighteenth and nineteenth century debates and ideologies"[7] in which women, because of their reproductive system, were viewed as closer to nature and more innately tied to the body than men. By contrast, men were connected to the soul/mind binary that has historically been associated with gender agency. In her writing, Wolff acknowledges the ways in which these preconceived stereotypes impacted the representation and reception of women in Western society; "[w]hen we recognize the great value put on the soul or the mind as against the body [...] the significance of the identification of women with the body is clear."[8] Undoubtedly influenced by these labels and associations, women artists working in the 1960s and 1970s found inspiration in these politics and incorporated empowerment and female emancipation as core themes in their work. As Wolff states, "Any body politics [...] must speak *about* the body, stressing its materiality and its social and discursive construction, at the same time as disrupting and subverting existing regimes of representation."[9]

In keeping with this, the *Woman Series* is a series of drawings that metaphorically and politically reconsiders the female body in Canadian modern art.

Like any woman artist working during the sixties, I will assume that Duncan was aware of the stirrings of the sexual revolution. For instance, works such as *Woman Series – Matron* (1965) and *Woman Series – Maiden* (1965) (cat. 46, p. 60 and cat. 45, p. 61) demonstrate that she was indeed exploring the *essential* woman in Western society. By creating these anonymous, truncated and headless bodies with such titles, the artist is stripping her depictions of women down to the idea that there is such a thing as "a" woman. Unlike the straight lines that characterize *Maiden* as a childlike rendering of a young woman with high breasts and a straight waist, *Matron* clearly suggests a mature woman's body with heavy breasts and broad hips. Through their titles, Duncan has linked this imagery to a critique of language and labeling. Moreover, I would posit that due to the closeness in time between Duncan's *Woman Series* and "dot" drawings (also from 1964), she was perhaps conscious of the relationship between the moon imagery of this latter series and the moon's traditional connection to menstrual cycles. Duncan's use of the circle in both these series evokes powerful feminine qualities and characteristics. Emphasized by the titles *Maiden* and *Matron*, the *Woman Series* drawings recall the ways in which women artists in Western society were materializing their feminist politics.

In the decades preceding the 1960s, Canadian Woman artists inserted themselves into all artistic movements. For example, Ghitta Caiserman and Paraskeva Clark began as Social Realists; Anne Savage and Florence Wyle were passionate about the national landscape æsthetic and mandate; and Marcelle Ferron and Rita Letendre embodied the trends of abstraction in Canada. Unique in theory and practice, Françoise Sullivan's *Dance in the Snow* (1948) figured as an interdisciplinary precursor to work that would overtly address the body two decades later. By the 1960s, Joyce Wieland was doing just this: renegotiating the gendered body. Wieland, a Toronto artist who moved to New York in 1962, like other protofeminist artists such as Louise Bourgeois and Eva Hesse, was creating work related to the female experience. To this day, Wieland remains an influential figure in contemporary art. She received national recognition in 1971 with the exhibition *True Patriot Love*, the National Gallery of Canada's first solo retrospective dedicated to the work of a woman artist.

Despite the rich feminist artistic activity that surrounded Duncan, she did not acknowledge its influence on her, or on her practice. Rather, she paid homage to abstraction. Duncan was a voracious student; she knew her art history. In a lecture in 1980, she references the Fauves, Henri Matisse and André Derain as examples of artists who "freed colour from its traditional role — to describe the colour of an object [...] on the way to colour as an expressive end in itself."[10] An avid traveller, she often returned to New York for artistic inspiration and kept up with current art theory. For example, in her notebook Duncan quotes the following excerpt from the article *The Primacy of Colour* (1964), in which critic Barbara Rose described the impact of Color Field painting on Washington-based painters: "Geometric painting can echo the underlying harmony of the universe, add optical stimulation to hard edge purity through pattern read as positive or negative."[11] In other notable mentions, Duncan singled out Karel Appel and Mark Rothko as quintessential abstract painters. She wrote that, "[Appel] would appear to be the antithesis of the great Rothko whose name comes to mind when I'm asked whose work I like but both relate to my experience, the physical one full of vitality [Appel] and the other transcendental [Rothko]."[12]

In terms of Canadian points of reference, Duncan was particularly taken by the Painters Eleven. After visiting an exhibition of their work in Ottawa in 1956, she credits the collective for influencing abstract painting in Canada: "Jack Bush, Oscar Cahén and William Ronald were among the eleven who were an important influence towards abstraction in Canada."[13] Duncan found Abstract Expressionism—in its lyrical and hard-edge formats and dynamic palette—the most inspiring work of the mid-twentieth century. In 1967, she emerged with a whole series of paintings where we directly see the influence of pure form and colour, such as *Untitled (Blue Tilt)* (1967) (cat. 55, opposite). In a 1966 lecture, Duncan said, " The artist works—not for decorative or storytelling reasons but for plastic reasons. He is concerned with the shapes in a purer way."[14] Clearly a modern artist at heart, it was colour, shape and scale that excited her. Duncan did engage in narrative creation through the subtle messages of her portraits, munitions drawings, puppets, and the explicit statement of her *Woman Series*. For instance, Duncan employed the form of her box-like torsos in two more series, *The Family* (1966) (cat. 47, p. 80 and cat. 48) and the *Lady Series* (1966–68) (cats. 49–52, pp. 72–74). The former are collage-on-canvas compositions that place three torsos into relation with one another: a male form and a female form with a child in its centre. That Duncan chose to depict the quintessential, nuclear family shows that the heteronormative model for the family was a reference point at this time. The *Lady Series* also mimics the shape of the *Woman Series*, but is done in watercolour and adds a textile pattern to each box-like torso. Duncan came by an interest in pattern honestly: her father, John Duncan, was a textile-firm engineer and so she grew up around textile factories. This background contributed to her interest in mixing realism with abstraction, and unlike the typically plainer forms of the *Woman Series*, the fabric patterns in these works add a personality to the body depicted. Duncan was evidently more interested in "storytelling" than she might have acknowledged in the sixties.

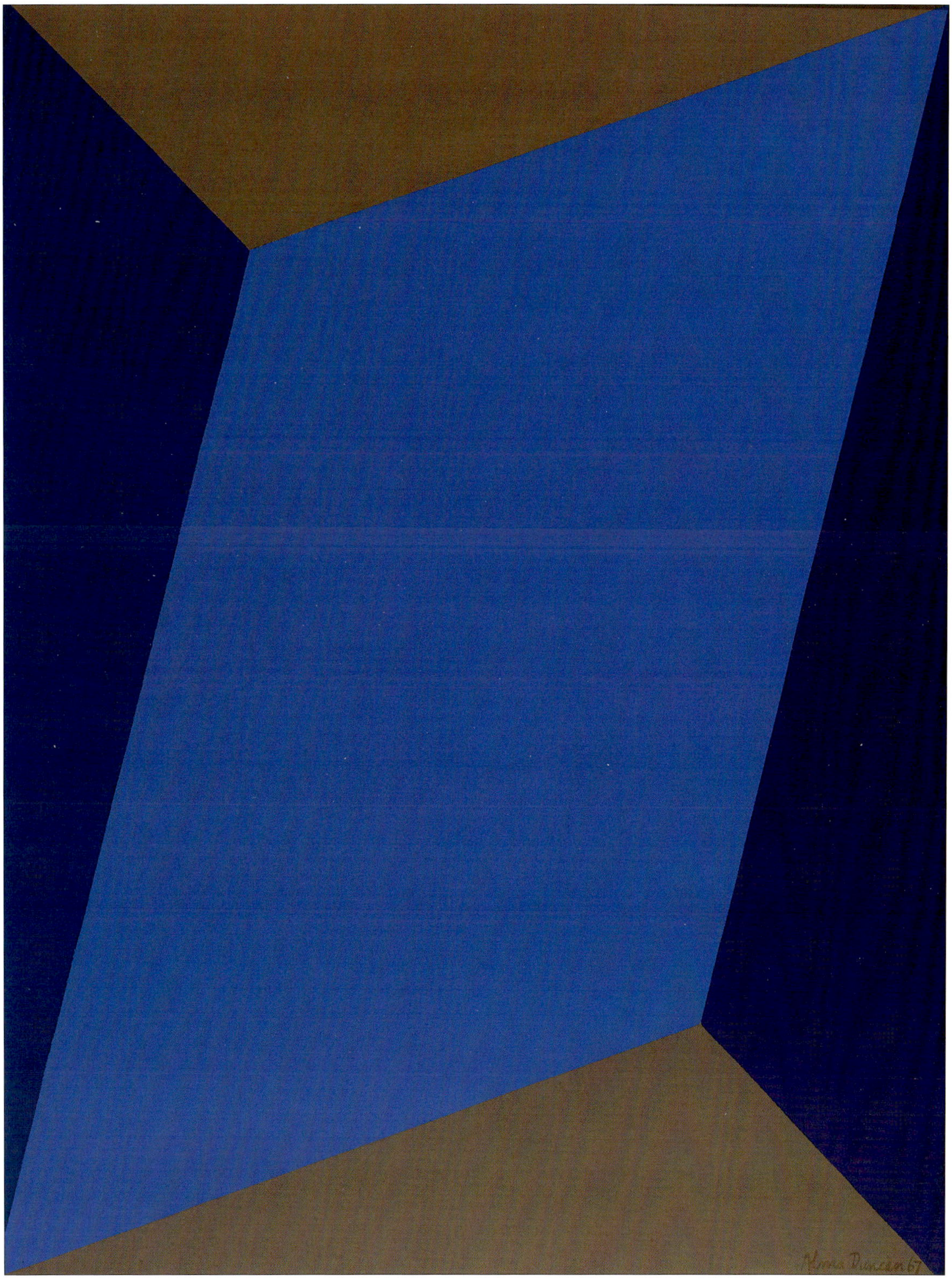

Untitled (Blue Tilt) | Sans titre (Inclinaison bleue) 1967 (cat. 55)
Courtesy of Renato Albino | Gracieuseté de Renato Albino

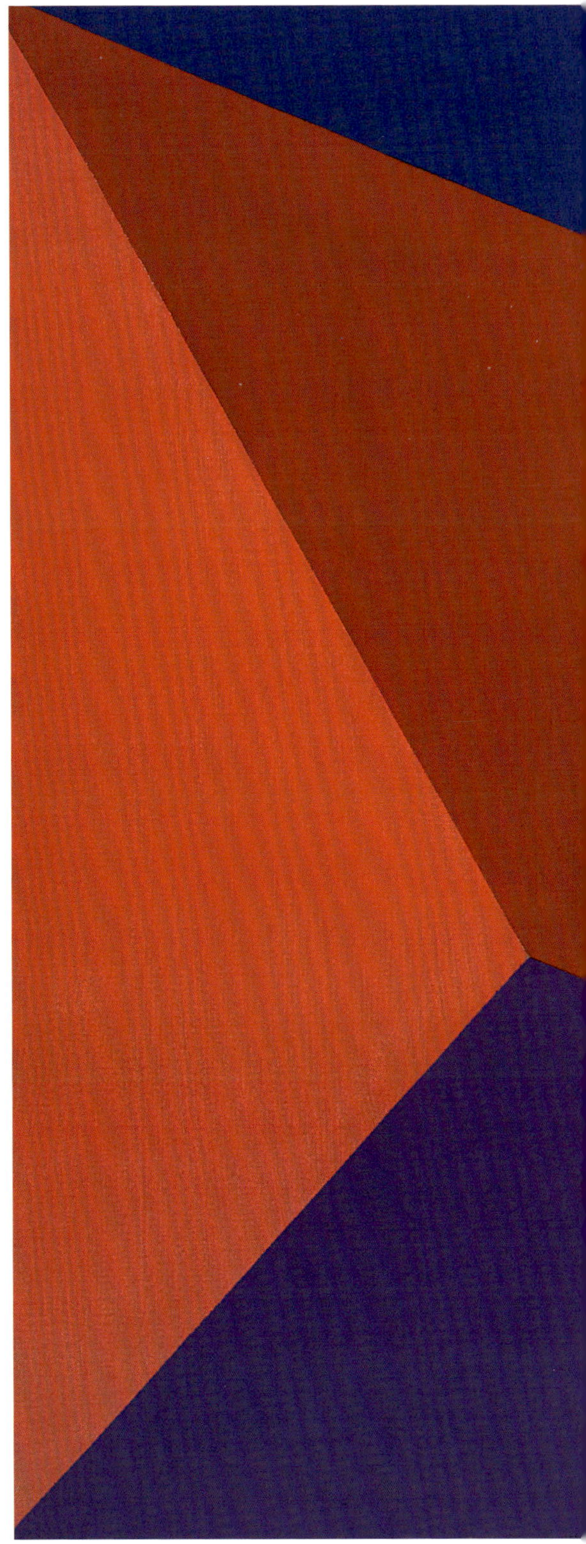

Untitled (Target) | Sans titre (Cible) 1967 (cat. 58)
Private Collection | Collection privée

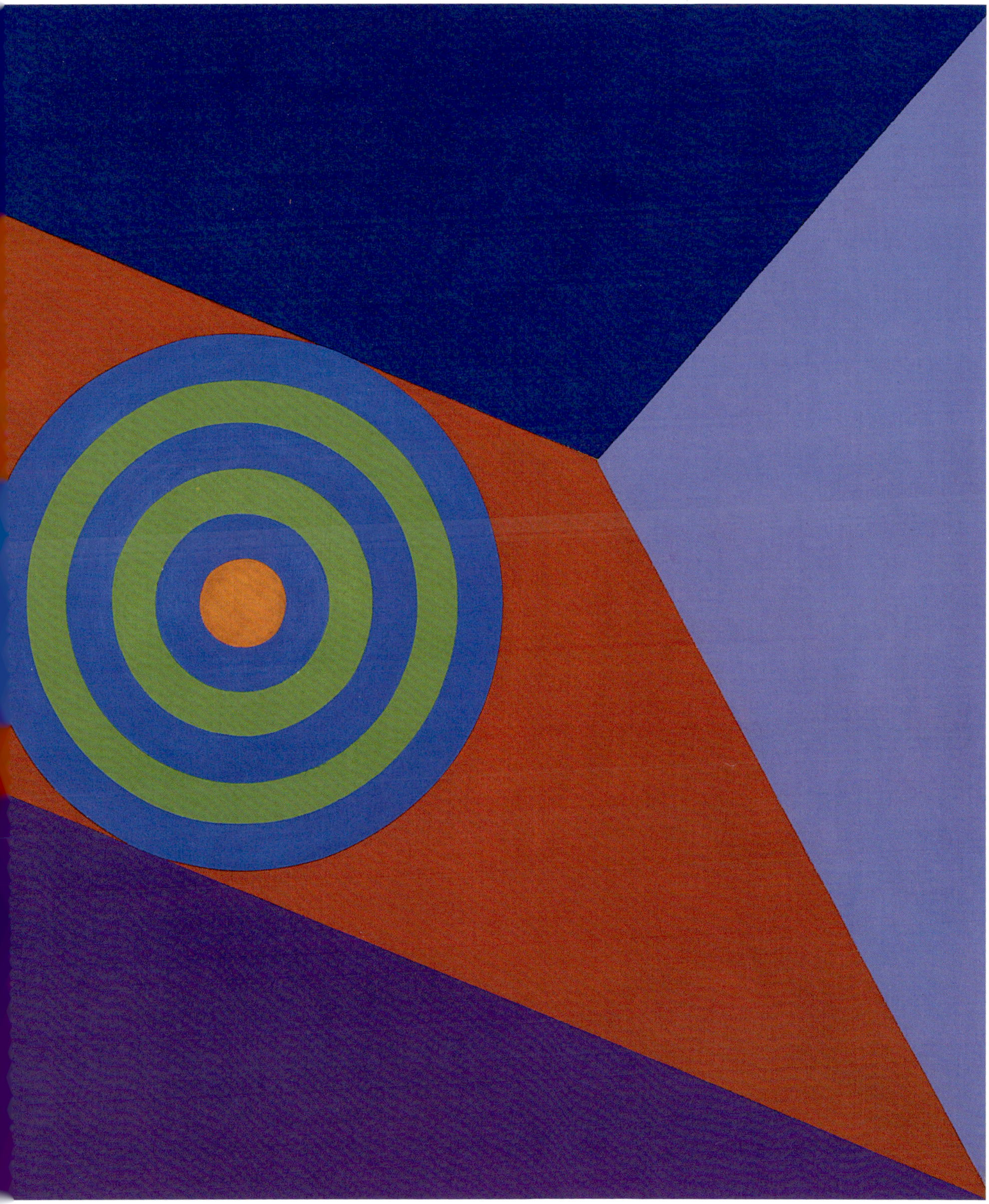

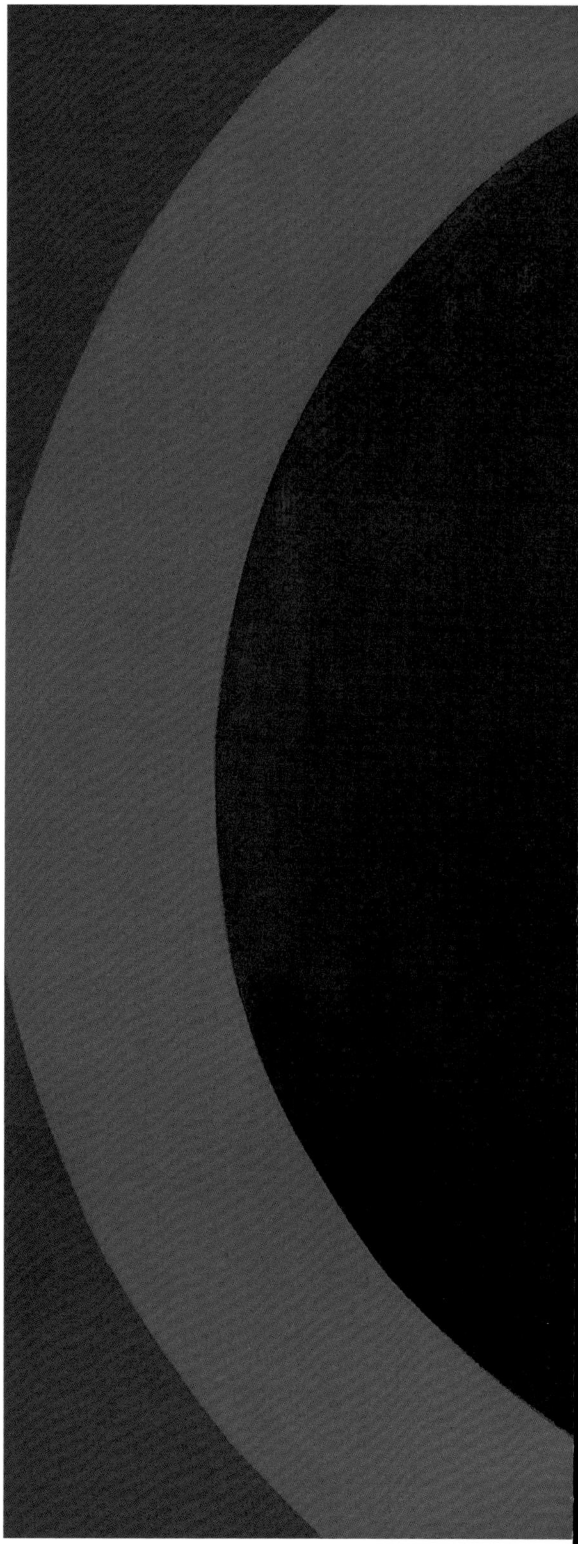

Untitled (Purple Circle) | Sans titre (Cercle violet) 1967 (cat. 59)
Courtesy of Renato Albino | Gracieuseté de Renato Albino

Contemporary feminist theory acknowledges the multiplicity of projects that grew out of the feminist movement. Misha Kavka states that such projects consist of "innumerable modes of doing—whether activist, practical, theoretical, or just 'quiet.'"[15] I see Duncan's contribution through the *Woman Series* as a project landing somewhere between Kavka's "activist" and "quiet." In the rest of her œuvre, her social commentaries exist, if only subtly. In the *Woman Series*, however, Duncan *actively* placed the women's essentialist roles on view for critique. Her direct dealing with such a politically loaded subject makes them an anomaly in her practice. In them, she frames and literally *cuts out* parts that distinguish the female body from that of the male. In doing so, she contributes to the deconstruction of normative views and the categorization of the female physical form, and as it changes with time. This contribution to Canadian feminist visual culture is also *quiet* insofar as she did not cite an overt allegiance to any cause. Yet despite her apparent lack of acknowledgement of the actual feminist movement, Duncan's works reference a time, a place, and a politic during which women artists were embodying an empowered sense of artistic freedom. As a result, Duncan's drawings make a strong statement about the stereotypes, prototypes, archetypes, and classifications in which women are placed. Therefore, in light of the multiple histories that make up the history of feminism (as described by theorists like Kavka), the postfeminist age rekindles a political need to identify what feminist activities and projects were about. Projects such as the *Woman Series* contributed to an overall culture that deconstructed notions such as the essential body, and this continues to inform today's feminism, showing why it is important to acknowledge the movement's history and to "tak[e] stock of where it has been."[16]

1 Joan Murray and Alma Duncan, " Tape Two," interview transcript, R.R.#2, Cumberland, ON, 13 February 1986, Babs McLaren personal archive, 7. **2** Alma Duncan, biographical notes, n.d., file "Biographies 1972–1992," box MG31 D245 15, 7, Library and Archives Canada, Ottawa (hereafter cited as LAC). **3** Two works, *Woman* (1964) and *Woman Series–Bouquet* (1965), were included in the exhibition *Canadian Water Colours, Drawings and Prints 1966*, held at the National Gallery of Canada and then circulated across Canada. *Donna della Serie 42* (c. 1965) was included in the international exhibition in Lugano, Switzerland, in 1966, and illustrated in the catalogue (see IX Mostra Internazionale di Bianco e Nero—Lugano, 8 Aprile–5 Giugno 1966). Works from this series also found their way into the collections of the Brooklyn Museum, the Canada Council Art Bank, and Museum London, to name a few. **4** Deanna Petherbridge, "Art and Anatomy: The Meeting of Text and Image," in *The Quick and the Dead: Artists and Anatomy* (Berkeley: University of California Press, 1997), 44. **5** Ibid., 85. **6** Ibid. **7** Janet Wolff, "Reinstating Corporeality: Feminism and Body Politics," in *The Feminism and Visual Culture Reader*, ed. Amelia Jones (London: Routledge, 2003), 417. **8** Ibid. **9** Ibid., 424. **10** Duncan, notes for "Arnprior Art Class," 1980, vol 3, file 20, LAC. **11** Duncan, file "Notebook 1957–1964 1/6", box MG31 D245 9, LAC. Curator Sue Scott describes that "In a 1964 article entitled 'The Primacy of Color,' critic Barbara Rose outlined what she considered to be the fundamental reasons for the emergence of this 'new sensibility,'—color field painting which included the work of the Washington painters. According to Rose, four factors played a role in influencing the rise of this new sensibility. These were 1) the opticality of works by Barnett Newman, Ad Reinhardt and Mark Rothko; works which engaged the eye rather than the mind, 2) the works and writings of Josef Albers on the use of complementary and discordant colors 3) Matisse's découpés published and later exhibited at the Museum of Modern Art and 4) the development of plastic-based paints which allowed experiments with technique as well as a broader palette of colors from which to choose." Sue Scott, "Washington Color Painters: The First Generation" (Orlando, FL: Orlando Museum of Art, 2014), www.suescottgallery.com, retrieved May 8, 2014. **12** Duncan, biographical notes, n.d., file "Biographies 1972–1992", box MG31 D245 15, 7, LAC. **13** Ibid. **14** Duncan, lecture notes "Talk on 'Collag' [sic] to Nat. Gall. Assoc.," 17 April 1966, vol 3, file 18 "Talk on Collage with demonstration for National Gallery Association," LAC. **15** Misha Kavka, "Introduction," in *Feminist Consequences: Theory for a New Century*, eds. Elisabeth Bronfen and Misha Kavka (New York: Columbia University Press, 2001), 11. **16** Ibid., 12.

Catherine Sinclair is Senior Curator at the Ottawa Art Gallery (OAG). She earned a Master's Degree in Canadian Art History from Carleton University (Ottawa) in 2006. At the OAG, she has contributed essays to numerous exhibition catalogues, including most recently *Natural Motif: Lorraine Gilbert and Natasha Mazurka* (2013) and *Pat Durr: Persistence of Chaos* (2012), and curated many exhibitions, such as *Sell Out?* (2013), *Explode: Marcelle Ferron and Rita Letendre* (2013), *Wally Dion: Star Blankets* (2011), and *Wyse Works: Exposing the Inevitable* (2011). Furthermore, she has presented on a variety of Canadian art historical topics in forums including the University Art Association Conference (UAAC) (Concordia University, Montreal, 2012), the Magnetic North Theatre Festival (Ottawa, 2011), an Ontario Association of Art Galleries (OAAG) panel at the Art Gallery of Hamilton (2011), the University of Ottawa (2009), and the Canadian Women Artists History Initiative Conference (CWAHI) (Concordia University, Montreal, 2008 and 2015).

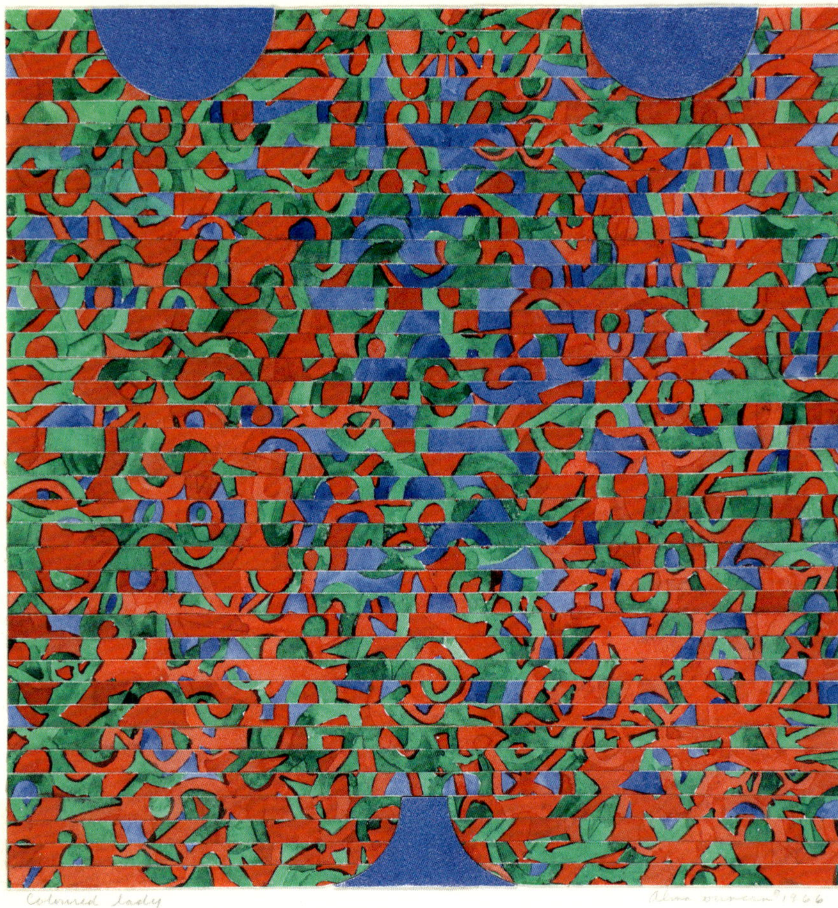

Coloured Lady | Dame de couleur 1966 (cat. 49)
Library and Archives Canada | Bibliothèque et Archives Canada

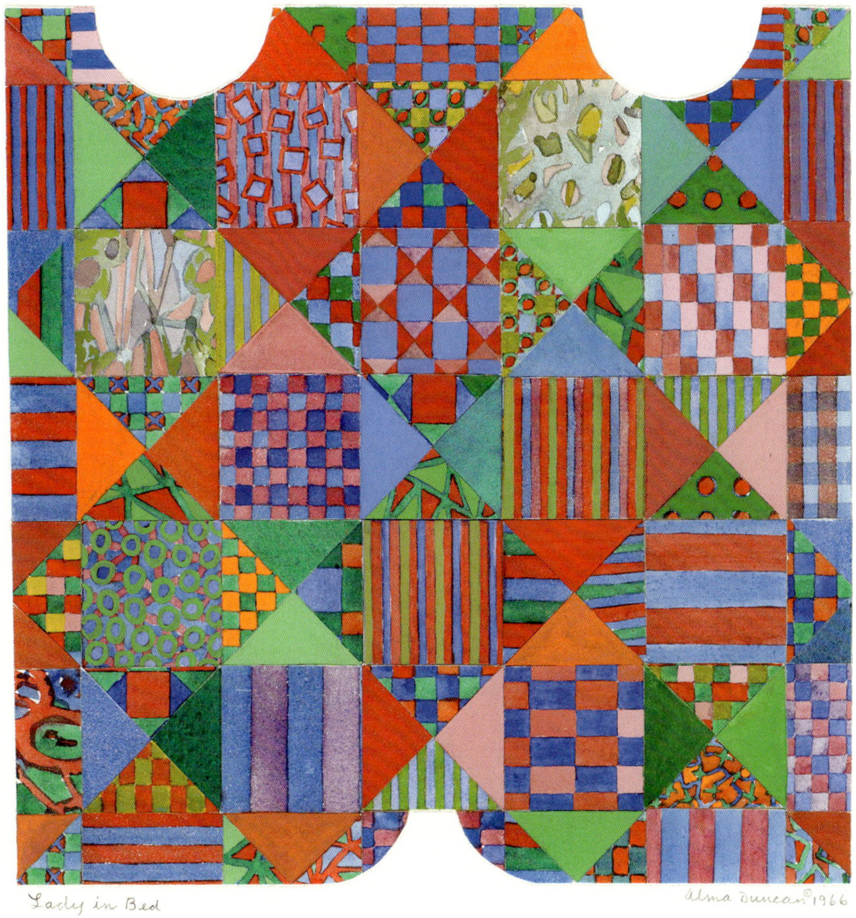

Lady in Bed | Dame au lit 1966 (cat. 50)
Library and Archives Canada | Bibliothèque et Archives Canada

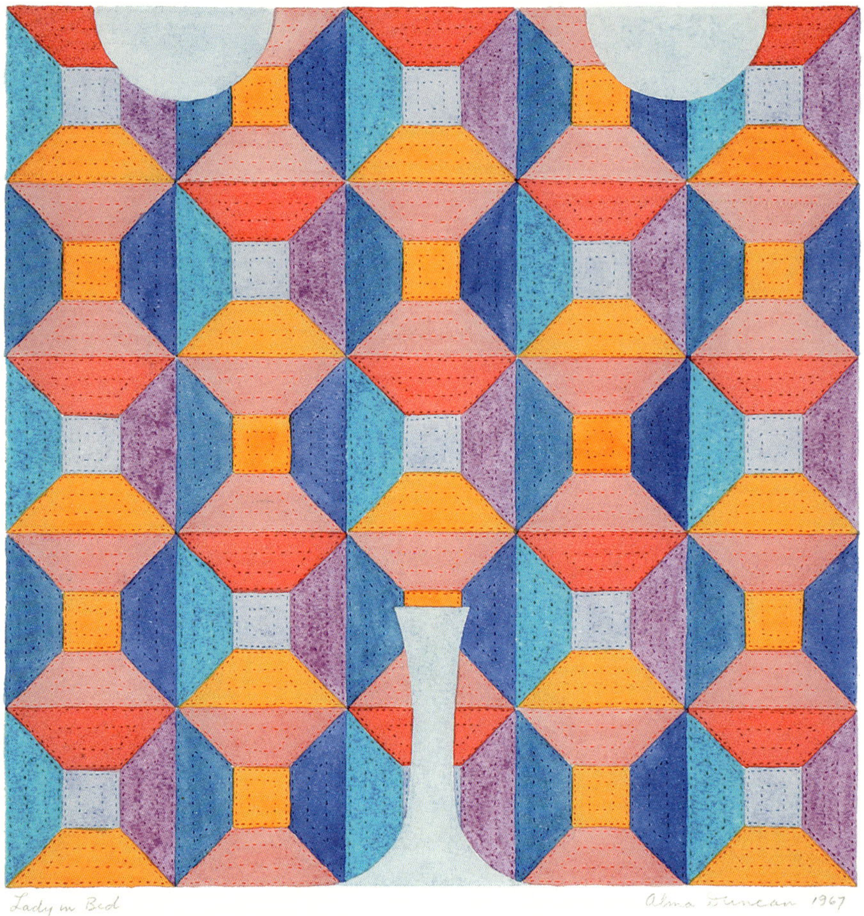

Lady in Bed | Dame au lit 1967 (cat. 52)
Courtesy of Brian Oickle | Gracieuseté de Brian Oickle

Encercler l'essentiel

Alma Duncan, l'abstraction et le féminisme discret

Catherine Sinclair

J'ai un faible pour les artistes canadiennes de l'après-guerre. Je trouve fascinant de voir le milieu de l'art au Canada, alors en plein changement, a été marqué par lesqui évoluaient dans un monde encore très masculin. Il leur fallait négocier le partage des responsabilités familiales, lutter pour se faire reconnaître à l'école d'art et demeurer pertinentes dans leur pratique artistique. Travaillant dans un environnement contemporain, je suis très consciente que les praticiennes et les professionnelles d'aujourd'hui sont encore influencées par les batailles qu'elles ont livrées. À cette époque, comme plusieurs femmes artistes de sa génération, Alma Duncan a contourné de nombreuses barrières sociales et de genres, que ce soit en dessinant dans des usines de munitions ou en travaillant à l'Office national du film du Canada. Ce que je trouve le plus curieux, c'est que Duncan ne s'est jamais identifiée comme féministe, bien qu'elle ait eu l'audace de déconstruire le corps féminin dans la *Série Femme*, une collection de dessins abstraits qui reflètent des préoccupations plus larges concernant les rôles domestique, sexuel et politique qui, aujourd'hui encore, cantonnent dans des stéréotypes les femmes artistes ou professionnelles.

La collection permanente de la Galerie d'art d'Ottawa comprend quatre portraits réalisés par cette artiste d'Ottawa. Dans *Autoportrait* (1943) (cat. 11, p. 102), mon préféré, Duncan se représente en jeune femme artiste jolie et pleine d'assurance. Lorsque Jaclyn Meloche et moi avons commencé à passer en revue ses œuvres pour monter cette exposition, j'ai découvert le corpus varié d'une artiste énergétique et prolifique. Outre ses portraits bien exécutés, Duncan pouvait rivaliser avec les meilleurs dessinateurs du pays; elle avait le sang-froid nécessaire pour se coiffer d'un casque et dessiner dans des fabriques de munitions et des usines industrielles; elle avait le talent ainsi que la volonté créatrice de monter de courts films d'animation image par image avec marionnettes à partir de rien.

Dans toute la variété de son travail, c'est sa manière de brouiller la frontière entre la représentation et l'abstraction qui m'a le plus frappée. C'est pour cette raison que j'ai su, en trouvant les grands et puissants dessins en noir et blanc de la *Série Femme* à Bibliothèque et Archives Canada, que nous étions tombées sur quelque chose d'extraordinaire. Simples et forts, ces dessins sont exécutés au crayon conté noir sur du papier blanc. Ils présentent des formes géométriques anthropomorphiques qui oscillent entre réalisme et abstraction, et qui, dans leur exploration de l'incarnation physique du corps féminin, sont truffés de significations conceptuelles.

La *Série Femme* de Duncan reflète les premiers remous de la deuxième vague de la révolution féministe, qui débuta dans les années 1960. Alors que la première vague, au tournant du siècle, s'articule autour du mouvement des suffragettes et de l'égalité des sexes, la deuxième vague se concentre plutôt sur la libération sexuelle et les enjeux politiques liés au corps. Des artistes féministes commencent à créer des œuvres qui s'élèvent contre les normes sociétales patriarcales. À l'époque, cependant, Duncan ne mentionne aucune influence féministe dans sa recherche, son œuvre ou ses écrits. Elle se concentre plutôt sur l'importance de la plasticité, portant une grande attention à la théorie de la couleur des expressionnistes abstraits. Pourtant, malgré cette absence d'adhésion à un objectif féministe formel, je considère que *Série Femme* de Duncan est sa déclaration féministe la plus ouverte, campée fermement au sein du féminisme de la deuxième vague, et représentative de la contribution discrète de l'artiste à la culture visuelle féministe du milieu du vingtième siècle.

C'est au début des années 1940 que Duncan a commencé à explorer les qualités expressives de la ligne et de la forme. Des œuvres telles que *Riveurs dans un atelier de montage de chaudières* (1943) (cat. 16, p. 42), effectuées à la craie, représentent des ouvriers au travail dans des usines de munitions et constituent sa première série de « dessins de munitions ». La commissaire Joan Murray les a très bien décrites en 1987 dans son catalogue d'exposition : plusieurs de ces œuvres présentent une « structure complexe en équilibre entre l'abstraction et le réalisme »[1]. Cependant, Duncan ne se lancera dans l'abstraction que dans les années 1960. Selon ses dires : « Les années 1960 étaient une époque merveilleuse pour l'expérimentation, et furent à l'origine de bien des choses »[2].

En 1964, année où elle crée la *Série Femme*, Duncan a 47 ans et habite la rue Somerset à Ottawa; elle passe cependant ses étés à Windrush, une demeure près de Galetta dans le haut de la vallée de l'Outaouais. Elle commence cette même année à combiner le réalisme et l'abstraction dans une série qu'elle nomme « dessins en pointillé », de délicates représentations à l'encre et à la plume de corps célestes flottant dans l'espace ou dans des paysages diffus. Un des dessins de cette série, *Sans titre n° 1* (1964) (cat. 39, p. 26), est la première œuvre de Duncan acquise par la Galerie nationale du Canada (ancien nom du Musée des beaux-arts du Canada). À cette époque, ses expériences avec la forme tournent surtout autour du cercle. Apparaissant dans ses dessins en pointillé, le cercle figure aussi dans les blocs à formes géométriques de la *Série Femme*, où il sert à représenter les principaux contours du corps féminin, comme on peut le voir dans *Série Femme – II* (1965) (cat. 42, p. 58). À l'instar des dessins en pointillé, la *Série Femme* obtiendra elle aussi une reconnaissance nationale et internationale[3]. Pourtant, la *Série Femme* se distingue largement du travail précédent de Duncan, tant par son usage de l'abstraction géométrique que par son expressivité conceptuelle.

La forme humaine est le premier sujet de Duncan, et elle y retourne souvent au fil des ans, dans ses portraits, autoportraits et marionnettes. En 1936, âgée de 19 ans, elle déménage à Montréal afin d'étudier l'économie politique à l'Université McGill. Elle y reste sept ans, jusqu'en 1943, et s'organise pour aller pendant l'été faire des croquis figuratifs dans les laboratoires d'anatomie de l'école de médecine. Quand elle conçoit la *Série Femme* en 1964, Duncan dessine le corps humain, sous forme de portrait et d'après modèles, depuis plus de vingt-cinq ans déjà. Cette série représente néanmoins sa première tentative de conceptualisation du corps et, plus précisément, du corps féminin.

Il est assez aisé de faire le lien entre les croquis effectués dans les laboratoires d'anatomie de la fin des années 1930 et les corps abstraits de la *Série Femme*. Par exemple, par leurs titres et leur sujet, *Série Femme – Torse carré* (1965) et *Série Femme – Torse* (1965) (cat. 44, p. 59 et 43, p. 54) rappellent de façon déroutante les cadavres tronqués que l'on pourrait trouver dans de tels laboratoires. Duncan suggère très réellement le corps humain féminin, évoquant les seins, la taille, les hanches, le triangle du pubis et les cuisses rondes. En présentant ainsi une forme féminine « universelle », ces dessins sont liés à l'histoire du débat « essentialiste », qui fut défait par le féminisme deuxième vague.

Les dessins de Duncan rappellent les dissections du corps humain que l'on retrouve ailleurs dans l'art occidental, particulièrement dans les célèbres tableaux peints au XVe et au XVIe siècles par Michel Ange et Léonard de Vinci. Ces « artistes-anatomistes » conservaient dans leur studio des squelettes et des crânes humains, et fabriquaient des modèles en cire de muscles dans diverses poses. Ces toiles n'étaient pas montrées au public vu leur nature préparatoire et à cause de tabous entourant les cadavres, mais elles démontrent l'intérêt scientifique qui est porté au corps à l'époque de la Renaissance italienne. De Vinci voyait notamment le corps comme « la mesure de toutes choses »[4]. Or, au XVIIIe siècle, l'intérêt scientifique porté à l'anatomie humaine devient synonyme de la représentation de la division des sexes. Selon l'historienne de l'art Deanna Petherbridge, « l'anatomie comparative des sexes devint très importante au XVIIIe siècle, de concert avec de nouveaux idéaux sur la maternité, les seins, l'allaitement, la responsabilité des femmes en matière d'habitudes de vie saines et leur confinement au rôle domestique des soins et de la maison »[5]. Des dessins de l'utérus maternel montrent souvent un corps de mère déconstruit et présenté en sections – un sujet bien illustré par Jan van Riemsdyck dans son célèbre dessin d'un torse de femme tronqué, avec un utérus, de la peau repliée et des cuisses amputées, publié dans *Anatomy of the Human Gravid Uterus* [Anatomie de l'utérus humain gravide] (1774) (voir p. 62) de William Hunter.

Le corps féminin est sans aucun doute une image lourde de sens. Dans son analyse du mouvement féministe de la deuxième vague – et des politiques liées au corps domestique qui l'accompagnent – Janet Wolff souligne le stéréotype qui relie le sexe au système reproductif. Ce stéréotype est « en grande partie le résultat des débats et idéologies des XVIIIe et XIXe siècles »[6] où les femmes, en raison de leur système reproductif, sont considérées comme étant plus près de la nature et ayant un rapport au corps plus inné que les hommes. En revanche, la division des genres traditionnelle veut que les hommes soient attachés à la relation âme/esprit. Dans ses écrits, Wolff admet que ces idées reçues ont eu un impact sur la façon dont les femmes sont représentées et perçues dans la société occidentale : « Quand on reconnaît que la valeur attribuée à l'âme ou à l'esprit est en opposition à celle du corps, la signification du rapport de la femme au corps est évidente »[7]. Les femmes artistes actives dans les années 1960 et 1970, sans doute influencées par ces étiquettes et ces idées, ont puisé leur inspiration dans les politiques de l'époque et ont incorporé la prise en charge et l'émancipation de la femme comme autant de thèmes au cœur de leur travail. Comme l'indique Wolff, « toute politique du corps [...] se doit de *parler du corps*, en mettant l'accent sur sa matérialité et les constructions sociales et discursives qui l'entourent, tout en bousculant et en renversant les modes de représentation actuels »[8]. En accord avec ces idées, la *Série Femme* propose un ensemble de dessins qui réexaminent, de manière métaphorique et politique, le corps féminin dans l'art moderne canadien.

Je présume que Duncan, comme n'importe quelle femme artiste évoluant dans les années 1960, était au courant des premiers signes de la révolution sexuelle. Des œuvres telles que *Série Femme – Madame* (1965) et *Série Femme – Demoiselle* (1965) (cat. 46, p. 60 et cat. 45, p. 61) démontrent bel et bien qu'elle explorait l'idée de l'*essence* de la femme dans la société occidentale. En représentant des corps anonymes tronqués et sans tête, et en les intitulant ainsi, l'artiste réduit ses images de femmes à l'idée improbable de « la » femme. À la différence des lignes droites qui font de *Demoiselle* la représentation enfantine d'une jeune femme aux seins hauts et à la taille droite, *Madame* suggère nettement le corps d'une femme mature, avec des seins lourds et des hanches larges. Par l'entremise de leurs titres, Duncan relie ces images à une critique du langage et des étiquettes. De plus, étant donné la proximité temporelle entre la *Série Femme* et les dessins en pointillé (aussi créés en 1964), j'imagine que Duncan consciente du lien entre les images de la lune de cette série et le rôle traditionnel de la lune dans les cycles menstruels. L'usage que Duncan fait du cercle dans ces deux séries suggère des qualités et des caractéristiques féminines puissantes. Couronnés de titres tels que *Demoiselle* et *Madame*, les dessins de la série *Femme* rappellent la façon dont les femmes artistes dans la société occidentale exprimaient alors leurs idées féministes.

Au cours des décennies précédant les années 1960, les artistes canadiennes s'étaient insérées dans tous les mouvements artistiques. Ghitta Caiserman et Paraskeva Clark, par exemple, firent leurs débuts parmi les socioréalistes, Anne Savage et Florence Wyle se passionnaient pour l'esthétique du paysage canadien et affirmaient la nécessité de le dépeindre, alors que Marcelle Ferron et Rita Letendre représentaient la tendance de l'abstraction au Canada. Unique sur le plan des idées et de la pratique, Françoise Sullivan, avec sa vidéo *Danse dans la neige* (1948), apparaît comme une artiste interdisciplinaire précurseure de celles qui traiteront ouvertement du corps vingt ans plus tard. C'est ce que fera Joyce Wieland dans les années 1960 : reconsidérer le corps sexué. Wieland, artiste torontoise qui s'est installée à New York en 1962, créait des œuvres reliées à l'expérience féminine, comme le faisaient d'autres artistes protoféministes telles que Louise Bourgeois et Eva Hesse. Encore aujourd'hui, Wieland est une figure de proue de l'art contemporain. Elle s'est fait connaître à l'échelle nationale en 1971 avec l'exposition *Véritable amour patriotique*, la première rétrospective que le Musée des beaux-arts du Canada consacre à une femme.

Malgré le foisonnement des activités féministes qui animent son environnement, Duncan ne reconnaît pas leur influence sur elle ou sur sa pratique; elle rend plutôt hommage à l'abstraction. Duncan était une étudiante avide et connaissait bien l'histoire de l'art. Elle mentionne, dans une conférence qu'elle donne en 1980, les Fauves, Henri Matisse et André Derain comme des artistes ayant « libéré la couleur de son rôle traditionnel – celui de décrire la couleur d'un objet [...] – vers la couleur comme moyen d'expression en soi »[9]. Elle est une voyageuse passionnée et retourne souvent à New York

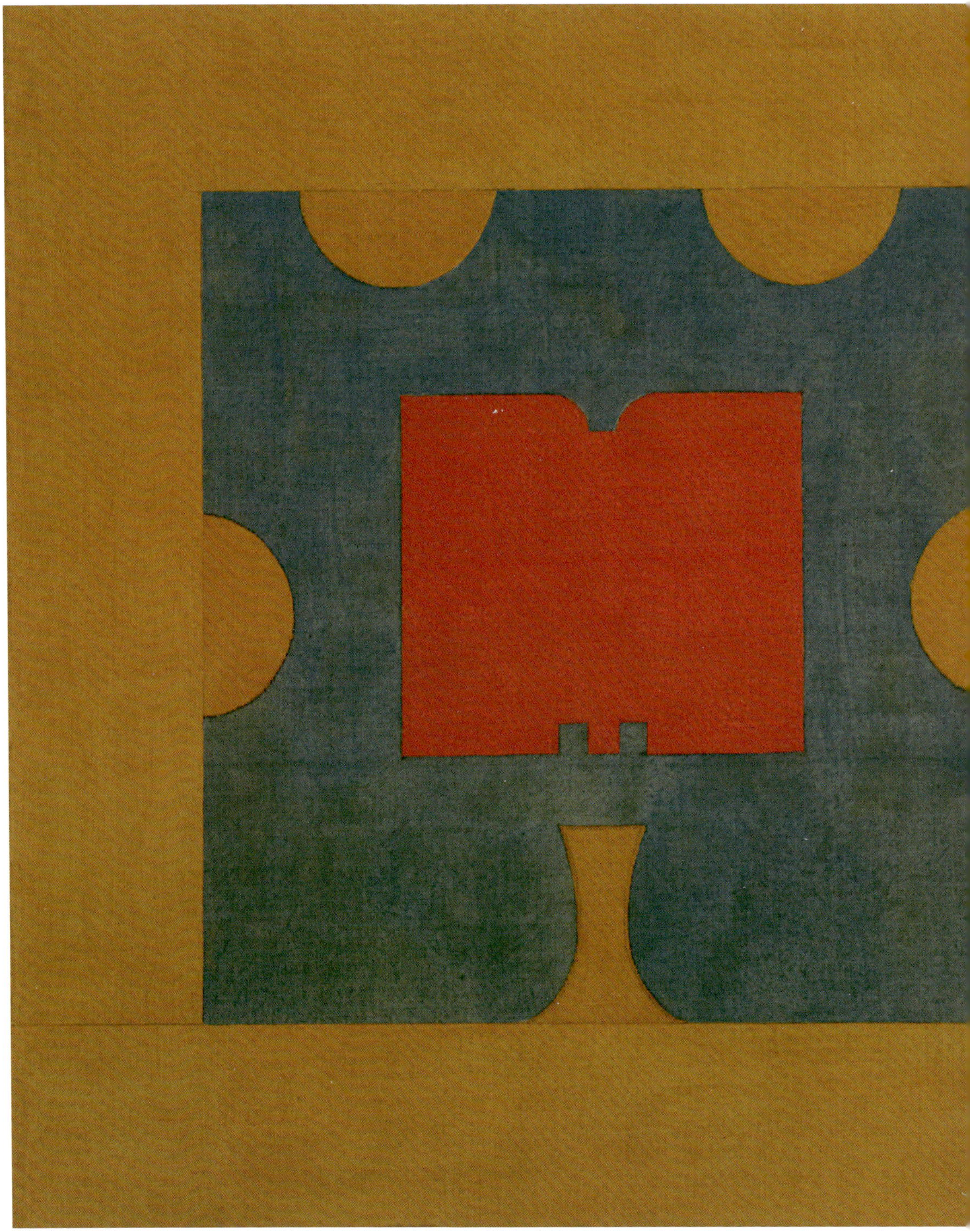

The Family | La famille 1966 (cat. 47)
Private Collection | Collection privée

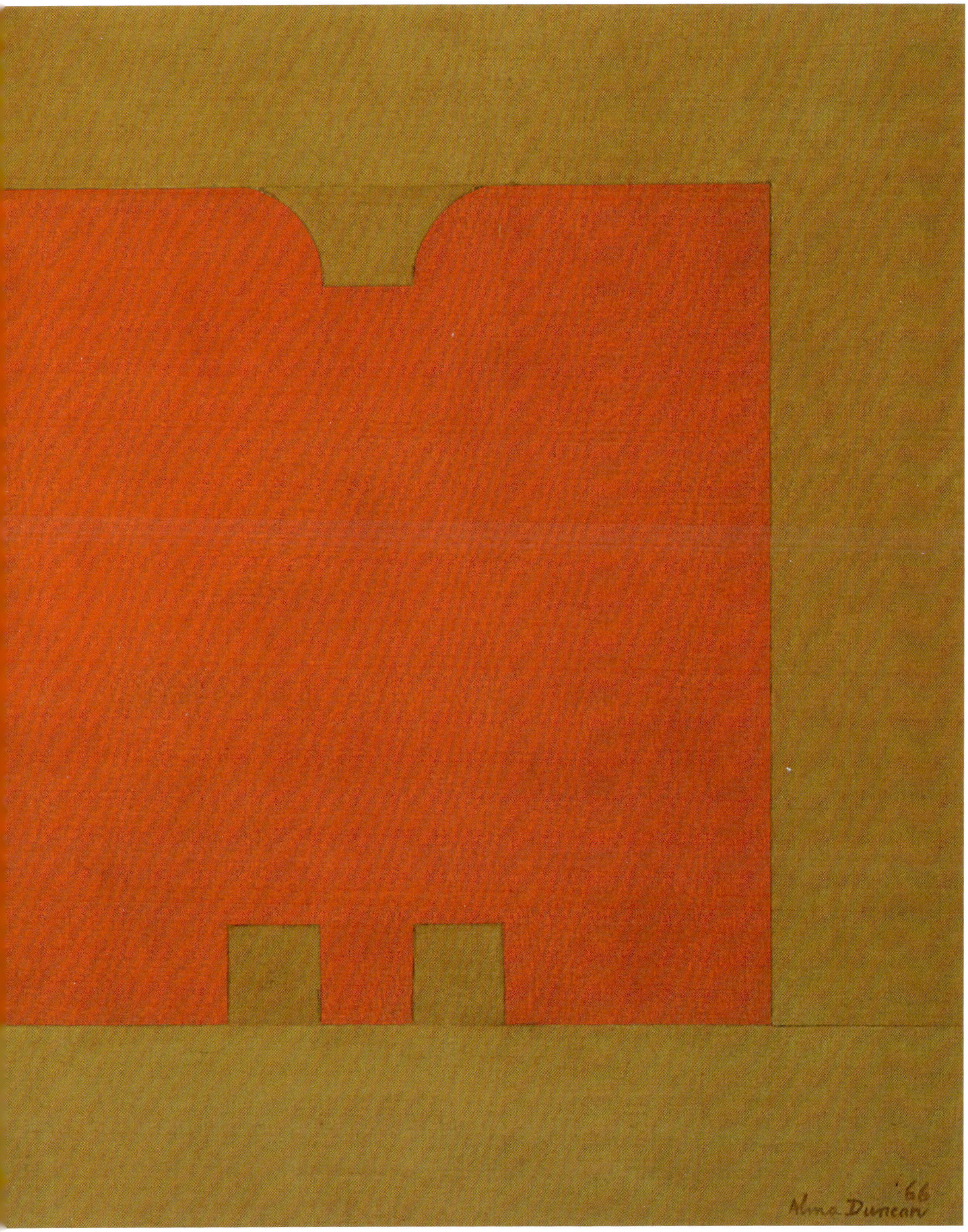
'66
Alma Duncan

y puiser de l'inspiration; elle se tient aussi au courant des nouvelles théories de l'art. Par exemple, elle note dans son carnet l'extrait suivant de l'article *The Primacy of Color* [La primauté de la couleur] (1964), où la critique Barbara Rose décrit l'impact de la peinture « color field » sur les peintres de Washington : « La peinture géométrique peut faire écho à l'harmonie sous-jacente de l'univers, ajouter des stimulations optiques à la pureté du hard-edge par le biais de motifs interprétés comme positifs ou négatifs »[10]. Dans d'autres commentaires dignes de mention, Duncan souligne que Karel Appel et Mark Rothko sont des peintres abstraits exemplaires. Elle écrit que « [Appel] peut sembler être à l'antipode du grand Rothko, dont le nom me vient toujours à l'esprit quand on me demande quel travail j'aime, mais les deux me rappellent mon expérience, l'une physique, pleine de vitalité [Appel], et l'autre transcendantale [Rothko] »[11].

En matière de références canadiennes, Duncan appréciait particulièrement le Groupe des Onze. Après avoir vu une de leurs expositions à Ottawa en 1956, elle attribue à ces peintres le mérite d'avoir influencé la peinture abstraite au Canada : « Jack Bush, Oscar Cahén et William Ronald font partie des onze qui ont exercé une influence importante vers l'abstraction au Canada »[12]. Duncan considérait que l'expressionnisme abstrait – dans ses manifestations tant lyriques que hard-edge et avec sa palette dynamique – produisait les œuvres les plus inspirantes du milieu du XXe siècle. En 1967, elle émerge avec une toute nouvelle série de toiles où l'on constate nettement l'influence de la couleur et de la forme pures, tel que *Sans titre (Inclinaison bleue)* (1967) (cat. 55, p. 65). Dans une conférence qu'elle donne en 1966, Duncan déclare que « l'artiste s'exécute non pas pour des raisons décoratives ou pour raconter des histoires, mais pour des raisons plastiques. Il se préoccupe des formes d'une manière plus pure »[13]. Artiste moderne dans l'âme, elle était captivée par la couleur, les formes, les proportions. Duncan s'adonne néanmoins à la création de récits par l'entremise des messages subtils qui émanent de ses portraits, de ses dessins de munitions et de ses marionnettes, et dans les messages plus explicites de la *Série Femme*. Par exemple, Duncan réutilise le format des torses carrés dans deux autres séries, *La famille* (1966) (cat. 47, p. 80 et cat. 48) et *Dame* (1966–68) (cat. 49–52, p. 72–74). La première série est composée de collages sur toile mettant en relation trois torses : une forme masculine et une forme féminine avec un enfant entre les deux. Duncan choisit de représenter la famille nucléaire standard, ce qui indique que le modèle hétéronormatif de la famille était une référence de base à cette époque. La *Série Dame* reprend aussi les formes de la *Série Femme*, mais ces œuvres-là sont exécutées à l'aquarelle, et des motifs textiles sont ajoutés à chaque torse carré. L'intérêt de Duncan pour les tissus lui vient de son père, John Duncan, qui était ingénieur dans une entreprise textile; elle a donc grandi autour des fabriques de textiles. Ce bagage familial a sans doute influencé son désir de mêler le réalisme et l'abstraction, et, contrairement aux formes unies de la *Série Femme*, les motifs en tissu de la *Série Dame* donnent une personnalité au corps représenté. De toute évidence, les œuvres de Duncan racontent plus d'histoires qu'elle-même ne s'en rend peut-être compte dans les années 1960.

La théorie féministe contemporaine reconnaît les multiples projets qui ont émergé du mouvement féministe. Misha Kavka déclare que ces projets regroupent « d'innombrables façons de faire – activiste, pratique, théorique ou même "discrète" »[14]. Je considère que l'apport artistique de Duncan, par l'entremise de sa *Série Femme*, est un projet qui se situe à mi-chemin entre les modes « activiste » et « discret » identifiés par Kavka. Le reste de son œuvre comporte certainement une critique sociale, mais elle est subtile. Dans la *Série Femme*, par contre, Duncan soumet *activement* à la critique les rôles des femmes considérés de manière « essentialiste ». Cette série constitue une anomalie dans sa pratique, car elle y traite directement d'un sujet très chargé sur le plan politique. Elle y cadre, et *coupe* littéralement, les parties du corps qui distinguent la femme de l'homme. Ce faisant, elle contribue à la déconstruction des points de vue normatifs et de la catégorisation de la forme physique féminine, qui évolue avec le temps. Cette contribution à la culture visuelle féministe canadienne est également *discrète*, pour autant que Duncan ne manifeste pas ouvertement son appui à une cause. Bien qu'elles ne semblent pas refléter les actions du mouvement féministe, les œuvres de Duncan font référence à une époque, à un lieu et à un moment politique où les femmes artistes incarnaient un sentiment de liberté artistique plein de force. En conséquence, ses dessins constituent une puissante critique des stéréotypes, prototypes, archétypes et classifications dont les femmes font l'objet. C'est pourquoi, à la lumière des multiples trames qui ont tissé l'histoire du féminisme (telles que décrites par des théoriciennes comme Kavka), l'ère postféministe ravive la nécessité politique d'identifier les enjeux des actions et des projets féministes du passé. Des projets comme la *Série Femme* ont contribué à un mouvement qui, de manière générale, s'attaquait à des idées telles que la notion « essentialiste » du corps, et ils continuent d'influencer le féminisme d'aujourd'hui, démontrant pourquoi il est important de reconnaître l'histoire de ce mouvement et de « faire le point sur le chemin parcouru »[15].

1 Joan Murray et Alma Duncan, « Deuxième cassette », transcription d'entrevue, RR2, Cumberland (Ontario), 13 février 1986, archives personnelles de Babs McLaren, p. 7. **2** Alma Duncan, notes biographiques, s.d., dossier « Biographies 1972–1992 », boîte MG31 D245 15, 7, Bibliothèque et Archives Canada, Ottawa (ci-après appelé BAC). **3** Deux œuvres, *Femme* (1964) et *Série Femme – Bouquet* (1965), sont incluses dans *Aquarelles, estampes et dessins canadiens, 1966*, une exposition présentée à la Galerie nationale du Canada (ancien nom du Musée des beaux-arts du Canada) et ensuite à travers le pays. *Donna della Serie 42* (v. 1965) est comprise dans l'Exposition internationale de dessins et de gravures de Lugano, en Suisse, en 1966, ainsi que dans le catalogue de l'exposition

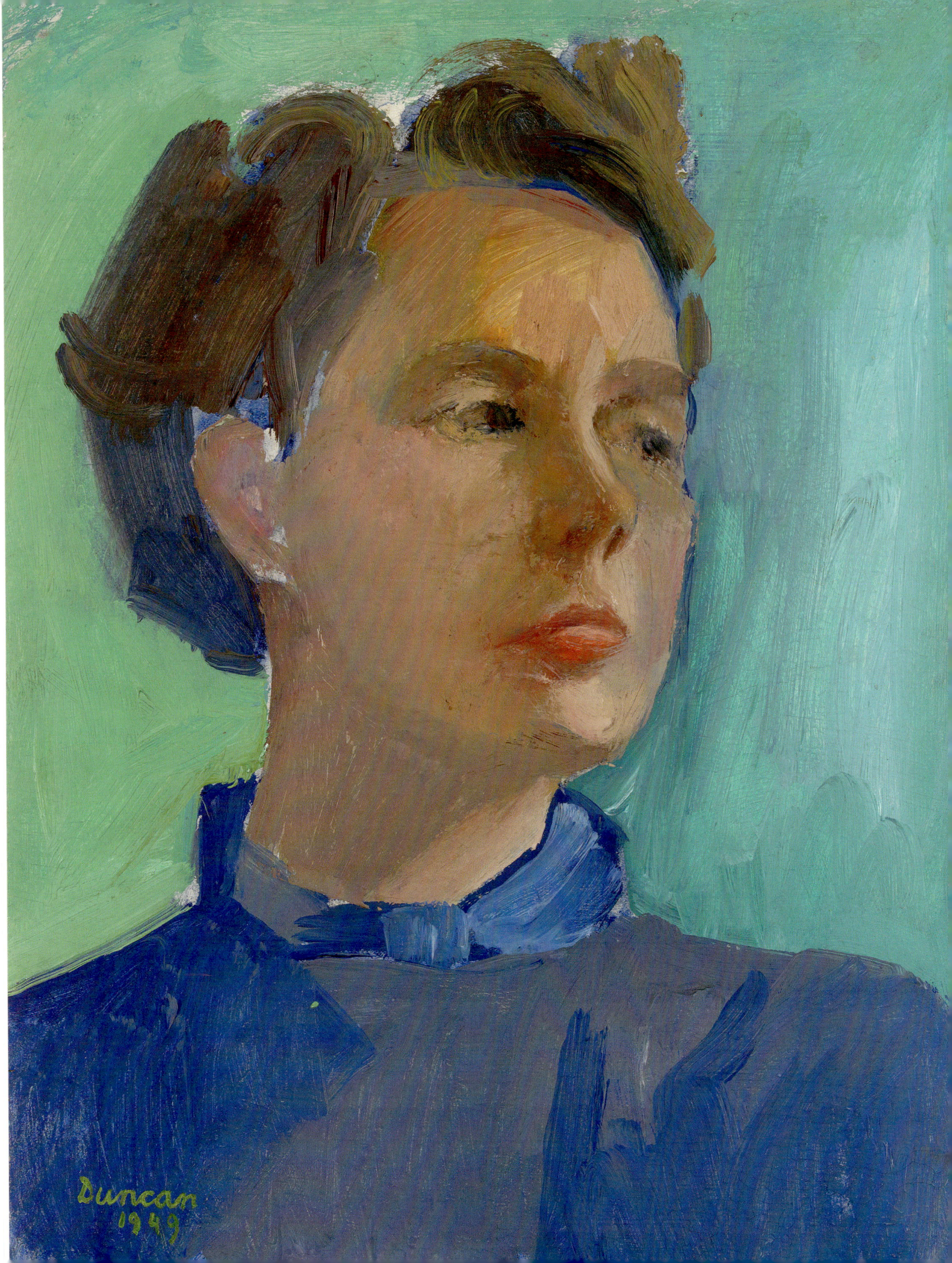
Duncan
1949

Facing a Canadian Cultural Heritage

The Politics of Portraiture

Jaclyn Meloche

A woman artist who is brave enough to perform her politics, strong enough to embrace her vulnerability, and curious enough to chance blurring the disciplinary boundaries in her practice is an artist worth celebrating. In the retrospective *Alma*, the Ottawa Art Gallery is recognizing Alma Duncan as a powerful voice who materialized Canadian visual culture on paper, on canvas, and in film. During the 1940s and 1950s, Duncan was an unofficial Canadian war artist, film animator at the National Film Board of Canada (NFB) and visual artist who captured, in portraits, the faces of cultural narrators Audrey (Babs) McLaren, P.K. Page, and Norman McLaren, to name a few. Drawing from Mikhail Bakhtin's theory of the dialogical body—the concept that meaning is the result of exchanges between characters in a performance—I interpret Duncan's art from this period as a relational collectivity that shapes a postwar national identity.[1] In part a celebration of female agency, this essay reclaims Alma Duncan's art within a single critical space where her works become a *performative archive* for the feminist and sociopolitical body.

Alma Duncan's relationship with the body is one that has always interested me, but also challenged me. How did she select her sitters?

Audrey (Babs) McLaren 1949 (cat. 22)
Library and Archives Canada | Bibliothèque et Archives Canada

On a formal level, how did she negotiate the æsthetics of portraiture? Although sometimes academic, her portraits are less about mimesis and technique than they are about forming a dialogical relationship with contemporary society. Duncan's figures transcend visuality, becoming instead embodiments of what feminist theorist Judith Butler calls *performativity*; "... performativity must be understood not as a singular or deliberate 'act,' but, rather, as the reiterative and citational practice by which discourse produces the effects that it names."[2] In other words, drawing from the theory that performance provides a space in which meaning is produced through an experiential exchange, Butler's model of performativity understands the (gendered) body as the result of a material, socio-cultural and embodied act of doing. In relation to Duncan's practice and the concept of dialogism, performativity offers a methodology through which to understand how her varied portraits become political acts of *doing* history, *doing* culture, and *doing* gender resistance.

In her survey *By a Lady: Celebrating Three Centuries of Art by Canadian Women*, Maria Tippett argues that women artists historically explored portraiture as a political act; "[women artists] also offered, through portraiture and figurative work, a new perception of Canadians — particularly of women — that served as a counterpoint to the landscape theme."[3] While she did paint some men, such as those depicted in *Ernst Neumann* (1942) (cat. 10, p. 20), *Grant Munro* (1947) (cat. 19, p. 95) and *Norman McLaren* (1947) (cat. 20, p. 108), the majority of her sitters were women, such as those of *Audrey (Babs) McLaren* (1949) (cat. 22, p. 88), *P.K. Page* (1947) (cat. 21, p. 96), *Isabel Jordon* (1947) (cat. 17, p. 94), and *Rosie with Badminton Racquet* (1943) (cat. 12, p. 92). Most notably, she painted herself. At times models or neighbours, Duncan's "women" were often cultural producers working as animators, photographers and poets. Indicative of the who's who of her professional milieu, her sitters were not selected out of convenience; instead, they represent the faces of a modern Canadian feminist narrative.

In the manifesto *The Second Sex*, Simone de Beauvoir understands the gendered body as a process of *becoming*, writing that "one is not born, but rather becomes a woman."[4] The distinction between being and becoming is relevant to the ways in which Duncan portrays her female sitters. In comparison to her nude studies that reflect the traditions of academic life drawing, such as *Female Nude Study* (1969) (cat. 62, p. 111) and *Male Nude Study* (1970) (cat. 63, p. 112), her portraits of women depict their professional *becomings* in society while also commenting on the changing status of women in the postwar era.

In the late 1940s, many women continued to work in professional roles at the NFB, regardless of its identity as a male-dominated bastion. For instance, along with Dorothy Macpherson and Audrey McLaren, Duncan was amongst a large group of women working at the Board. According to McLaren, "[T]here were lots of women [working at the NFB].

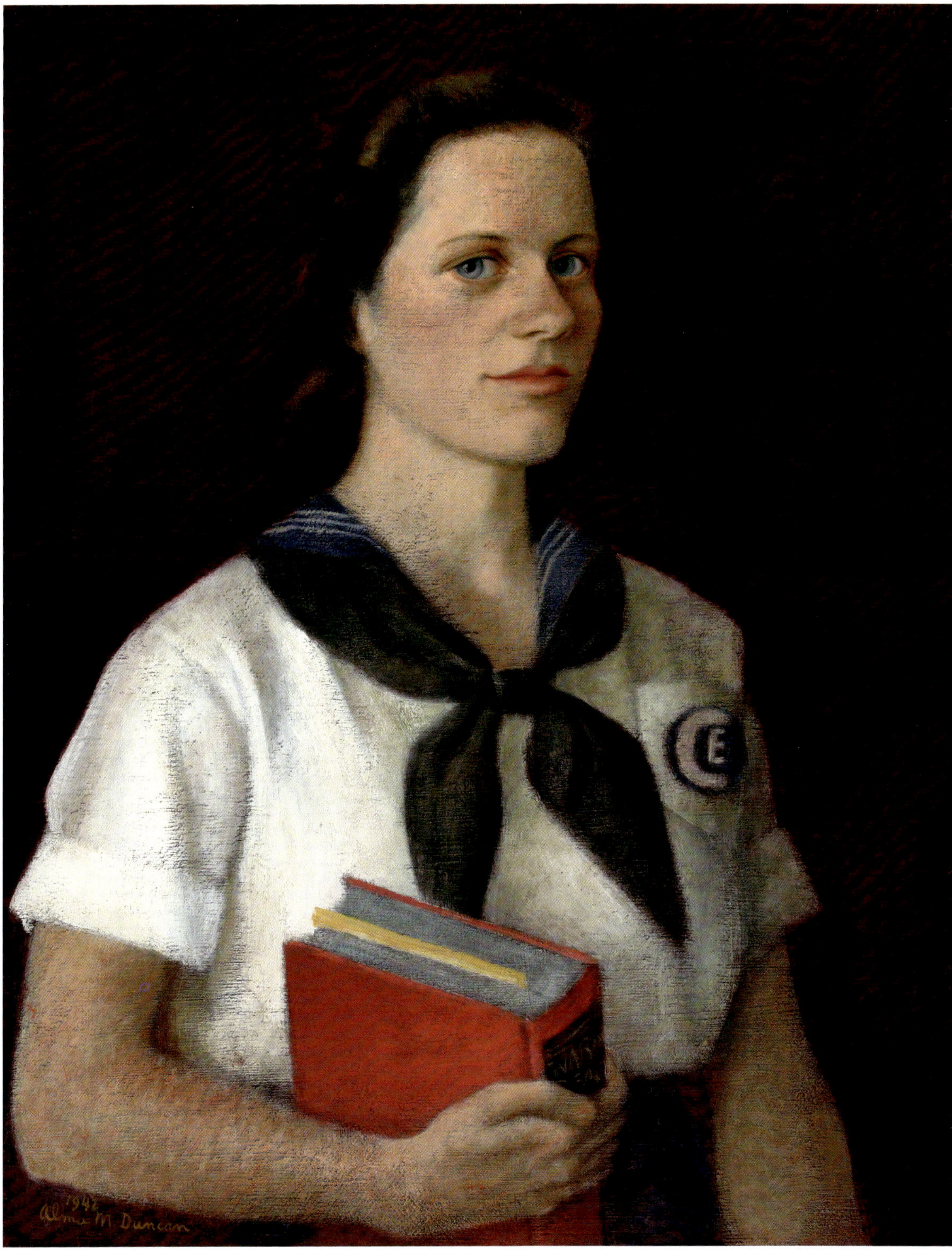

Joan Wilkie 1942 (cat. 9)
Library and Archives Canada | Bibliothèque et Archives Canada

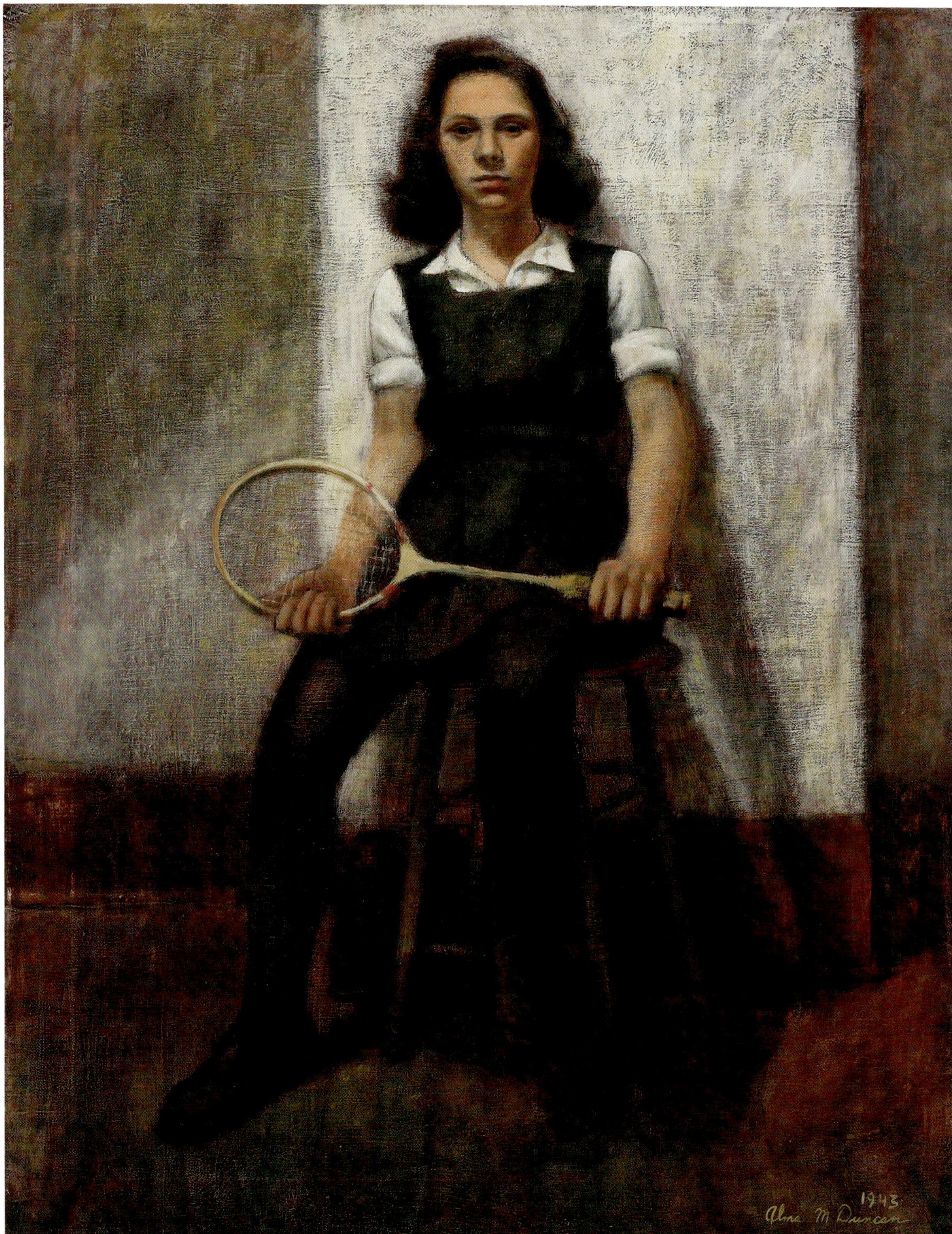

Rosie with Badminton Racquet | Rosie avec une raquette de badminton 1943 (cat. 12)

Art Gallery of Ontario | Musée des beaux-arts de l'Ontario

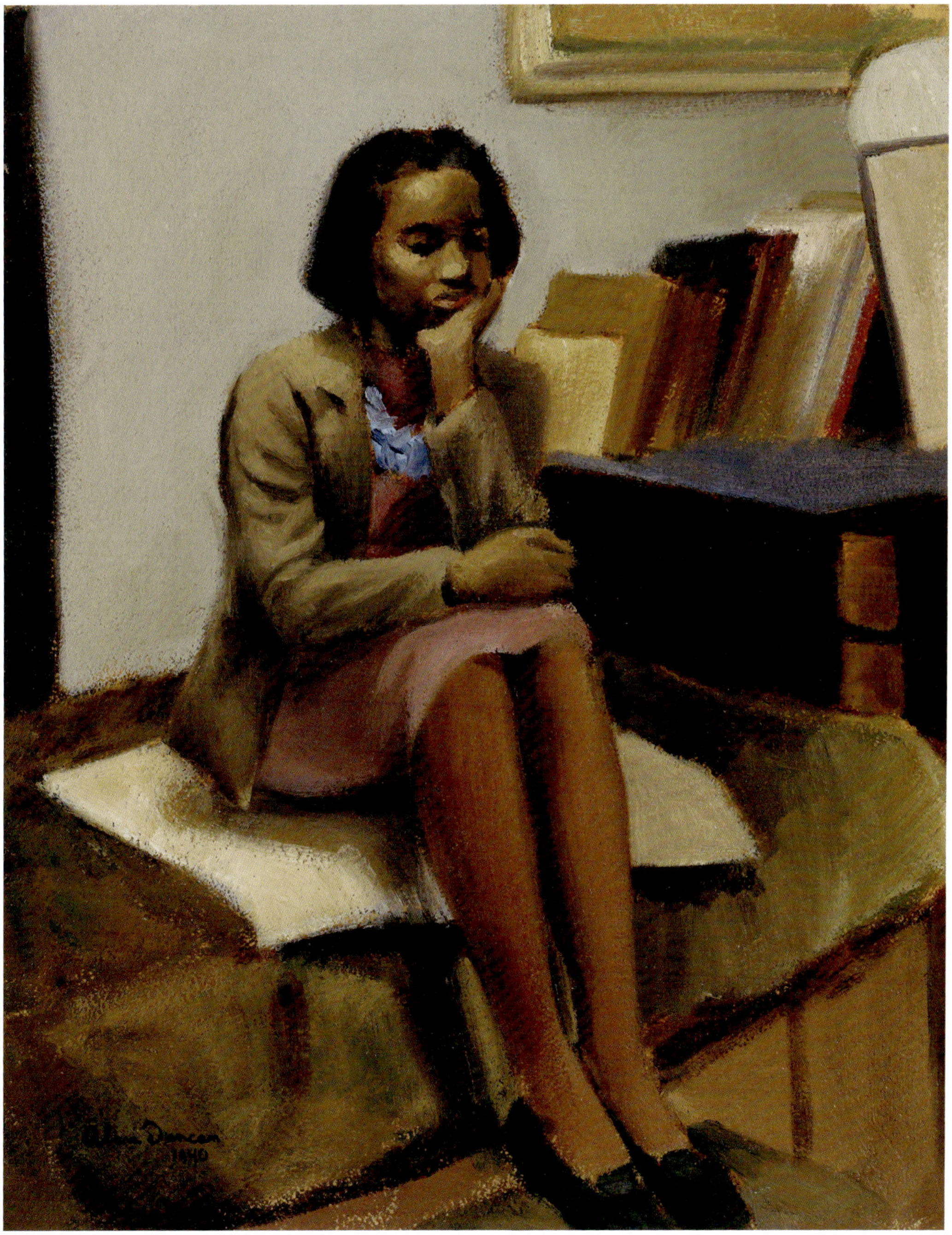

Young Black Girl | Jeune fille noire 1940 (cat. 7)
Art Gallery of Ontario | Musée des beaux-arts de l'Ontario

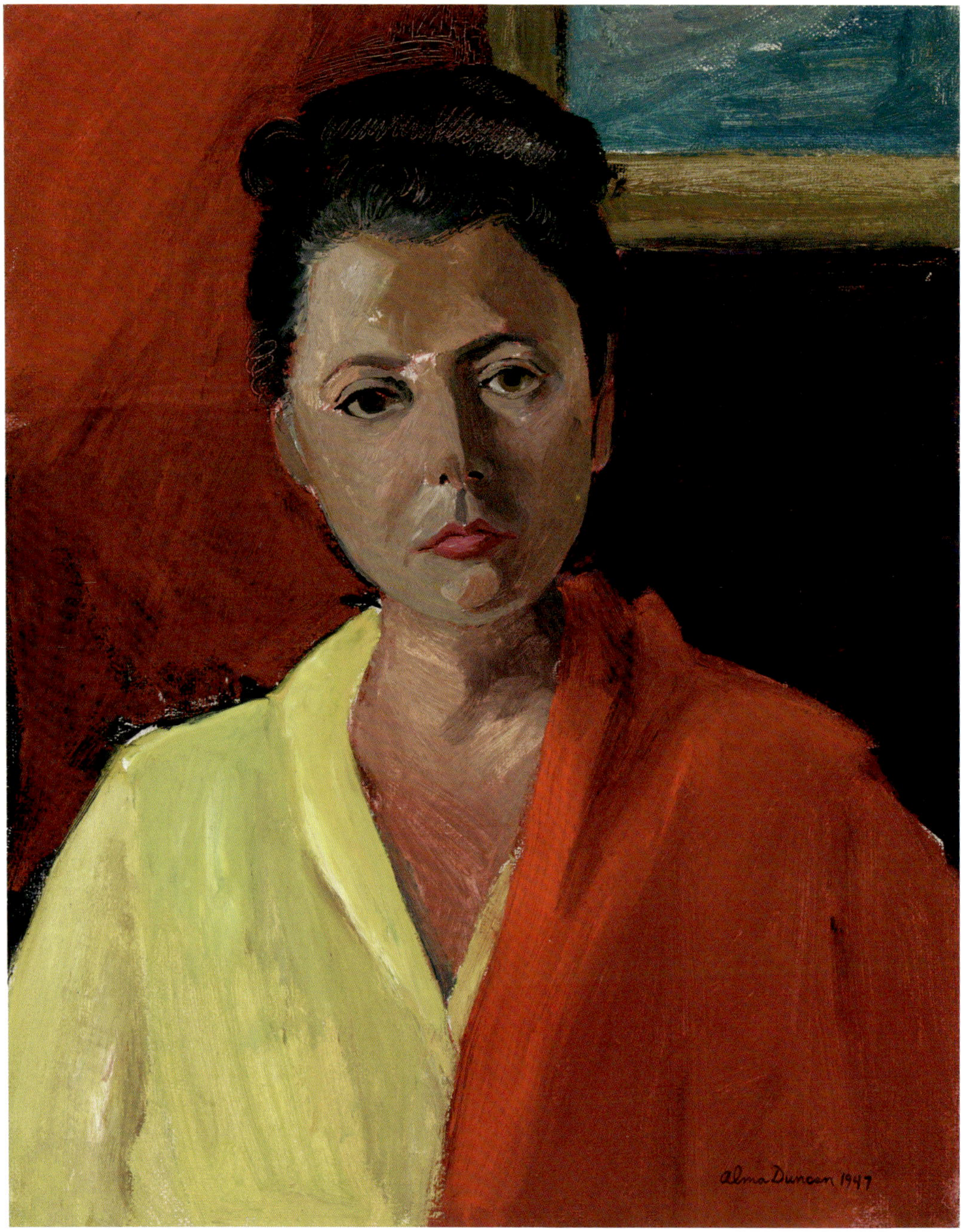

Isabel Jordon 1947 (cat. 17)
Library and Archives Canada | Bibliothèque et Archives Canada

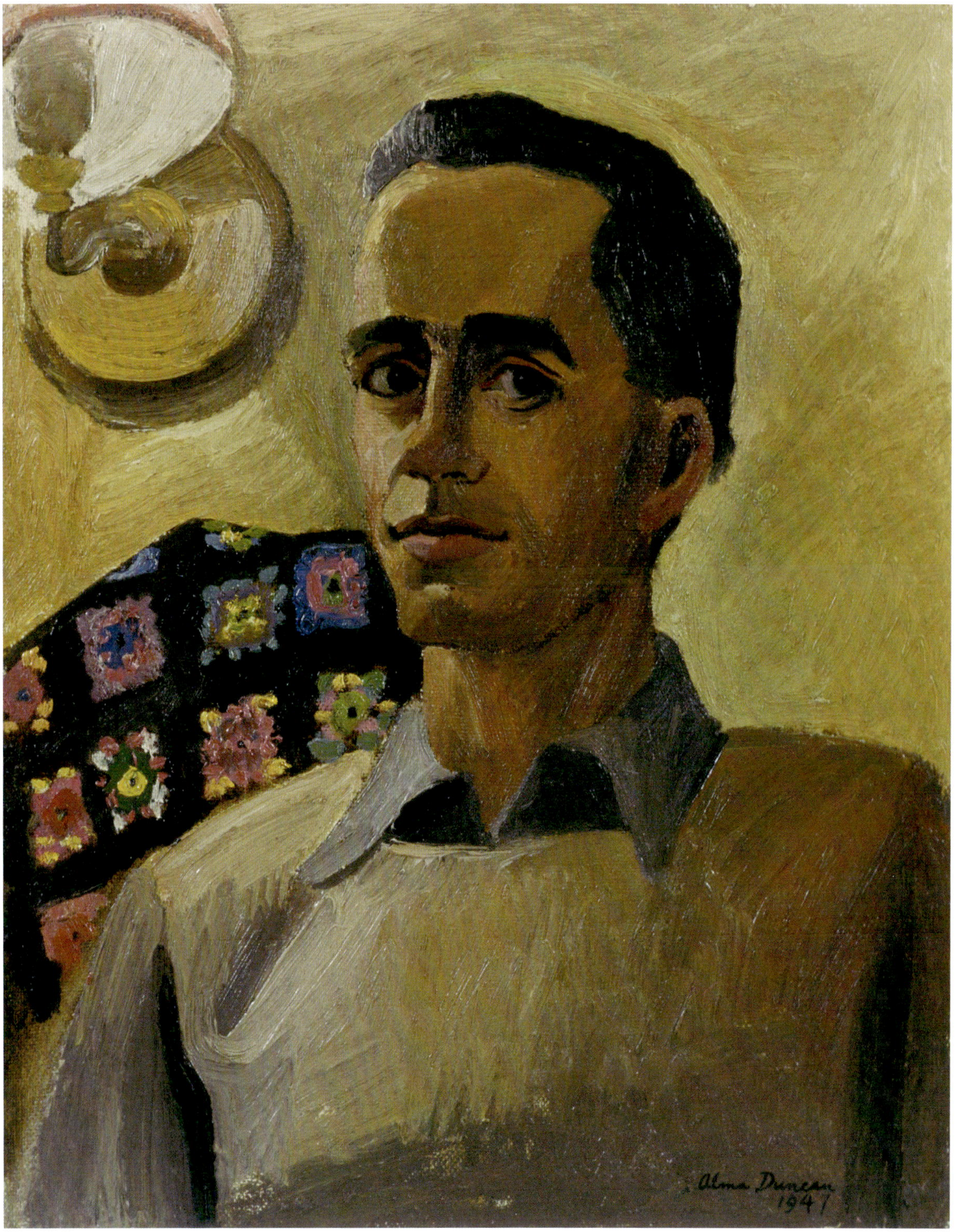

Grant Munro 1947 (cat. 19)
Ottawa Art Gallery | Gallery d'art d'Ottawa

McLaren, *Grant Munro* and *Norman McLaren* are executed with expressive brush strokes, a limited palette and exaggerated features. Reminiscent of Color Field painting, the spaces in which her figures sit recall Mark Rothko's blurred renderings of space, colour, and the experiential. Telling of a spontaneity and freedom that is characteristic of art produced during the postwar era, Duncan's figures from this period become evidence of her abstract influences. In comparison to her earlier "polished" portraits, her turn to the conceptual influenced a formal shift in her later representations of the body, both on canvas and in film. For example, in her film *Hearts and Soles* (1955), bodies become shoes. Likened to actors, Duncan's "new" portraits from this era perform the changing æsthetics of the time and the gender politics that overshadowed Canadian visual culture.

Throughout her career, Alma Duncan painted several self-portraits beginning with *Self-Portrait* (1939) (cat. 2, opposite). Habitually representing herself as a working artist, her self-portraits become powerful feminist statements that challenge the ways in which women were regarded in the larger sphere of contemporary society. According to art historian Marsha Meskimmon, self-portraits by women artists have often been used as vehicles for social intervention to articulate both professionalism and competence. By challenging the socially preconceived limitations of women's roles in society, women artists started to appropriate portraiture as a space in which they could question "traditional" representations of women in art, as well as the role of the female artists. As Meskimmon states, "[T]he author of the self-portrait is both subject and object. For women, this interaction is particularly critical. Woman has been the object of art for centuries, while women have remained marginalized as producers. To act in both roles, simultaneously, is to stage a crucial intervention."[10] Thus, through self-portraiture, women artists, like Duncan, have been able to counter the conventions of Western culture, which have for many years overlooked their recognition.

Conceptually, women artists' self-portraits function as platforms for sociopolitical commentary. In the catalogue *Self-Portraits by Women Painters*, editors Liana De Girolami Cheney, Alicia Craig Faxon, and Kathleen Lucey Russo note that, "female self-portraiture in painting is a source of revelation, not merely a signature. It is not meant as an exercise in iconographical reference, but rather an interpretation or statement of the artist's character and self-definition and her relationship to her milieu."[11] Constituting more than a mirrored image of herself, Duncan's self-portraits become her way of asserting her professional skills and challenging the limitations placed upon women by society. For example, by depicting herself in the act of painting in *Self-Portrait with Braids* (1940) (cat. 6, p. 100), she asserts her desire to be taken seriously both as a professional artist and as an individual regardless of her childlike demeanor. Through self-portraiture, women

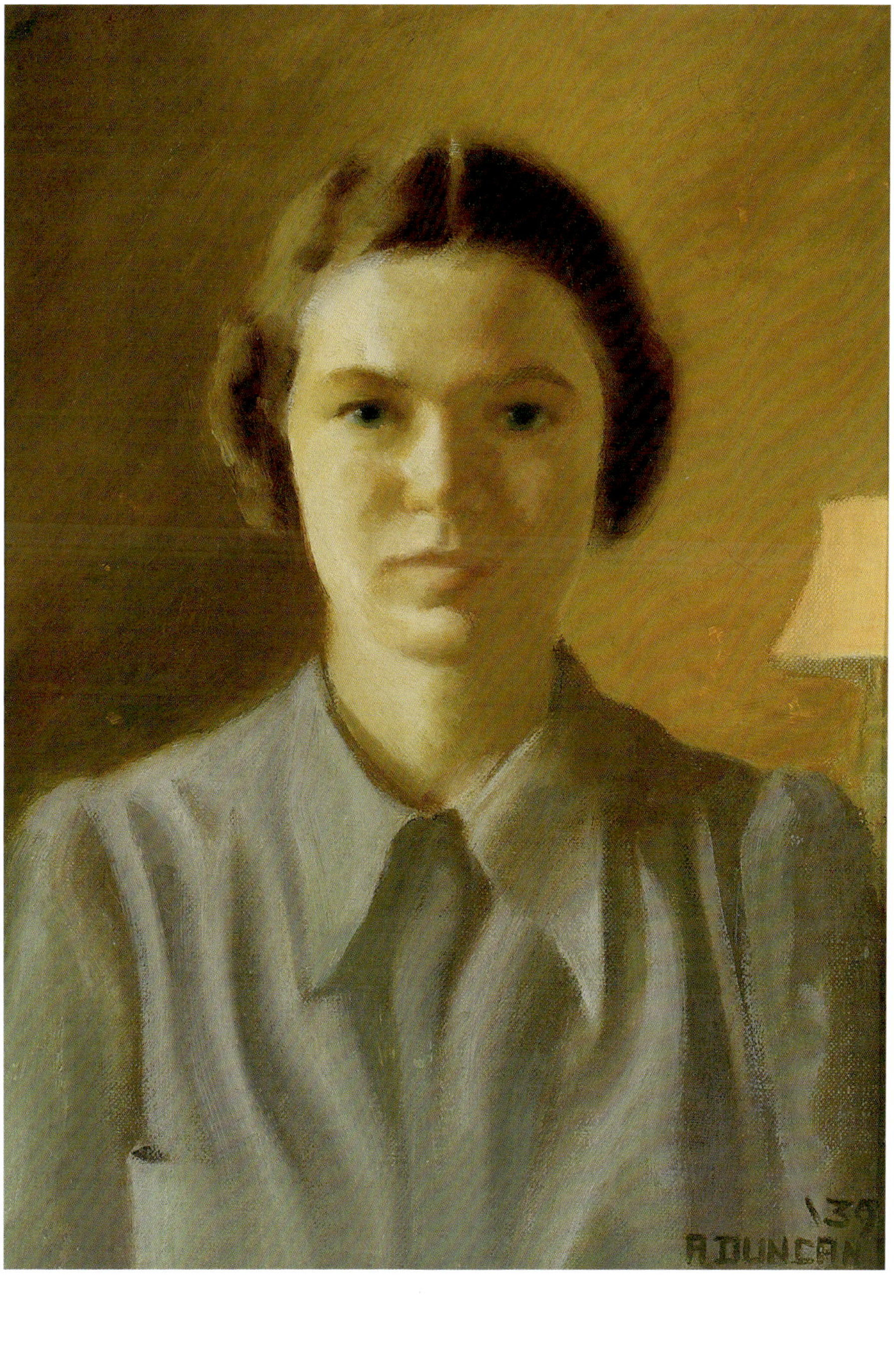

Self-Portrait | Autoportrait 1939 (cat. 2)
Private Collection | Collection privée

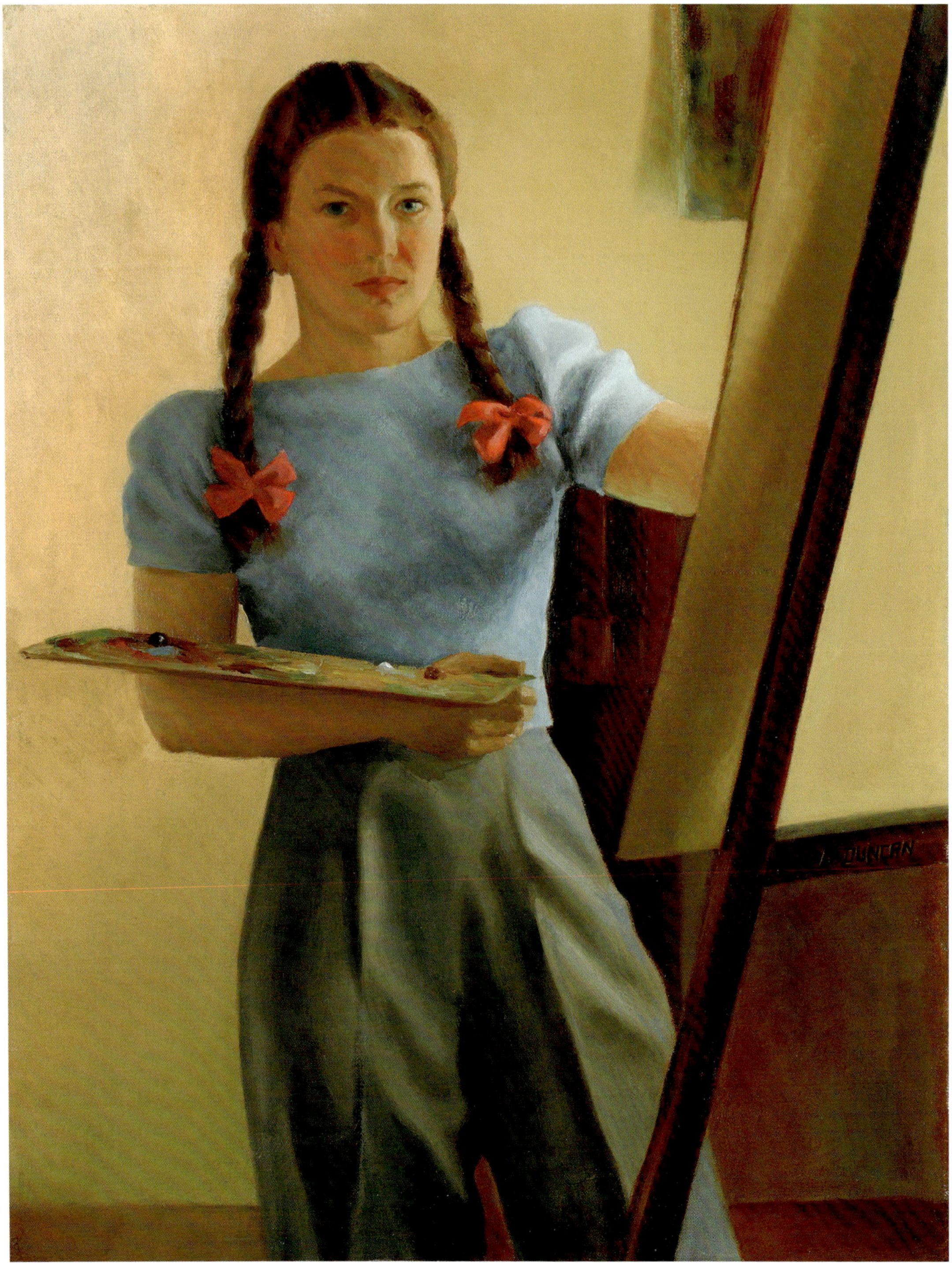

Self-Portrait with Braids | Autoportrait avec tresses 1940 (cat. 6)
Library and Archives Canada | Bibliothèque et Archives Canada

artists could undermine the conventions of art history by introducing evidence of their professional expertise into their paintings to assert their talent and their commitment.

Because self-portraiture represents an artist's talent as a metaphorical space for a multiplicity of meanings, one cannot overlook the significance of pose and dress as features of self-representation. The decision to sit for a portrait or undertake a self-portrait is a conscious act, so what the sitter wears is extremely telling of self-identity. In *The Fashion System*, Roland Barthes argues that attire can be interpreted as a system of signs that creates meaning. He states,

Fashion becomes an autonomous cultural object, with its own original structure and, probably, with a new finality; other functions are substituted for or added to the social functions usually acknowledged by vestimentary Fashion; these functions are analogous to those found in all literature and can be summarized by saying that, through the language which henceforth takes charge of it, Fashion becomes narrative.[12]

The idea that fashion can tell a story or create meaning is vital in the context of self-portraiture. In many of Duncan's self-portraits, such as *Self-Portrait with Braids*, and *Self-Portrait with Red Stripes* (1958) (cat. 32, p. 104), her clothing and coiffure become indicators of her self-image, her status, and her personality. Thus, in addition to constituting a part of the sitter's identity, fashion is ultimately a self-conscious vehicle for self-narration.

Historically, it was unacceptable for a woman artist to depict herself in the act of painting or in a manner that made her appear to engage in a "masculine" profession. In response to the pressures of having to conform to society's preconceived notions of femininity, women artists traditionally portrayed themselves not as artists but as women in fashionable and "feminine" attire. In *Self-Portrait with Braids*, however, Duncan is wearing trousers — commonly associated with men or "liberated" women — and depicts herself as an artist in front of her easel. In keeping with Barthes' analysis, a sitter's clothing and coiffure narrate a range of issues including personality, gender, class, race and social aspirations. The decision to represent herself wearing a pair of what were then regarded as "masculine" pants consequently denotes a challenge to "conventional" definitions of femininity in self-portraiture.

Alma Duncan's clothes are not the only signifiers suggesting that she was challenging contemporary conventions. What about her braids? Childlike in their simplicity, her braids, and particularly their red bows negate the idea of the artist's professionalism in both the portrait and in reality. In 1940 Duncan was twenty-three years old. She had not yet reached "professional" status and the braids remind the viewer that she was at an early stage of her career in this portrait. Ideologically and politically, she used the representation

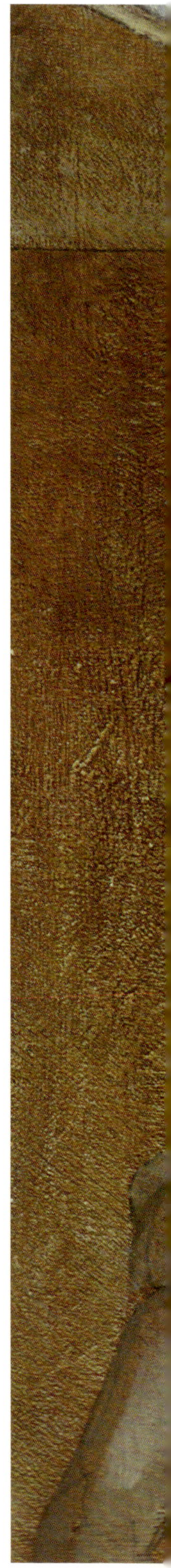

Self-Portrait | Autoportrait 1943 (cat. 11)
Ottawa Art Gallery | Galerie d'art d'Ottawa

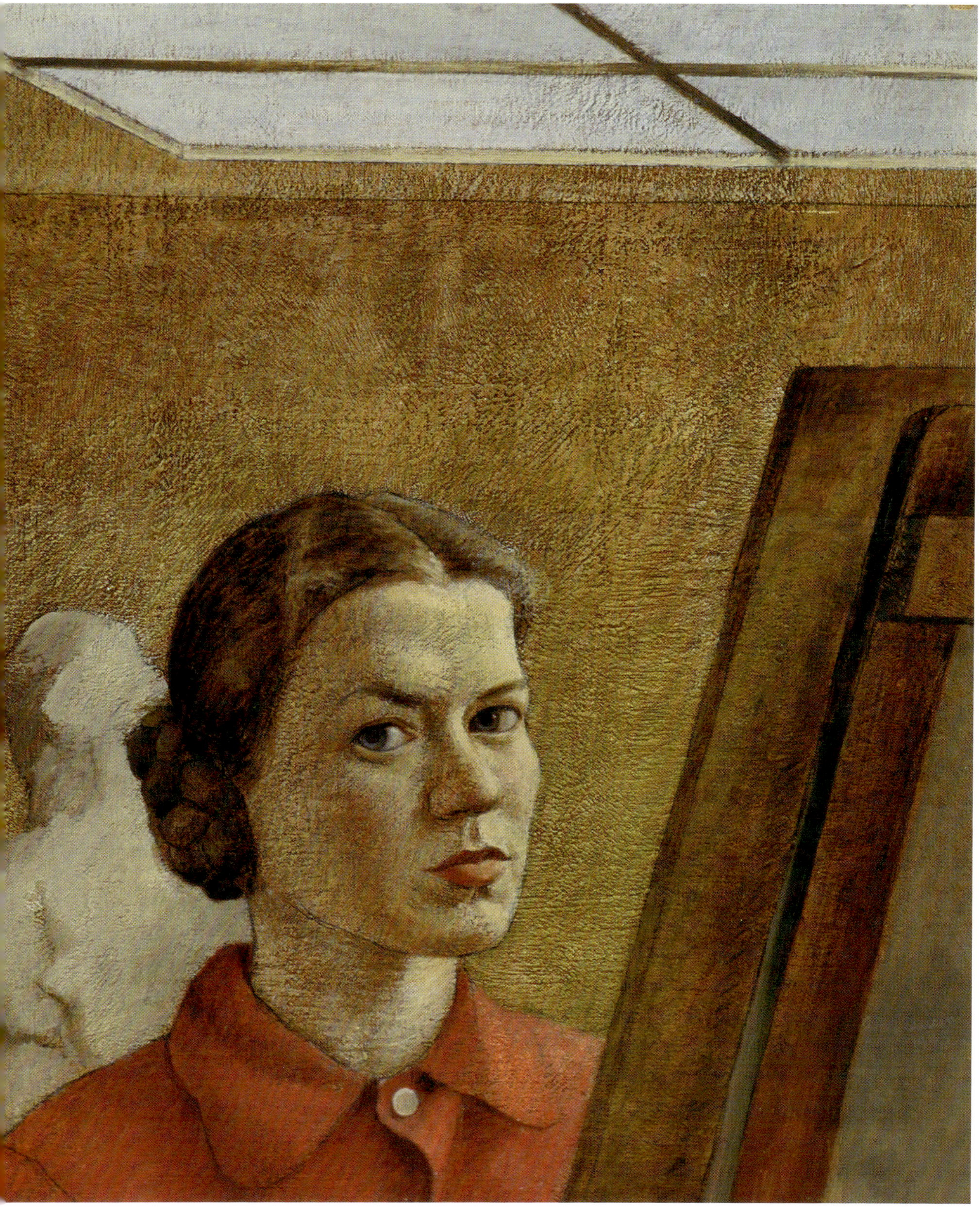

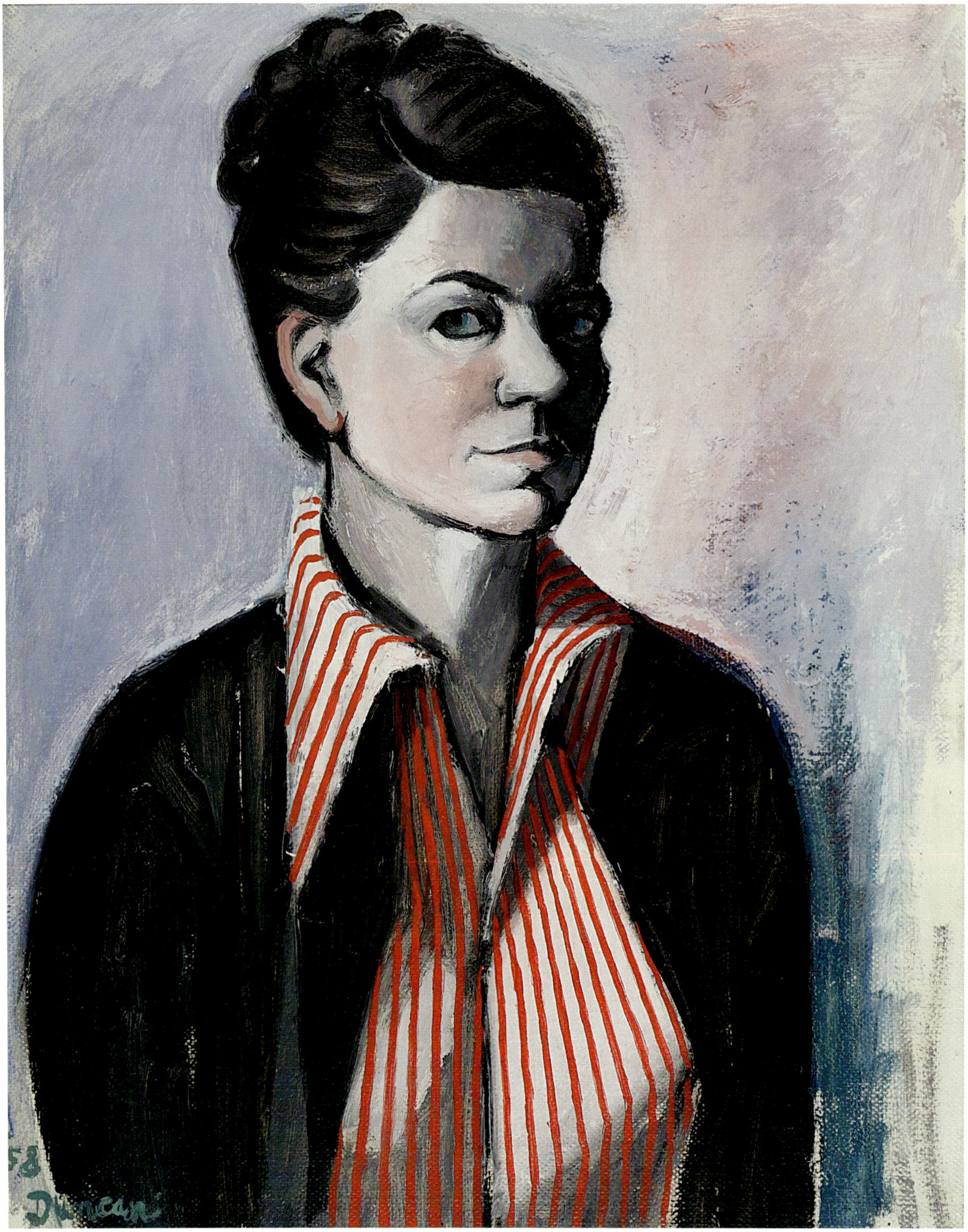

Self-Portrait with Red Stripes | Autoportrait avec rayures rouges 1958 (cat. 32)

Courtesy of D & E Lake Ltd. Fine Arts | Gracieuseté de D & E Lake Ltd. Fine Arts

of self as a vehicle to assert her talent and to challenge the obstacles posed by age and gender. Therefore, not only do her signature braids remind the viewer that she is still a young woman, they emphasize the notion that age should not be a determining factor in recognizing her talent.

Alma Duncan's negotiation of the professional body vis-à-vis the body-in-play is a theme that is echoed in her portraits in the 1950s. While working under the direction of Norman McLaren at the NFB, she experimented with film animation using puppets, a newly popular technique in Canadian film. According to John Grierson, cartoons "... are by far the most valuable way of putting over public messages."[13] If you consider its appeal to the general public, and its ability to be mass-produced, this playful form of animation can be considered a highly practical vehicle to communicate ideas to both children and adults. In *Cartoon Capers: The History of Canadian Animators*, Karen Mazurkewich comments on the NFB's interest in puppetry noting that this particular pedagogical device compares to *political mouthpieces*; "[T]he NFB's original mandate was to operate as the government's mouthpiece during World War II."[14] In this context, the films were not only intended to entertain the public, they were also meant to educate the public. Representing voices that are not their own on stage, but rather the voices of their creators, puppets become metaphors that begin to teach and communicate meaning.

Apart from Evelyn Lambart, whom Mazurkewich names "Canada's first lady of animation,"[15] Alma Duncan was one of the few women to work for the animation department. In 1951, she produced her first animated film for the Board, *Folksong Fantasy*. Based on three folk tales, *The Riddle Song*, *Who Killed Cock Robin?* and *The Cooper of Fife*, the film addresses abuse, death, gender roles, patriarchy, and power in Western culture. For instance, in *The Cooper of Fife*, Duncan used her puppets as a vehicle to editorialize against domestic violence. As the cooper begins to beat his wife, the artist's puppet quickly transforms into a devil (cat. 24, p. 121). Two horns appear on his head while a pointed white foam beard materializes on his chin turning him into a caricature of evil. These physical changes were not part of the original tale, so one can only assume that they were indicative of Duncan's own opinions.

Alma Duncan withdrew from the Board in 1951 and formed a partnership with Audrey McLaren called Dunclaren Productions. Together the pair produced three animated films: *Kumak the Sleepy Hunter* (1953) (cat. 25, p. 123), *Hearts and Soles* (1955) (cat. 26, p. 124) and *Friendly Interchange* (1958) (cat. 34, p. 127). Although at work in many different mediums, Duncan's art from this period remains connected in its references to contemporary stereotypes and sociological issues. For instance, in their first collaborative film, *Kumak the Sleepy Hunter*—a tale of a narcoleptic Inuit hunter named Kumak—Dunclaren used handmade puppets, papier mâché masks, hand-stitched leather clothing, and numerous stage props, such as seals and hunting kayaks (cat. 27, p. 122) to narrate their interpretation of the Canadian north.

Akin to mouthpieces, the puppets in the award-nominated short film bring to life a culture and community that the artist was excited about. Influenced by her scientist friends who worked in the Arctic.[16] Duncan, (who eventually travelled to the North in 1975 for artistic research) drew inspiration from fellow members of the Arctic Circle, a local club formed in 1947 for Ottawans interested in "everything Arctic." In her own words, "[S]everal of the members very patiently answered questions and gave advice."[17] Although Duncan and McLaren were not in direct communication with Inuit communities, they did acknowledge that theirs was a contemporary and personal interpretation of Inuit culture told through the eyes of passionate observers. Therefore, echoing Mazurkewich's argument that puppets are anthropological objects that enact meaning, I interpret Duncan's characters as metaphorical stand-ins for the narration of "other" cultures, histories, and traditions in early Canadian animated film using puppets.

In *Hearts and Soles*, Dunclaren appropriated shoes as the mouthpiece for the exploitation and deconstruction of gender hierarchies. In the opening scene a pair of women's red high heels begin to dance with a pair of men's brown dress shoes. A third pair of men's shoes join in and the dancing quickly becomes a competition. Like indexical references to people, the shoes become symbols of the absent body. But as the plot develops, "her" first dancing partner becomes very protective and begins to shield "her" from the second pair of shoes. *Hearts and Soles* enfolds the gender stereotyping of the era; the red shoes act out the role of the "weaker sex" while the men's shoes portray the competitive battle for male dominance. By 1955, the year the film was produced, a decade had elapsed since the Second World War ended, and women's resumption of their domestic roles reinstated their status as "other." According to Ruth Roach Pierson, "[T]he war's slight yet disquieting reconstruction of womanhood in the direction of equality with men was scrapped for a full-skirted and redomesticated postwar model, and for more than a decade feminism was once again sacrificed to femininity."[18] Therefore, the red shoes' allure in the film reintegrates the woman's role as sex object, over whom men contest.

Today, ten years after Alma Duncan's passing, it is necessary to state that she was truly a woman artist ahead of her time who did not shy away from pursuing politically charged themes. As powerful examples of feminist visual culture, her portraits find strength in their layered entanglements. Reflecting on contemporary gender stereotypes and the shifting æsthetics in Canadian modern art, Duncan's works from the 1940s and 1950s become visual documents that chronicle the artist's relationship to her cultural and social climate as well as to the development of Canadian art during the postwar era. Therefore, by placing Alma Duncan's art within a dialogical framework, Canadian art history can begin to understand her portraits, self-portraits, puppets and masks as a timeless *performative archive.*

1 The argument in this essay draws from my MA thesis in Canadian Art History. See Jaclyn Meloche, "Braiding the Boundaries: A Dialogical Study of Alma Duncan's Art from the 1940s and 1950s" (master's thesis, Carleton University, 2004). **2** Judith Butler, *Bodies That Matter: On the Discursive Limits of Sex* (New York: Routledge, 1993), xii. **3** Maria Tippett, *By a Lady: Celebrating Three Centuries of Art by Canadian Women* (Toronto: Penguin Books, 1992), 105. **4** Simone de Beauvoir, *The Second Sex*, trans. E.M. Parshley (New York: Vintage Books, 1989), 267. **5** Audrey McLaren, interview with Jaclyn Meloche, tape recorded in Ottawa, November 18, 2002. **6** Richard Brilliant, *Portraiture* (London: Reaktion Books Limited, 1991), 10. **7** Joan Rivière, " Womanliness as a Masquerade" in *Formations of Fantasy*, eds. Victor Burgin, James Donald, and Cora Kaplan. (London and New York: Methuen, 1986), 38. **8** Ibid. 35–6. **9** See Efrat Tseëlon, *Masquerade and Identities: Essays in Gender, Sexuality and Marginality* (London and New York: Routledge, 2001). **10** Marsha Meskimmon, *The Art of Reflection: Women Artist's Self-Portraiture in the Twentieth Century* (New York: Columbia University Press, 1996), 14. **11** Liana De Girolami Cheney, Alicia Craig Faxon and Kathleen Lucey Russo, *Self-Portraiture by Women Painters* (Farnham, UK: Ashgate Publishing Limited, 2000), xxvi. **12** Roland Barthes, *The Fashion System*, trans. Matthew Ward and Richard Howard. New York: Farrar, Straus & Giroux, 1983, 244. **13** John Grierson, "Interview with John Grierson," 1972, vol. C12, C2527, 116, McGill University Archives, Montreal. Helen Brimmell, "The Beauty of Industrial Work is Shown in Current Exhibit by Artist Alma Duncan," *The Daily Mercury*, January 18, 1988, n.p. **14** Karen Mazurkewich, *Cartoon Capers: The History of Canadian Animators* (Toronto: McArthur & Company, 1999), 10. **15** Ibid. 196. **16** Alma Duncan, biographical notes n.d., file "Biography 1972–1992," box 15, Library and Archives Canada, Ottawa (hereafter cited as LAC). **17** Dunclaren Productions' notes for the 1954 screening of *Kumak the Sleepy Hunter* (for the Arctic Circle), Ottawa, January 6, 1954, vol. 3, file 9, LAC. **18** Ruth Roach Pierson, *They're Still Women After All: The Second World War and Canadian Womanhood* (Toronto: McClelland and Stewart, 1986), 220.

Jaclyn Meloche is a visual artist and art historian interested in recovering women artists' bodies of work through a feminist and poststructuralist lens. Currently working to complicate the æsthetic and conceptual boundaries of performance and performativity vis-à-vis a discourse of matter in her research and writing, she is also engaged with a creative practice that entangles drawing, performance and photography. She has earned a Bachelor of Fine Arts (University of Ottawa), a Master of Arts in Canadian Art History (Carleton University), a Master of Fine Arts (School of Visual Arts) and is currently pursuing a research-creation-led PhD in Humanities (Fine Arts) at Concordia University. Meloche is a part-time professor in the Department of Visual Arts at the University of Ottawa, and is currently based in Ottawa.

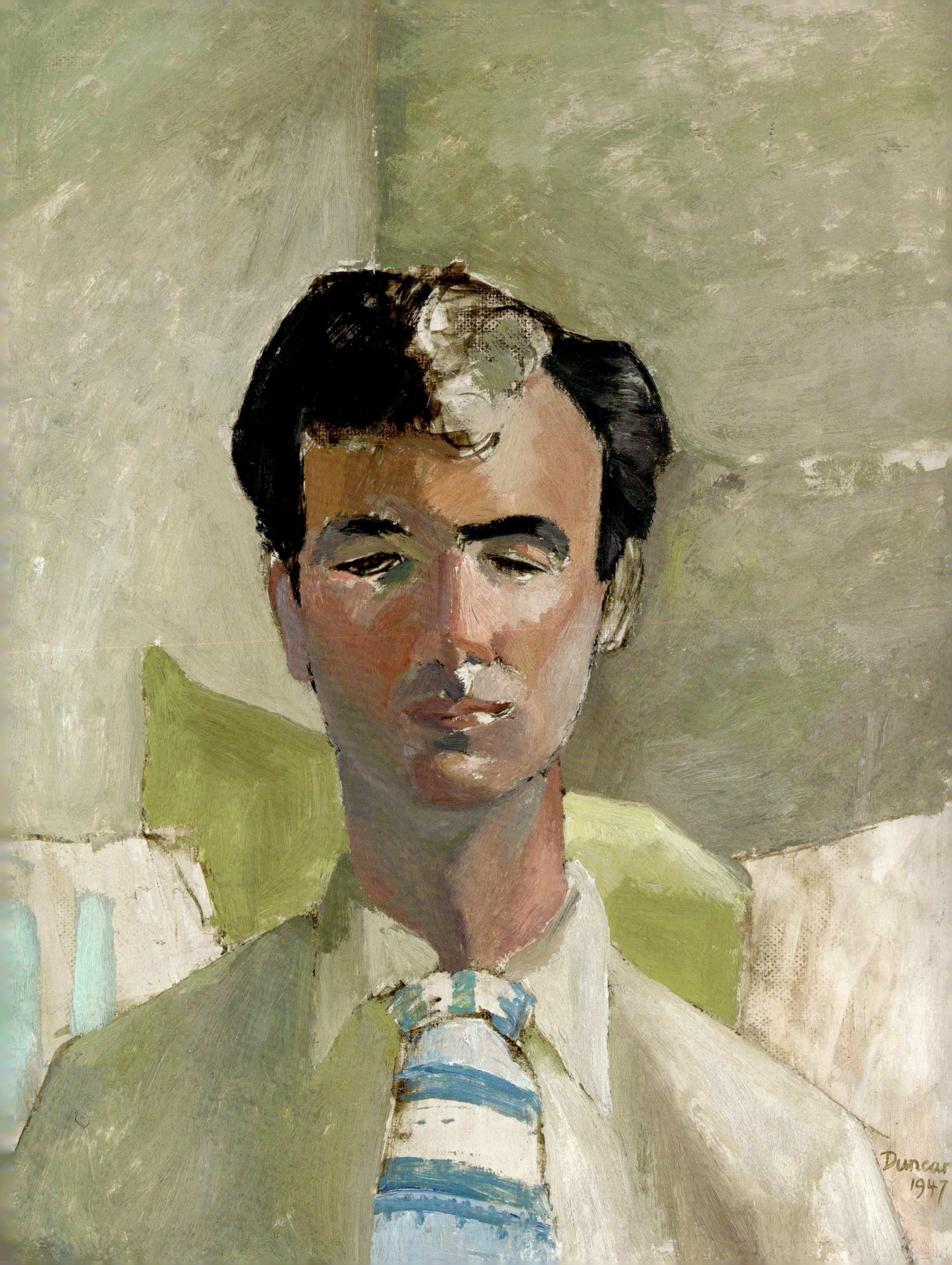
Duncan
1947

Faire face à un héritage culturel canadien

Les politiques du portrait

Jaclyn Meloche

Une femme artiste qui a le courage de mettre ses opinions politiques en action, la force d'accepter sa vulnérabilité et assez de curiosité pour courir le risque de brouiller les frontières disciplinaires au sein de sa pratique, voilà une artiste digne d'être célébrée. En présentant l'exposition rétrospective *Alma*, la Galerie d'art d'Ottawa reconnaît la voix puissante d'Alma Duncan; une voix qui a incarné – sur papier, sur toile et sur pellicule – la culture visuelle du Canada. Durant les années 1940 et 1950, Duncan a été une artiste de guerre non officielle, une cinéaste d'animation œuvrant à l'Office national du film du Canada (ONF) et une artiste visuelle capturant dans ses portraits les visages de chroniqueurs culturels tels qu'Audrey « Babs » McLaren, P.K. Page et Norman McLaren, entre autres. En m'inspirant de la théorie du corps dialogique de Mikhaïl Bakhtine – selon laquelle le sens naît d'échanges entre des personnages dans une performance –, j'interprète l'œuvre de Duncan à cette époque comme une collectivité relationnelle participant à créer l'identité nationale d'après-guerre[1]. Cet essai est en partie une célébration de la volonté (ou *agentivité*, *capacité* ou *puissance d'agir*) féminine, et une tentative de recadrer l'art d'Alma Duncan dans un espace critique tel que son œuvre devient une *archive performative* du corps féministe et sociopolitique.

Norman McLaren 1947 (cat. 20)
Library and Archives Canada | Bibliothèque et Archives Canada

Le rapport au corps qu'Alma Duncan entretient en est un qui m'a toujours intéressée et mise à l'épreuve. Comment choisissait-elle ses modèles ? D'un point de vue formel, comment abordait-elle l'esthétique du portrait ? Bien que parfois académiques, ses portraits ne sont pas tant affaire de mimétisme et de technique qu'une tentative d'établir une relation dialogique avec la société contemporaine. Les portraits de Duncan dépassent le visuel pour incarner ce que la théoricienne féministe Judith Butler nomme *performativité* : « [...] il ne faut pas comprendre la performativité comme un "acte" singulier ou délibéré, mais, plutôt, comme la pratique réitérative et citationnelle par laquelle le discours produit les effets qu'il nomme »[2]. En d'autres mots, en s'inspirant de la théorie selon laquelle la performance fournit l'espace dans lequel le sens est produit par le biais d'un échange expérientiel, le modèle de la performativité de Butler conçoit le corps (sexué) comme le résultat d'« actes de faire » matériels, socioculturels et corporels. Pour ce qui est de la pratique de Duncan en lien avec le concept du dialogisme, la notion de performativité offre un cadre méthodologique qui permet de comprendre comment les portraits de Duncan sont autant de façons de *faire* l'histoire, de *faire* la culture et de *faire* de la résistance face à la catégorisation des genres.

Dans son étude *By a Lady: Celebrating Three Centuries of Art by Canadian Women* (Fait par une dame. Une célébration de trois siècles d'art créé par des femmes canadiennes), Maria Tippett fait valoir que, au cours de l'histoire, le fait d'explorer le portrait était pour les femmes artistes un acte politique : « Les femmes artistes offraient aussi, par l'entremise du portrait et du travail figuratif, une nouvelle perception des Canadiens – et particulièrement des Canadiennes – qui servait de contrepoint au thème du paysage »[3]. Duncan a beau avoir peint quelques hommes, comme dans *Ernst Neumann* (1942) (cat. 10, p. 20), *Grant Munro* (1947) (cat. 19, p. 95) et *Norman McLaren* (1947) (cat. 20, p. 108), la majorité de ses modèles demeure des femmes, comme dans *Audrey « Babs » McLaren* (1949) (cat. 22, p. 88), *P.K. Page* (1947) (cat. 21, p. 96), *Isabel Jordon* (1947) (cat. 17, p. 94) et *Rosie avec une raquette de badminton* (1943) (cat. 12, p. 92). En premier lieu, elle se peignait elle-même. Tour à tour modèles ou voisines, les « femmes » de Duncan étaient souvent des productrices culturelles œuvrant comme animatrices, photographes ou poètes. Ses modèles, qui représentaient le gratin de son milieu professionnel, n'étaient pas sélectionnés par souci de commodité – elles représentaient plutôt les visages du féminisme moderne canadien.

Dans son manifeste *Le deuxième sexe*, Simone de Beauvoir parle du corps sexué comme étant un processus en devenir – « On ne naît pas femme : on le devient »[4]. Cette distinction entre être et devenir explique la manière dont Duncan représente ses modèles féminins. Contrairement à ses études de nu empreintes de la tradition académique du dessin d'après modèle, comme *Étude de nu – Femme* (1969) (cat. 62, page suivante) et *Étude de nu – Homme* (1970) (cat. 63, p. 112), ses portraits de femmes représentent

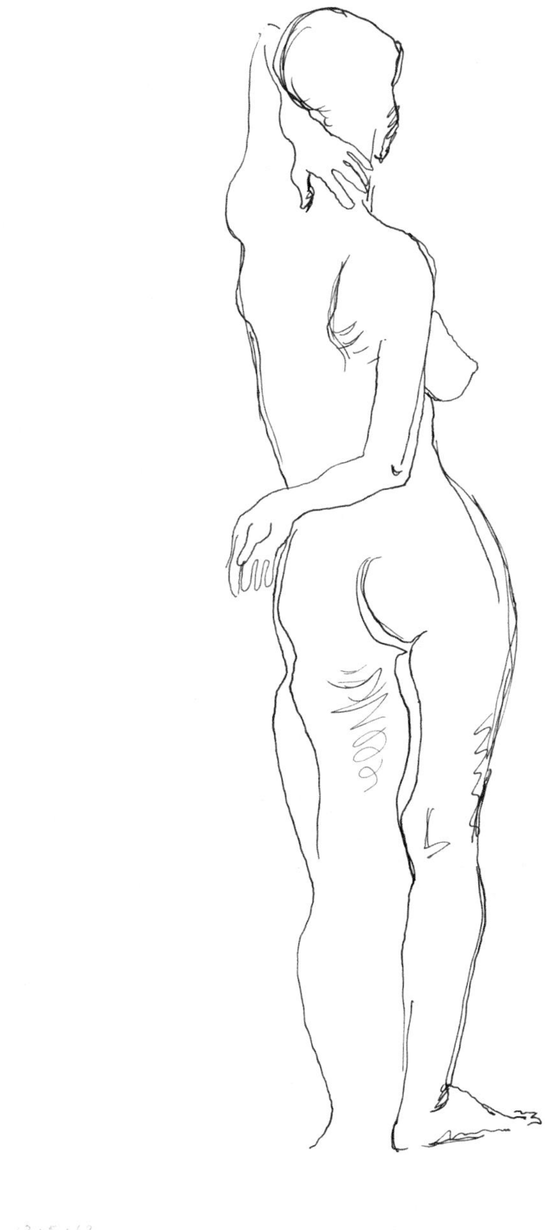

Female Nude Study | Étude de nu–Femme 1969 (cat. 62)
Library and Archives Canada | Bibliothèque et Archives Canada

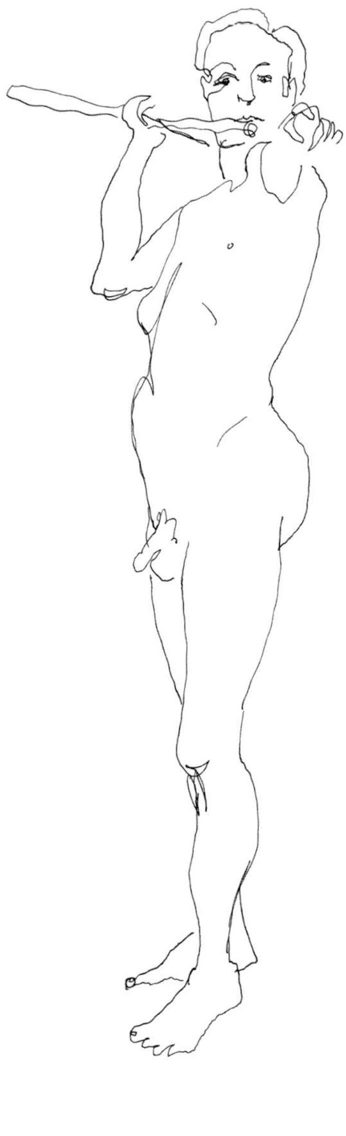

Male Nude Study | Étude de nu – Homme 1970 (cat. 63)
Library and Archives Canada | Bibliothèque et Archives Canada

leurs *devenirs* professionnels dans la société, tout en commentant le statut changeant de la femme dans l'après-guerre.

À la fin des années 1940, plusieurs femmes ont continué d'occuper des postes professionnels à l'ONF, malgré sa réputation de bastion de la domination mâle. Par exemple, Duncan faisait partie d'un grand groupe de femmes, avec Dorothy Macpherson et Audrey McLaren, qui travaillaient à l'Office. Selon McLaren, « il y avait beaucoup de femmes [qui travaillaient à l'ONF]. Presque plus de femmes que d'hommes. Mais un bien grand nombre de femmes »[5]. Elle souligne que peu d'entre elles étaient impliquées dans le département d'animation, mais que plusieurs occupaient des postes professionnels, comme P.K. Page, qui était commis et scénariste, et McLaren, assistante technique. En représentant certaines des femmes qui ont contribué à la reconstruction culturelle du Canada après la Deuxième Guerre mondiale, les portraits de Duncan des années 1940 capturent les visages des femmes et des hommes qui étaient activement impliqués dans la promotion de la culture canadienne, au pays comme à l'étranger.

Dans le portrait *P.K. Page*, Duncan représente Patricia Kathleen Page en femme du monde hautement sophistiquée. Selon l'historien de l'art Richard Brilliant, les portraits de personnes professionnelles en disent long sur leurs rôles publics :

Les portraits de gens qui occupent des postes importants aux yeux du public – élus, intellectuels, artistes créatifs, héros de guerre et champions respectés – portent habituellement les fondements de leurs rôles publics exemplaires; ils proposent des images d'hommes et de femmes sérieux, méritant le respect – des gens qui devraient aussi être pris au sérieux par les spectateurs.[6]

Affublée de vêtements, de bijoux et de maquillage raffinés, Page est représentée en femme professionnelle d'un certain statut social. Habitant à l'époque à Montréal, ses poèmes commencent à recevoir l'approbation du public et sont publiés dans des magazines tels que *Contemporary Verse*, *Unit of Five* et *Poetry*. Dans ce portrait, la coiffure élégante et les bijoux éclatants de Page marquent sa position sociale et sa réputation croissante. C'est la couleur de ses lèvres, cependant, qui est la plus frappante. Son rouge à lèvres cardinal évoque un pouvoir (sexué) qui renseigne sur la construction de son identité.

Dans son essai « La féminité en tant que mascarade », la psychanalyste britannique Joan Rivière stipule que le « masque féminin » de la femme sert à distinguer son identité de celle de l'homme. La féminité peut donc être assumée et portée comme un masque, dit-elle, aussi bien pour cacher le fait qu'elle possède une certaine masculinité que pour se prémunir contre des représailles si l'on découvrait cela[7]. En d'autres mots, les femmes qui exercent des rôles professionnels tendent parfois à exagérer leur féminité afin de masquer des traits estimés comme masculins par la société, comme le pouvoir et l'intelligence[8].

Étant donné le succès professionnel de Page, son portrait devient une représentation de ce que Rivière qualifie de « succès masculin ». En comparaison à l'argument butlerien d'Efrat Tseëlon[9], selon qui le masque est une méthode de performance, Rivière complique la relation entre genre et maquillage, postulant que ce dernier sert en réalité à exagérer l'identité de la personne tout en exagérant sa différence avec le corps masculin. Dans *P.K. Page*, le « masque féminin » de la poète est approprié en tant que signifiant d'une *re*-construction sociale et d'une *re*présentation professionnelle.

Si ses premiers portraits sont très représentationnels, Duncan adopte à la fin des années 1940 un style plus expressionniste. Par exemple, les portraits *Audrey « Babs » McLaren*, *Grant Munro* et *Norman McLaren* sont exécutés avec des coups de pinceau expressifs, une palette restreinte et des traits exagérés. Rappelant la peinture « color field », les espaces dans lesquels elle situe ses modèles évoquent les représentations floues que Mark Rothko fait de l'espace, de la couleur, de l'expérience. Exprimant la spontanéité et la liberté qui caractérisent l'art de l'après-guerre, les figures que Duncan peint à cette époque prouvent l'influence de l'art abstrait sur sa pratique. Ce virage vers le conceptuel, en comparaison aux portraits « polis » de ses débuts, a influencé un changement dans ses représentations futures du corps, sur la toile et sur la pellicule. Dans le film *L'amour pas-à-pas* (1955), par exemple, les corps deviennent des chaussures. Tels des acteurs, ces « nouveaux » portraits de Duncan performent les esthétiques changeantes de l'époque et les politiques de genres qui ont dominé la culture visuelle canadienne.

Alma Duncan a peint plusieurs autoportraits au fil de sa carrière, en commençant par *Autoportrait* (1939) (cat. 2, p. 99). Elle se représente habituellement en artiste au travail; ses autoportraits sont ainsi des déclarations féministes puissantes qui défient la façon dont les femmes sont généralement perçues dans la société contemporaine. Selon l'historienne de l'art Marsha Meskimmon, les autoportraits de femmes artistes ont souvent servi de véhicules d'intervention sociale pour démontrer leur professionnalisme et leurs compétences. En confrontant les limites préconçues des rôles des femmes dans la société, les femmes artistes ont commencé à s'approprier le portrait comme un espace où elles pouvaient remettre en question les représentations « traditionnelles » des femmes dans l'art, ainsi que le rôle de l'artiste femme. Comme l'indique Meskimmon, « la personne qui signe un autoportrait en est à la fois le sujet et l'objet. Pour les femmes, cette interaction est particulièrement significative. *La* femme a été l'objet de l'art pendant des siècles, alors que *les* femmes sont restées dans les marges de la production. Agir dans les deux rôles en même temps, c'est organiser une intervention de première importance »[10]. C'est donc grâce à l'autoportrait que les femmes artistes, comme Duncan, ont pu aller à l'encontre des conventions de la culture occidentale qui, pendant tant d'années, avait maintenu leurs apports dans l'ombre.

Sur le plan conceptuel, les autoportraits de femmes artistes servent de plateformes à des observations sociopolitiques. Dans le recueil *Self-Portraits by Women Painters* (Autoportraits de femmes artistes), les auteures Liana De Girolami Cheney, Alicia Craig Faxon et Kathleen Lucey Russo mentionnent que « l'autoportrait féminin en peinture est une révélation, pas juste une signature. Il ne s'agit pas d'un exercice de références iconographiques, mais plutôt d'une interprétation ou d'une déclaration du caractère et de la quête de soi de l'artiste et de son rapport à son milieu »[11]. Plus qu'une simple image renvoyée dans un miroir, les autoportraits de Duncan constituent sa manière de déclarer son adresse professionnelle et de défier les limites que la société impose aux femmes. Par exemple, en se représentant dans l'acte de peindre dans *Autoportrait avec tresses* (1940) (cat. 6, p. 100), elle proclame son désir d'être prise au sérieux en tant qu'artiste professionnelle et en tant qu'individu, malgré son apparence juvénile. Grâce à l'autoportrait, les femmes artistes bouleversent les conventions de l'histoire de l'art en présentant dans leurs tableaux des preuves de leurs habiletés professionnelles, de leur talent et de leur engagement dans leur métier.

Puisque, dans l'autoportrait, le talent d'un artiste sert d'espace métaphorique ouvert à une multiplicité de sens, nous ne pouvons ignorer la signification de la pose et de l'habillement comme autant de facettes de la représentation de soi. Choisir de prendre la pose pour un portrait ou d'entreprendre un autoportrait est un acte conscient; les vêtements du modèle sont donc très révélateurs de sa vision de soi. Dans *Système de la mode*, Roland Barthes explique que la tenue vestimentaire peut être interprétée comme un système de signes qui créent du sens :

La Mode devient un objet culturel autonome, pourvu d'une structure originale et probablement d'une finalité nouvelle; aux fonctions sociales, reconnues d'ordinaire à la Mode vestimentaire, se substituent ou s'ajoutent d'autres fonctions, analogues à celles de toute la littérature, et que l'on peut résumer d'un mot en disant qu'à travers la langue qui la prend désormais en charge, la Mode devient récit.[12]

L'idée que la mode peut raconter une histoire et créer du sens est importante dans le contexte de l'autoportrait. Dans plusieurs autoportraits de Duncan, comme *Autoportrait avec tresses* et *Autoportrait avec rayures rouges* (1958) (cat. 32, p. 104), sa tenue et sa coiffure sont des indicateurs de son image de soi, de son statut et de sa personnalité. Par conséquent, en plus de former une grande partie son identité, la mode est finalement un moyen très conscient pour le modèle de se raconter.

Par le passé, il était inacceptable qu'une femme artiste se représente dans l'acte de peindre, ou d'une quelconque autre manière qui donne l'impression qu'elle exerçait une profession « masculine ». Afin de répondre au besoin de se conformer aux idées préconçues de la féminité, les femmes artistes se représentaient habituellement non pas comme des artistes, mais comme des femmes habillées de manière « féminine » et à la mode. Cependant, dans *Autoportrait avec tresses*, Duncan porte un pantalon – associé aux hommes ou aux femmes « libérées » – et se représente en artiste, assise à son chevalet. Conformes à l'analyse de Barthes, la tenue et la coiffure du modèle touchent à plusieurs sujets, y compris la personnalité, le genre, la classe, l'ethnie et les ambitions sociales. La décision de se représenter en pantalons considérés comme « masculins » fait donc de l'autoportrait un défi lancé aux définitions « conventionnelles » de la féminité.

Les vêtements d'Alma Duncan ne sont pas les seuls signifiants qui suggèrent qu'elle affrontait les normes contemporaines; qu'en est-il de ses tresses ? Simples et enfantines, ses tresses – et surtout les boucles rouges qui les nouent – contredisent l'idée du professionnalisme de l'artiste tant dans le portrait qu'en réalité. En 1940, Duncan a 23 ans. Elle n'a pas encore obtenu le statut de « professionnelle » et dans ce portrait ses tresses nous rappellent qu'elle est au début de sa carrière. D'un point de vue idéologique et politique, elle se sert de la représentation de soi pour affirmer son talent et défier les obstacles posés par son âge et son sexe. Ses tresses nous rappellent qu'elle est toujours une jeune femme, mais elles mettent de l'avant l'idée selon laquelle l'âge ne devrait pas influer sur la reconnaissance de son talent.

La négociation entre le corps professionnel et le corps en action à laquelle se livre Alma Duncan est un thème qui revient souvent dans ses portraits des années 1950. Alors qu'elle travaille à l'ONF sous la direction de Norman McLaren, elle fait des expériences avec le film d'animation en se servant de marionnettes, une technique nouvellement populaire dans le cinéma canadien. Selon John Grierson, les dessins animés sont « … de loin la meilleure façon de faire passer des messages publics »[13]. Compte tenu de leur attrait auprès du grand public et de la possibilité d'une production en série, cette forme d'animation amusante peut en effet être vue comme un moyen très pratique de communiquer des idées aux enfants et aux adultes. En parlant de l'intérêt que l'ONF porte aux marionnettes, Karen Mazurkewich souligne, dans *Cartoon Capers: The History of Canadian Animators* (Aventures animées. L'histoire des cinéastes d'animation canadiens), qu'elles sont des outils pédagogiques comparables à des *porteparoles politiques* : « Le mandat original de l'ONF était de servir de porte-parole pour le gouvernement lors de la Deuxième Guerre mondiale »[14]. Vu dans ce contexte, l'objectif des films n'était pas seulement de divertir le public, mais aussi de les éduquer. En représentant sur scène une voix qui n'est pas la leur, mais plutôt celle de leurs créateurs et créatrices, les marionnettes deviennent des métaphores qui enseignent et communiquent du sens.

Mis à part Evelyn Lambart, que Mazurkewich qualifie de « première dame du cinéma d'animation au Canada »[15], Alma Duncan était une des rares femmes à travailler au département d'animation de l'ONF. Elle produit *Fantaisie folklorique* en 1951, son premier film d'animation pour l'Office. Basé sur trois contes folkloriques – *The Riddle Song* (La chanson-devinette), *Qui a tué le rouge-gorge ?* et *The Cooper of Fife* (Le tonnelier de Fife) – le film aborde les thèmes de l'abus, de la mort, des rôles sexuels, du patriarcat et du pouvoir dans la culture occidentale. Par exemple, dans *Le tonnelier de Fife*, Duncan utilise sa marionnette pour se prononcer contre la violence conjugale. Alors que le tonnelier bat sa femme, la marionnette se transforme rapidement en démon (cat. 24, p. 121); deux cornes apparaissent sur sa tête, et de la mousse blanche forme une barbiche pointue sur son menton, transformant la marionnette en caricature du Malin. Ces changements physiques ne font pas partie de l'histoire originale, alors nous pouvons présumer qu'ils traduisent les opinions de Duncan.

Alma Duncan se retira de l'Office en 1951 afin de former une compagnie en partenariat avec Audrey McLaren, qu'elles nommèrent Dunclaren Productions. Ensemble, elles réalisèrent trois films animés : *Kumak le chasseur somnolent* (1953) (cat. 25, p. 123), *L'amour pas-à-pas* (1955) (cat. 26, p. 124) et *Échange amical* (1958) (cat. 34, p. 127). Bien que réparti dans divers moyens d'expression, le travail de Duncan à cette époque présente une constante dans ses références aux stéréotypes et aux questions sociologiques propres à la société contemporaine. Par exemple, dans leur premier film collaboratif, *Kumak le chasseur somnolent*, qui raconte l'histoire d'un pêcheur inuit narcoleptique nommé Kumak, Duncan et McLaren utilisent des marionnettes faites à la main, des masques en papier mâché, des vêtements en cuirs cousus à la main ainsi que de nombreux accessoires tels que phoques et kayaks de chasse (cat. 27, p. 122) pour communiquer leur vision du Nord canadien.

Dans ce court-métrage nominé aux prix de la British Academy of Film and Television Arts, les marionnettes servent de porte-parole pour témoigner d'une culture et d'une communauté qui intéressaient l'artiste. Influencée par ses amis et amies scientifiques qui travaillaient dans l'Arctique[16], et avant de faire son propre voyage dans le Nord à des fins de recherche artistique en 1975, Duncan s'inspire de ses collègues du « Arctic Circle », un club local formé en 1947 pour les Ottaviens intéressés par « tout ce qui a rapport à l'Arctique ». Dans ses propres mots : « Plusieurs membres ont fait preuve de patience et de générosité en répondant à mes questions et en me portant conseil »[17]. Bien qu'elles ne fussent pas en communication directe avec des communautés inuites, Duncan et McLaren reconnaissaient que leur film était une interprétation contemporaine et personnelle de la culture inuite, racontée du point de vue d'observatrices passionnées. À la lumière de l'argument de Mazurkewich, selon lequel les marionnettes sont des objets

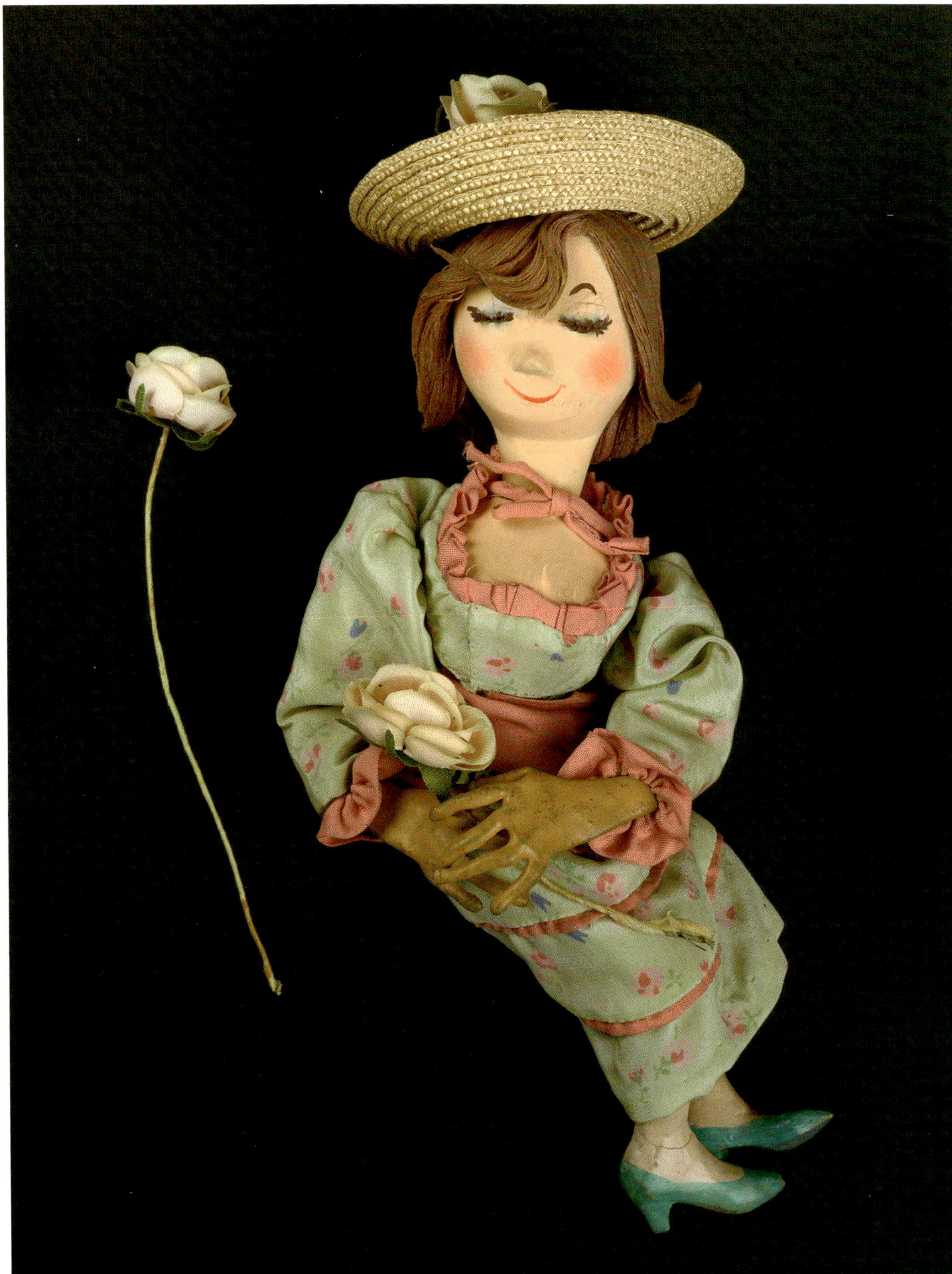

Folksong Fantasy | Fantaisie folklorique 1951 (cat. 27)
puppet and film prop | marionnette et accessoire de film
Library and Archives Canada | Bibliothèque et Archives Canada

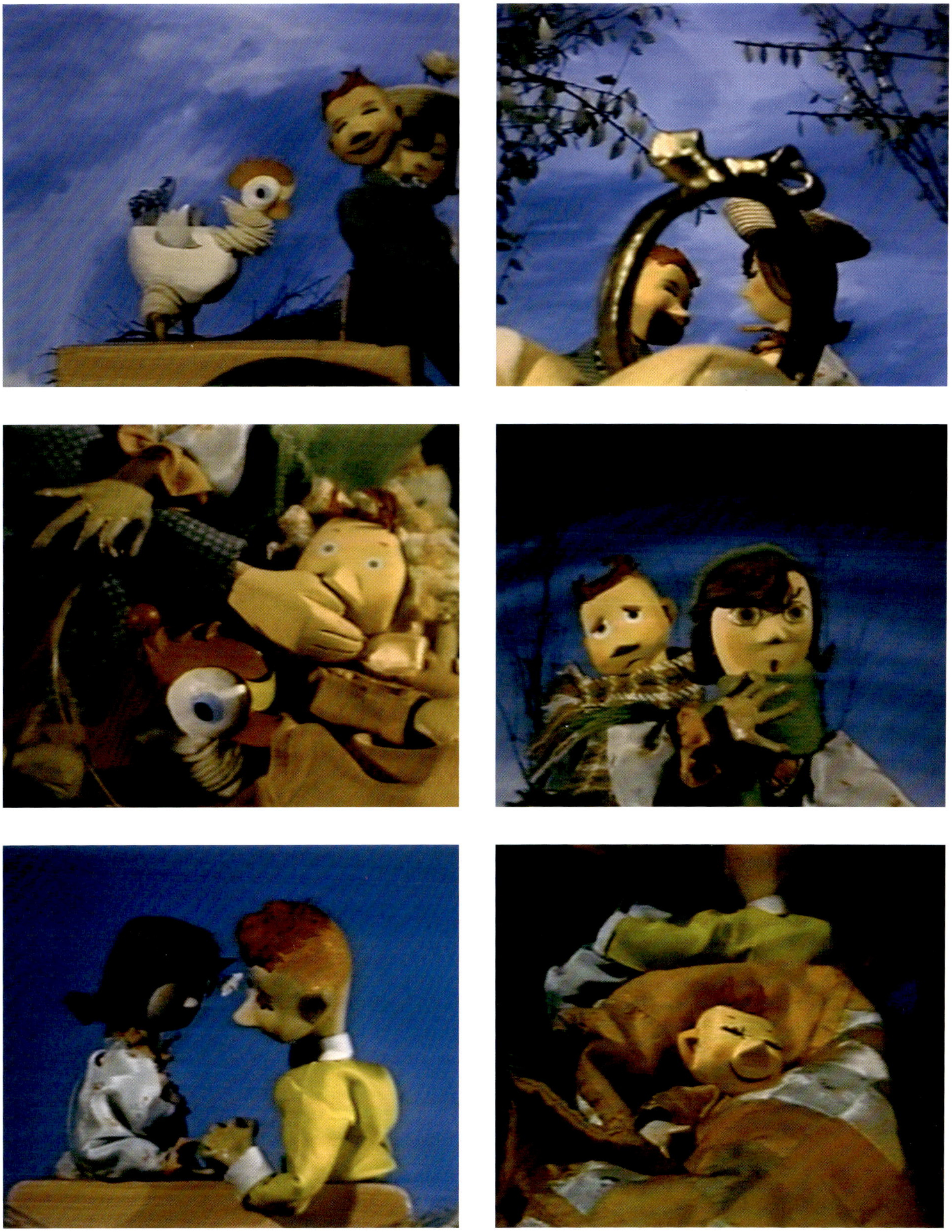

Folksong Fantasy | Fantaisie folklorique 1951 (cat. 24)
film stills from *The Riddle Song* | photographies tirées du film *La chanson-devinette*
National Film Board of Canada | Office national du film du Canada

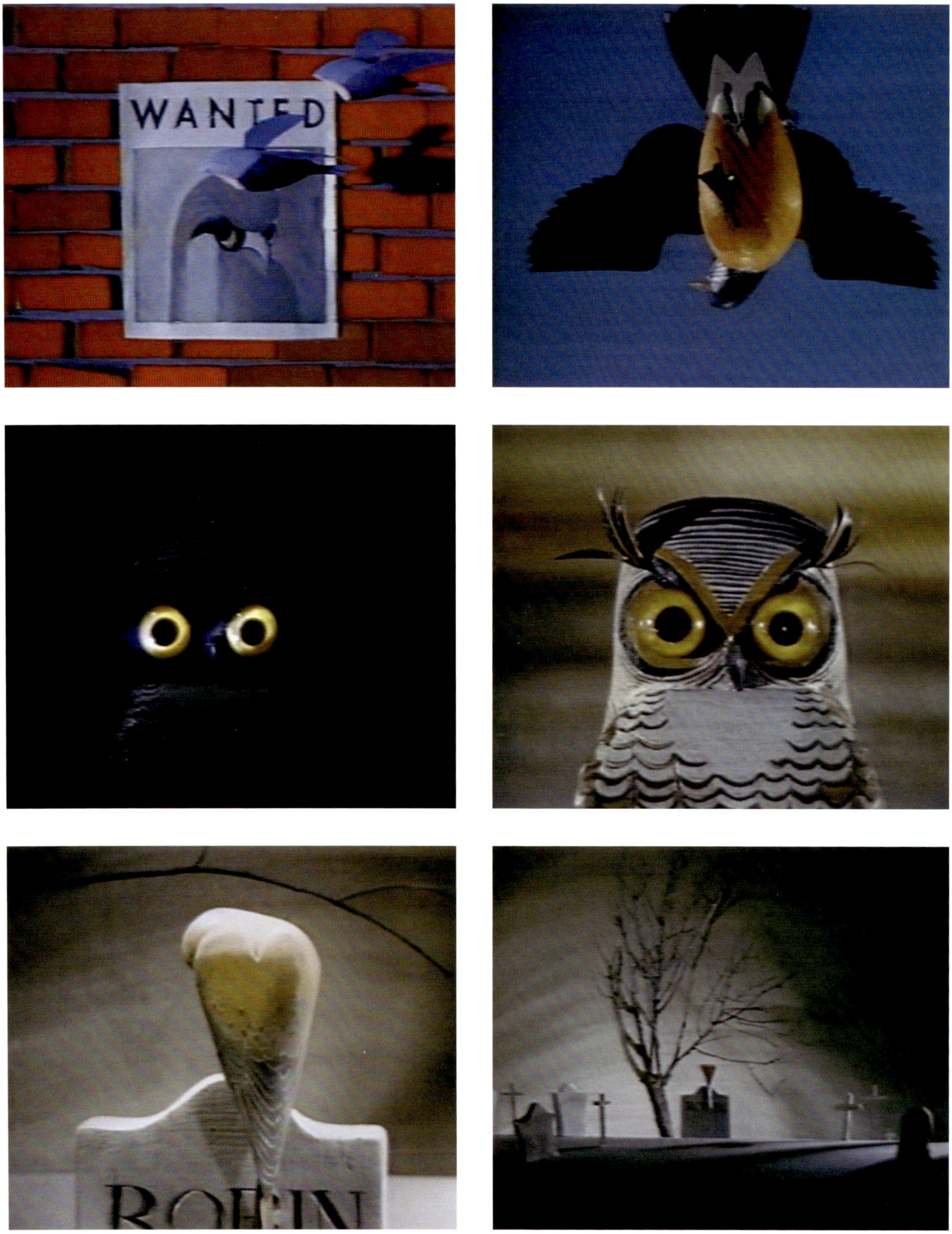

Folksong Fantasy | Fantaisie folklorique 1951 (cat. 24)
film stills from *Who Killed Cock Robin?* | photographies tirées du film *Qui a tué le rouge-gorge ?*
National Film Board of Canada | Office national du film du Canada

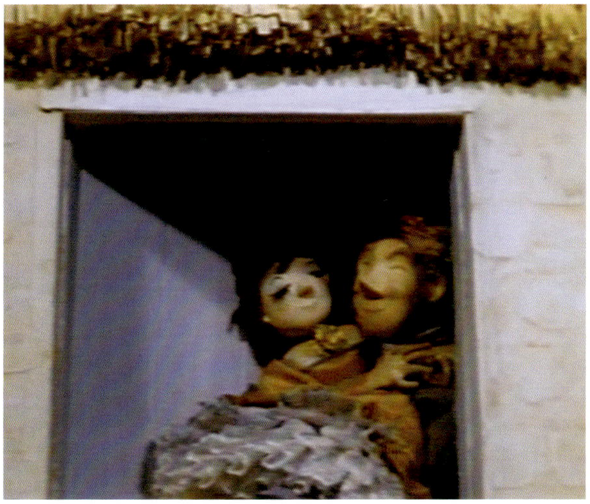
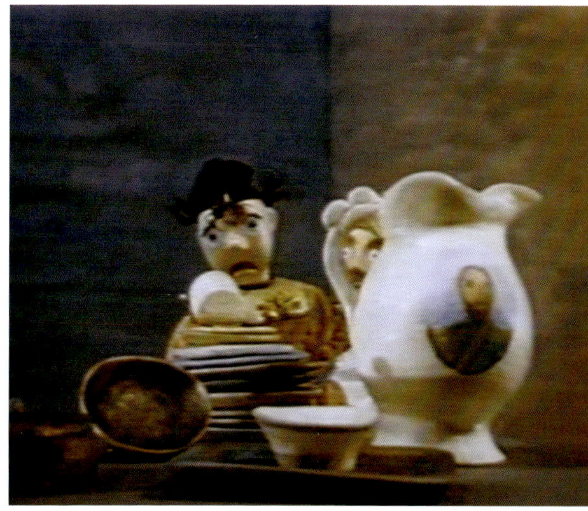
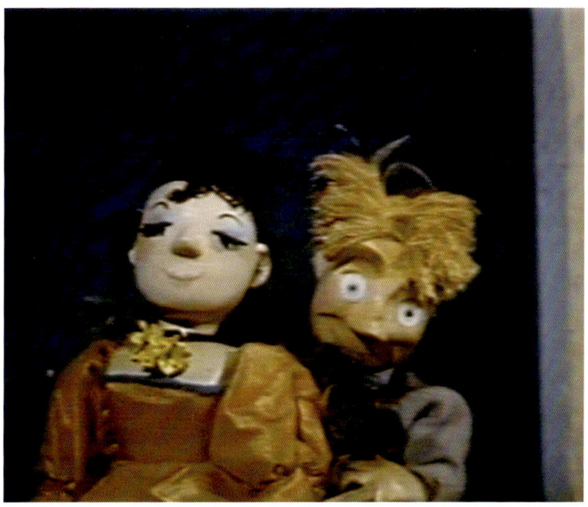
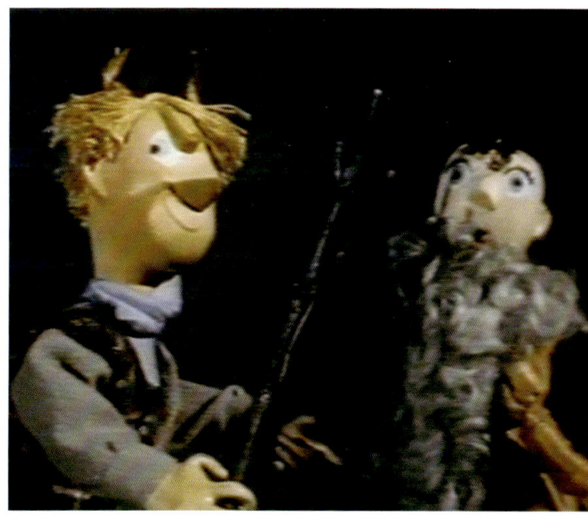
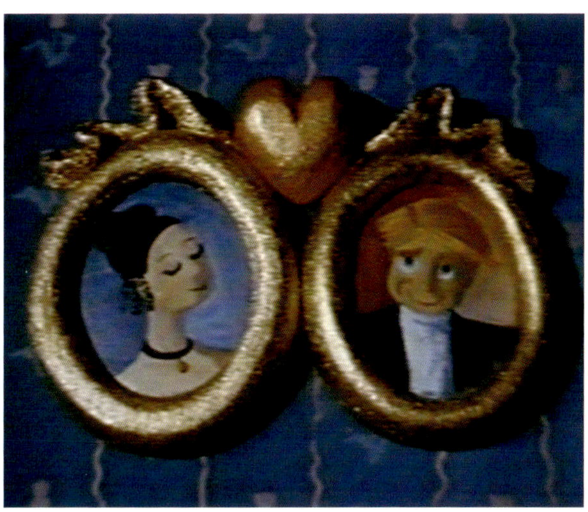
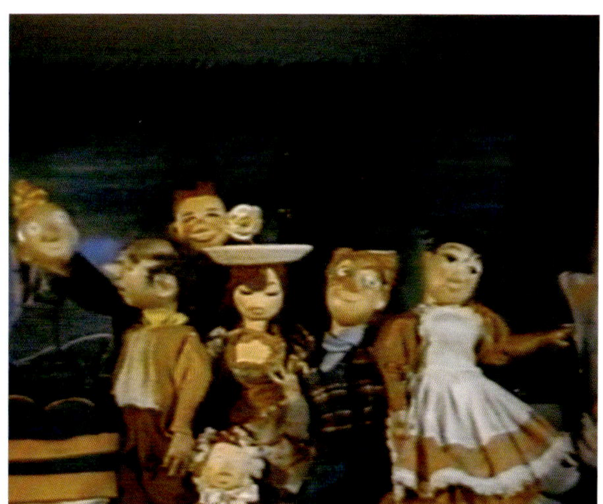

Folksong Fantasy | Fantaisie folklorique 1951 (cat. 24)
film stills from *The Cooper of Fife* | photographies tirées du film *Le tonnelier de Fife*
National Film Board of Canada | Office national du film du Canada

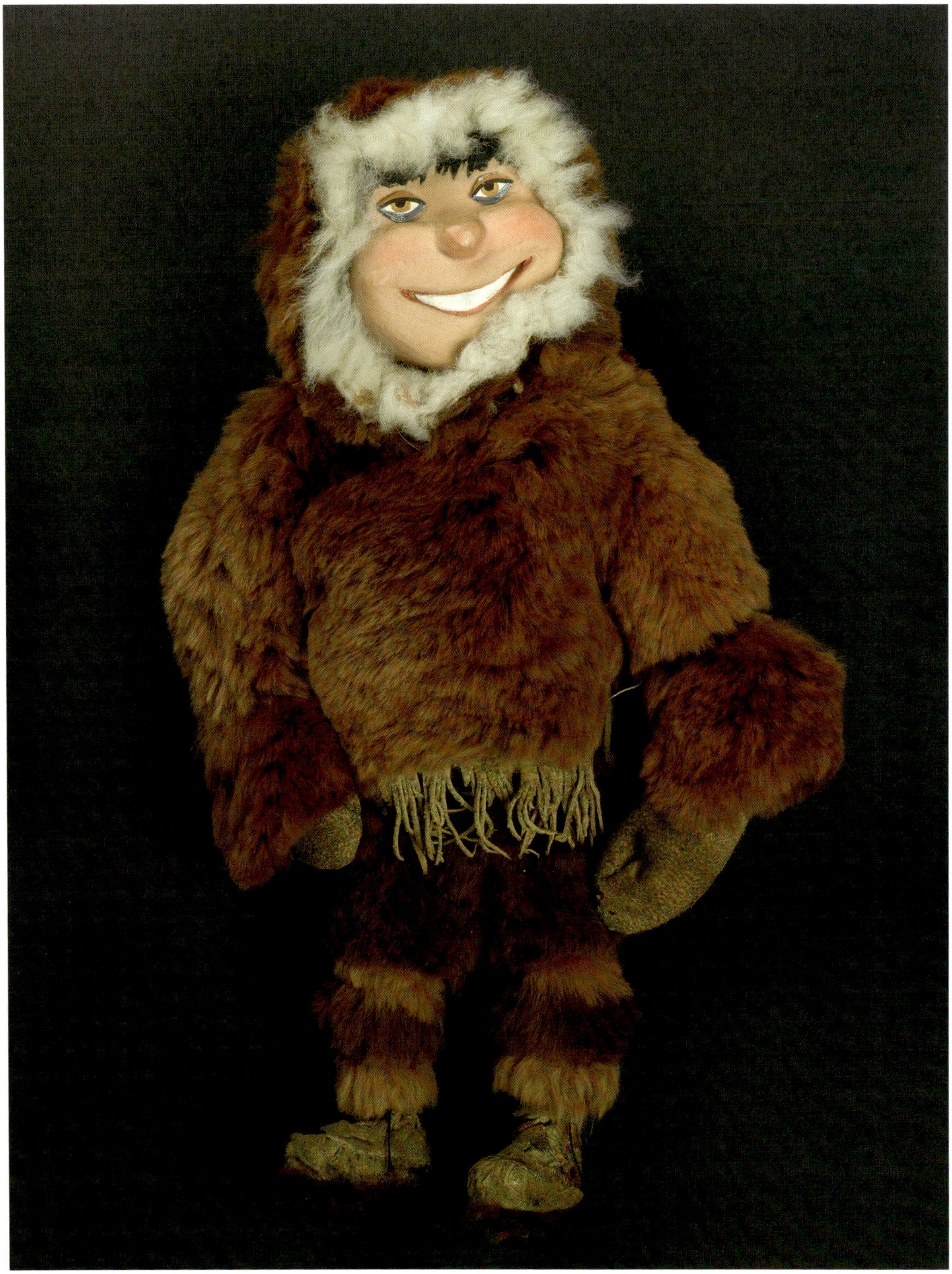

Kumak the Sleepy Hunter | Kumak le chasseur somnolent 1953 (cat. 27)
puppet | marionnette
Library and Archives Canada | Bibliothèque et Archives Canada

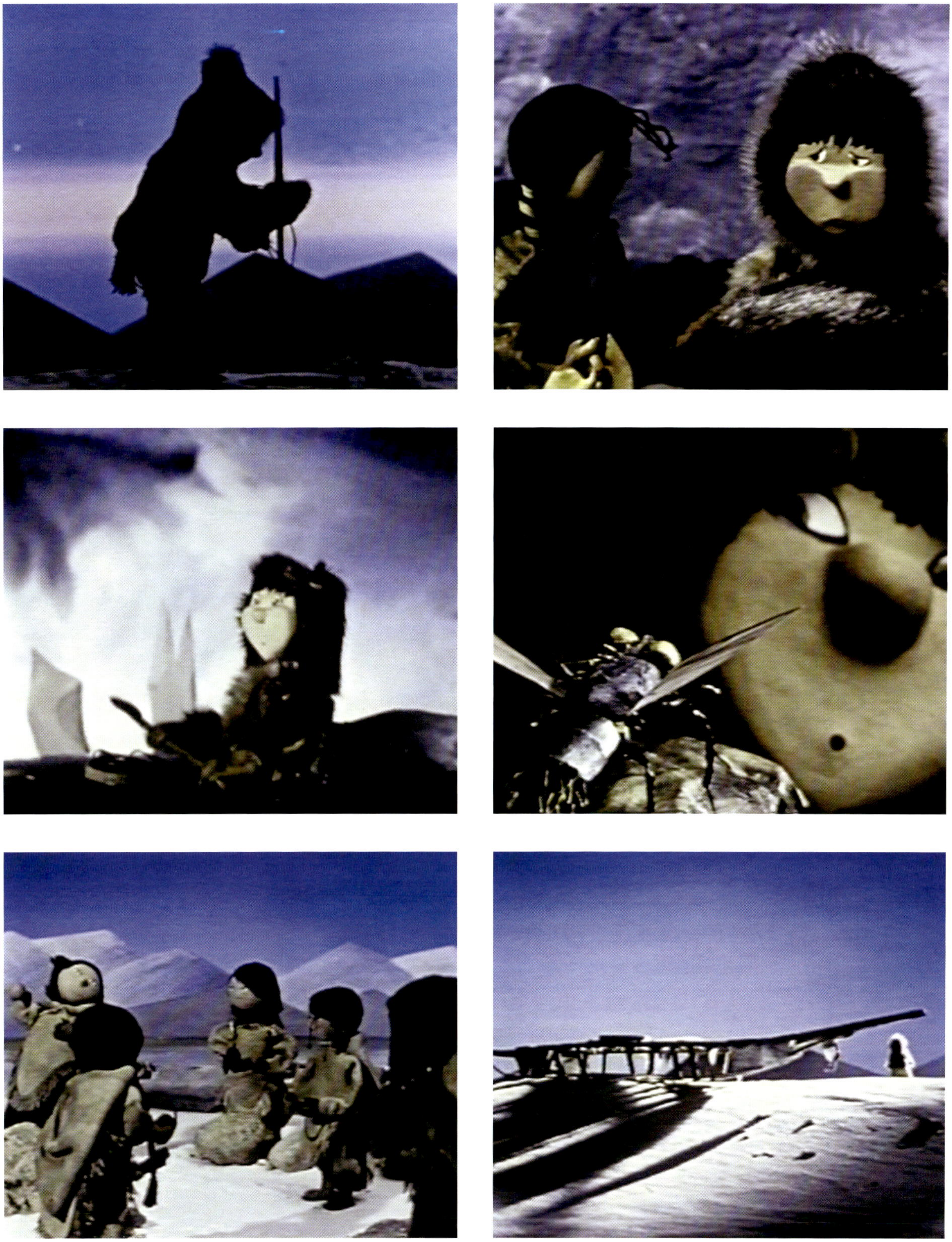

Kumak the Sleepy Hunter | Kumak le chasseur somnolent 1953 (cat. 25)
film stills | photographies tirées du film
Courtesy of Dunclaren Productions | Gracieuseté de Dunclaren Productions

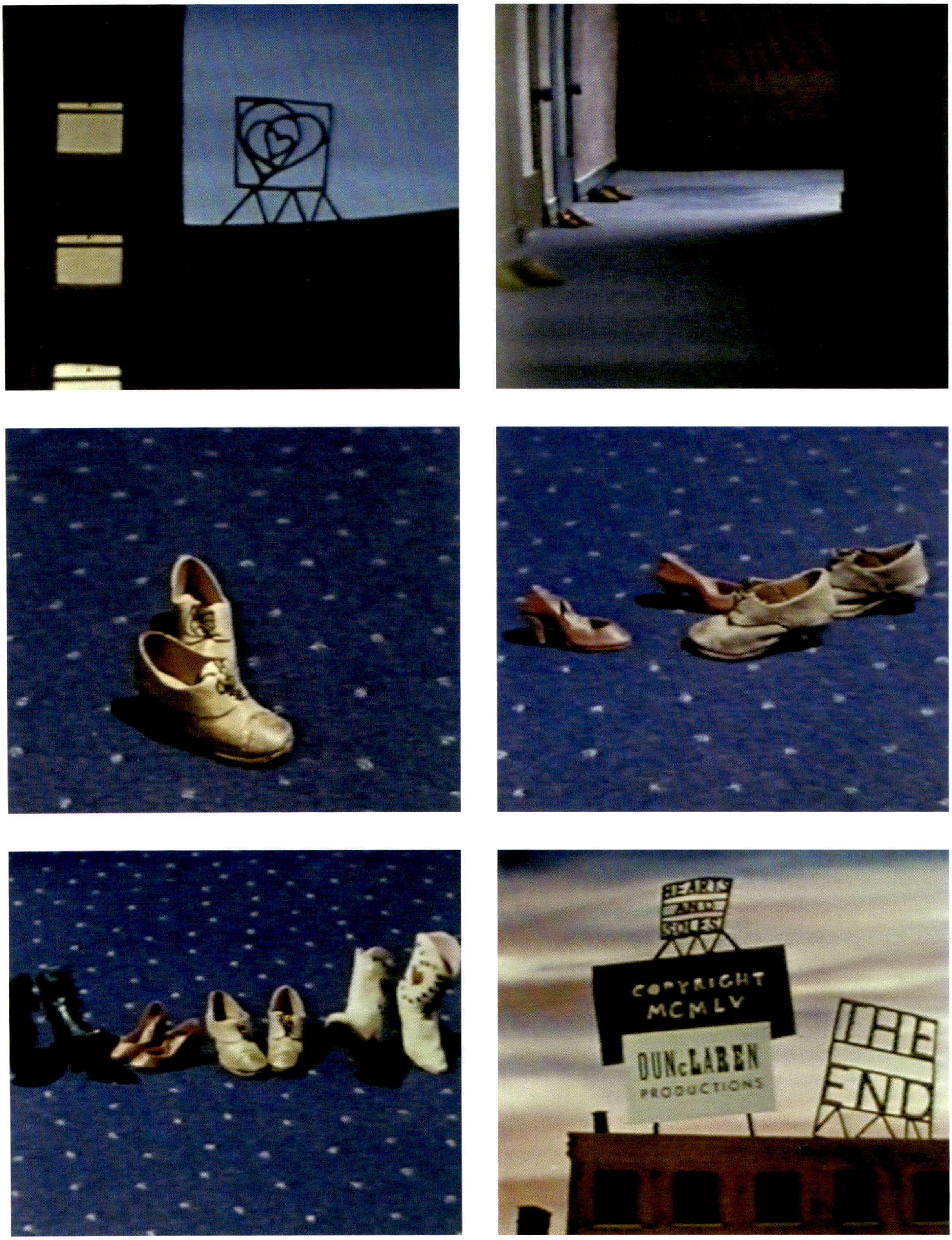

Hearts and Soles | L'amour pas-à-pas 1955 (cat. 26)
film stills | photographies tirées du film
Courtesy of Dunclaren Productions | Gracieuseté de Dunclaren Productions

anthropologiques qui créent du sens, je perçois les personnages de Duncan comme des doubles métaphoriques qui témoignent d'« autres » cultures, d'« autres » histoires et d'« autres » traditions dans les premiers films d'animation canadiens avec marionnettes.

Dans *L'amour pas-à-pas*, Dunclaren se sert de chaussures pour dénoncer l'exploitation et la hiérarchisation des genres. Le film débute avec une paire de talons hauts rouges qui commence à danser avec des chaussures d'homme brunes. Une troisième paire, des chaussures d'hommes, se joint au duo et la danse tourne rapidement à la compétition. Indices de références à des personnes, les chaussures deviennent les symboles du corps absent. Au fil du récit, le premier partenaire de danse devient très protecteur à l'égard d'« elle » et s'acharne à « la » protéger de la deuxième paire. *L'amour pas-à-pas* présente les stéréotypes sexuels de l'époque : les chaussures rouges jouent le rôle du « sexe faible », alors que les chaussures d'homme symbolisent la lutte féroce pour la domination masculine. En 1955, date à laquelle le film est réalisé, la Deuxième Guerre mondiale est terminée depuis dix ans, et les femmes, en reprenant leurs rôles domestiques, ont du même coup réintégré la position d'« autre ». Selon Ruth Roach Pierson, « la guerre a eu l'effet léger mais dérangeant d'orienter la population féminine vers une position d'égalité avec les hommes, mais cet effet est remplacé par le modèle d'après-guerre en jupe évasée et à nouveau domestiqué, et, pendant plus de dix ans, le féminisme est de nouveau sacrifié en faveur de la féminité »[18]. Les chaussures rouges du film marquent donc le retour de la femme-objet que les hommes s'arrachent.

Aujourd'hui, dix ans après son décès, il importe de déclarer qu'Alma Duncan était une artiste réellement en avance sur son époque, qui ne se gênait pas pour traiter de thèmes à forte connotation politique. Ses portraits sont de puissants exemples de la culture visuelle féministe, et ils puisent leur force dans les multiples enchevêtrements qu'ils contiennent. Reflétant les stéréotypes de genres de l'époque, ainsi que les changements esthétiques qui se sont produits dans l'art moderne canadien, les œuvres de Duncan des années 1940 et 1950 sont des documents visuels qui relatent son rapport au climat culturel et social ainsi qu'au développement de l'art canadien d'après-guerre. Donc en interprétant l'œuvre de Duncan à la lumière du dialogisme, l'histoire de l'art canadien pourra commencer à considérer ses portraits, ses autoportraits, ses marionnettes et ses masques comme autant d'*archives performatives*.

1 L'argumentaire de cet essai découle de mon mémoire de maîtrise en histoire de l'art canadien; Jaclyn Meloche, *Braiding the Boundaries: A Dialogical Study of Alma Duncan's Art from the 1940s and 1950s* (Tresser les frontières. Une étude dialogique de l'art d'Alma Duncan dans les années 1940 et 1950), Mémoire de maîtrise, Ottawa, Université Carleton, 2004. **2** Judith Butler, *Ces corps qui comptent. De la matérialité et des limites discursives du sexe*, traduction de Charlotte Nordmann, Paris, Éditions Amsterdam, 2009, p. 27 (ouvrage original publié en 1993). **3** Maria Tippett, *By a Lady: Celebrating Three Centuries of Art by Canadian Women* (Fait par une dame. Une célébration de trois siècles d'art créé par des femmes canadiennes), Toronto, Penguin Books, 1992, p. 105. **4** Simone de Beauvoir, *Le deuxième sexe. Tome II*, Paris, Gallimard, 1949, p. 13. **5** Audrey McLaren, entrevue avec Jaclyn Meloche, enregistré à Ottawa, le 18 novembre 2002. **6** Richard Brilliant, *Portraiture* (Le portrait), London, Reaktion Books Limited, 1991, p. 10. **7** Joan Rivière, « Womanliness as a Masquerade » (La féminité en tant que mascarade), dans *Formations of Fantasy*, Victor Burgin, James Donald et Cora Kaplan (dir.), Londres/New York, Methuen, 1986, p. 38. **8** Ibid., p. 35–36. **9** Efrat Tseëlon, *Masquerade and Identities: Essays in Gender, Sexuality and Marginality* (Mascarade et identités. Essais sur le genre, la sexualité et la marginalité), Londres/New York, Routledge, 2001. **10** Marsha Meskimmon, *The Art of Reflection: Women Artist's Self-Portraiture in the Twentieth Century* (L'art de la réflection. Les autoportraits de femmes artistes au XXe siècle), New York, Columbia University Press, 1996, p. 14. **11** Liana De Girolami Cheney, Alicia Craig Faxon et Kathleen Lucey Russo, *Self-Portraiture by Women Painters* (Autoportraits de femmes artistes), Farnham (RU), Ashgate Publishing Limited, 2000, p. xxvi. **12** Roland Barthes, *Système de la mode*, dans *Œuvres complètes. Tome II*, Paris, Seuil, p. 357, 1994 (1967). **13** John Grierson, « Interview with John Grierson » (Entrevue avec John Grierson), 1972, vol. C12, C2527, 116, Archives de l'Université McGill, Montréal, dans Helen Brimmell, " The Beauty of Industrial Work is Shown in Current Exhibit by Artist Alma Duncan" (La beauté du travail industriel est dévoilée dans une exposition de l'artiste Alma Duncan), *The Daily Mercury*, 18 janvier 1988, s.p. **14** Karen Mazurkewich, *Cartoon Capers: The History of Canadian Animators* (Aventures animées. L'histoire des cinéastes d'animation canadiens), Toronto, McArthur & Company, 1999, p. 10. **15** Ibid., p. 196. **16** Alma Duncan, notes biographiques, s.d., dossier « Biographies 1972–1992 », boîte 15, Bibliothèque et Archives Canada, Ottawa (ciaprès appelé BAC). **17** Notes de Dunclaren Productions pour le visionnement de *Kumak le chasseur somnolent* en 1954 (devant le « Arctic Circle »), Ottawa, Ontario, 6 janvier 1954, vol. 3, dossier 9, BAC. **18** Ruth Roach Pierson, *They're Still Women After All: The Second World War and Canadian Womanhood* (Après tout, elles sont toujours femmes. La Deuxième Guerre mondiale et la population féminine canadienne), Toronto, McClelland and Stewart, 1986, p. 220.

Jaclyn Meloche est une artiste visuelle et historienne de l'art qui cherche à recadrer dans un contexte féministe et poststructuraliste les corpus de femmes artistes. Elle travaille actuellement, dans ses recherches et dans ses écrits, à compliquer les limites esthétiques et conceptuelles de la performance et de la performativité vis-à-vis d'un discours sur la matière. Elle est aussi engagée dans une pratique artistique où s'entremêlent le dessin, la performance et la photographie. Elle détient un baccalauréat en arts visuels de l'Université d'Ottawa, une maîtrise ès arts en histoire de l'art canadien de l'Université Carleton, une maîtrise en arts visuels de la School of Visual Arts, et elle est présentement doctorante dans un programme de recherche-création en sciences humaines (arts visuels) à l'Université Concordia. Meloche enseigne dans le département des arts visuels à l'université d'Ottawa et habite Ottawa.

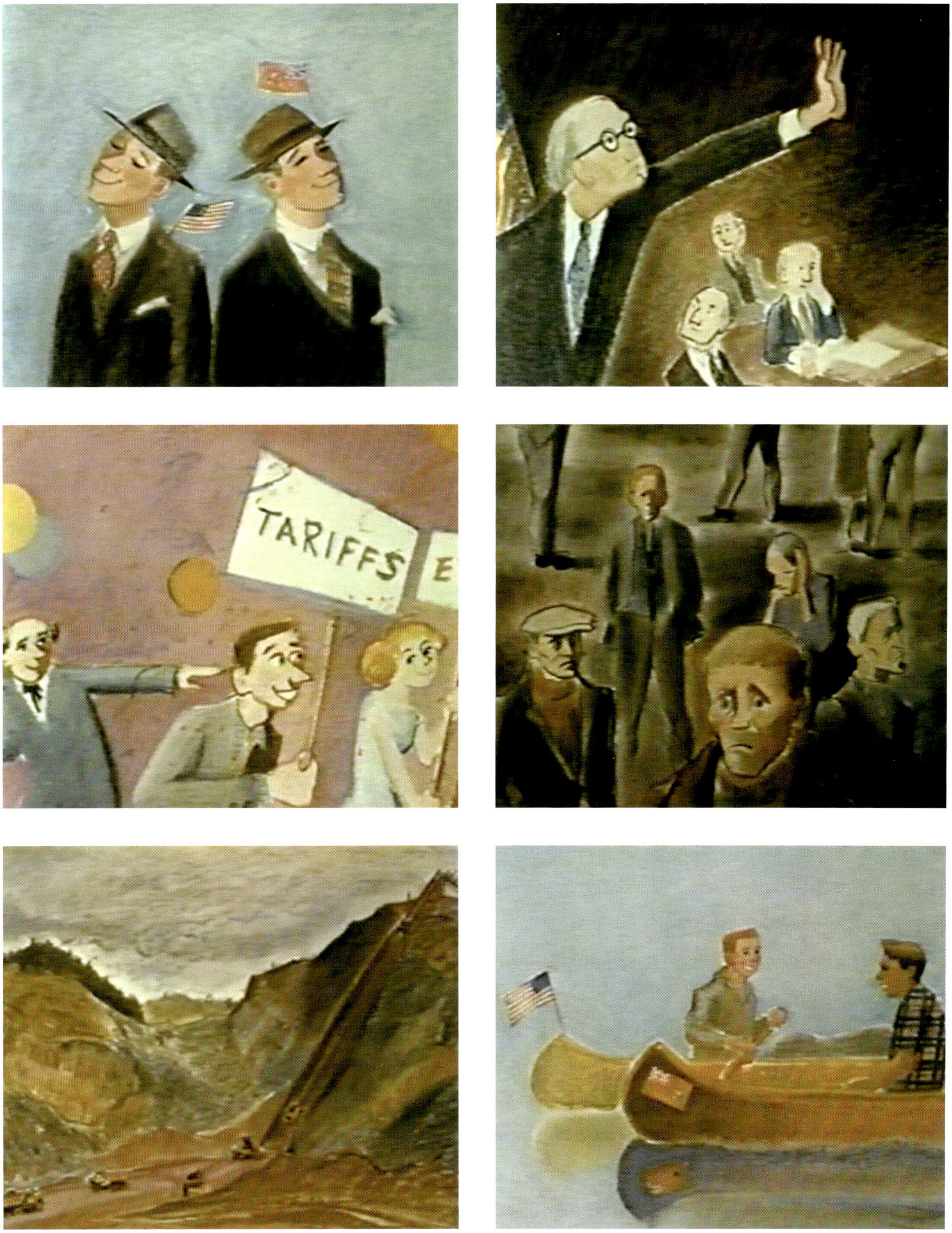

Friendly Interchange | Échange amical 1958 (cat. 34)
film stills | photographies tirées du film
Courtesy of Dunclaren Productions | Gracieuseté de Dunclaren Productions

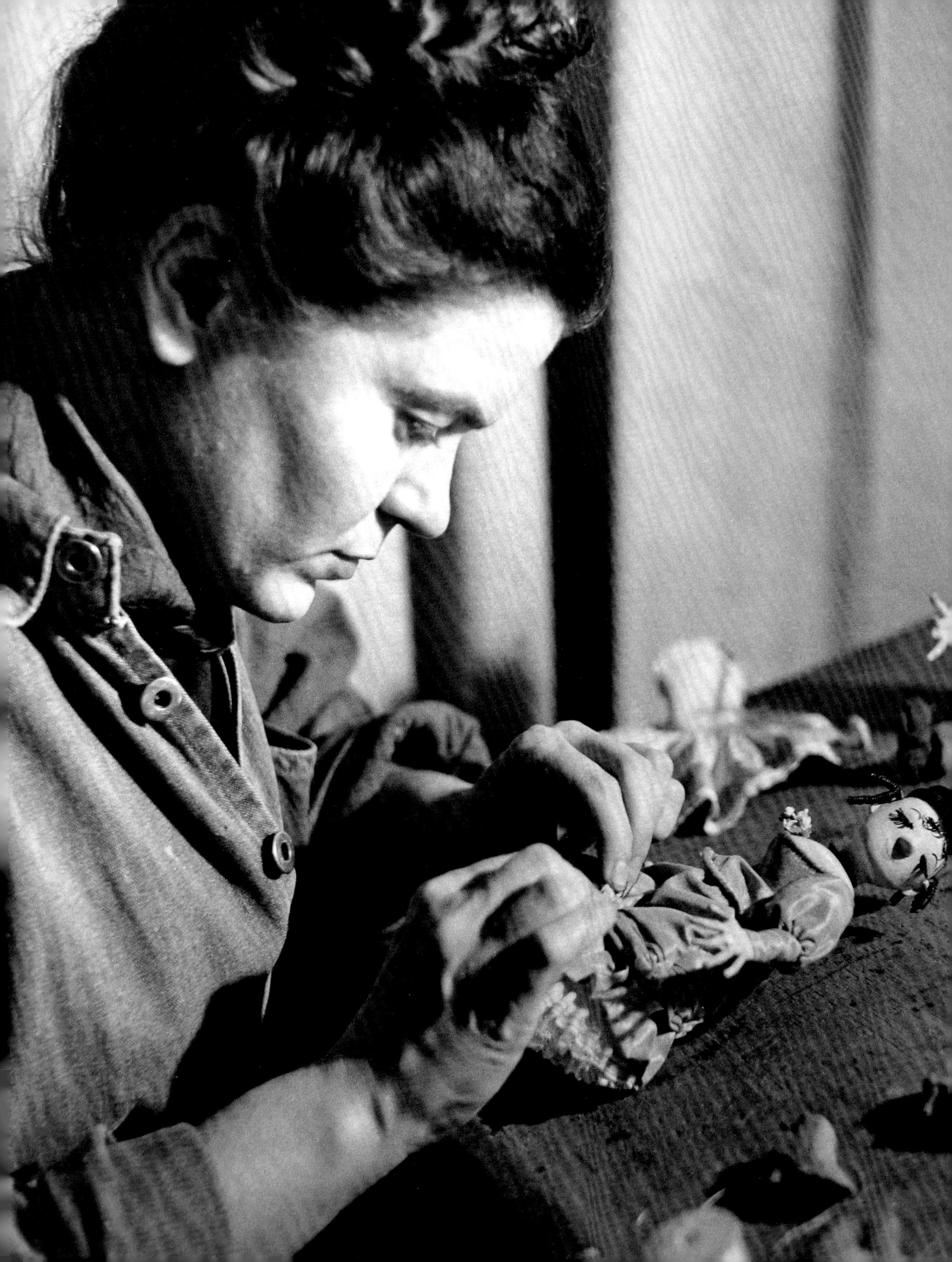

Marginal Experiments

Canadian Cinema 1939–1959

Tom McSorley

Strange as it might seem, in order to truly understand Canadian cinema history we must travel to pre-cinematic, pre-revolutionary Mexico of the nineteenth century. A dictator of that era, president Porfirio Díaz, made a famous declaration about his country that also applies to Canada, and in particular Canadian film: "Poor Mexico! So far from god, so close to the United States."[1] While rich, fortunate Canada is not at all, even metaphorically speaking, "far from god"—it is very close indeed to the United States. Economically and culturally dominated by its powerful and attractive southern neighbour, Canadian film has struggled to define itself against Hollywood's overwhelming cinematic presence. Since the dawn of filmmaking in Canada in the early twentieth-century, the stories imagined of ourselves were markedly different from the glossy, ruggedly individualist, conquering narratives of the American cinema. In Canadian movies we dream, but we dream differently. For those working in the industry, the dominant dream for much of the century was to leave Canada, and to make it in Hollywood. Canada exported literally hundreds of talented filmmakers and performers. Consequently, Canada has a considerable presence in the world's most powerful film industry,

Alma Duncan working on the making of the film *Folksong Fantasy*, 1951
Alma Duncan travaillant à la réalisation du film *Fantaisie folklorique*, 1951

but has been slow to develop its own. The chief cause has been the continuous American corporate ownership of distribution and exhibition systems in Canada since the 1920s. Now, as then, over 95% of moving images seen in Canada are made in Hollywood, and our absence from our own cinema screens is a persistent symptom of being "so close."

Cinema arrived in Canada in the late nineteenth century with images made and about elsewhere. The first public screening in Canada was held in Montreal in June 1896, a reel of short films by the Lumière Brothers of France and by the Edison Company of the United States. Later, films were screened in Ottawa and moved westward, enchanting and in a certain sense colonizing Canada with moving images. The consumption of images created elsewhere largely defines the cultural practice of going to the movies for Canadians to this day. This is not to suggest that no films were made here. In the early 1900s, film travelogues extolling the natural wonders of Canada were produced by the Canadian Pacific Railway. By 1918, the Canadian government recognized cinema's potential as a source of public education and national development. In 1923, it established the Canadian Government Motion Picture Bureau. The purpose of such state film institutions was to educate Canadians with didactic, information-based short documentaries. No thoughts of film as a medium of entertainment were considered. This Canadian tendency, coupled with the emergence of Hollywood film industry hegemony, contributed to the almost total marginalization of Canadian feature filmmaking.

Out of this lamentable absence, however, eventually emerged the possibilities of alternative film practices and cinematic æsthetics. As a result of its marginality within its own borders, the Canadian cinema has developed outside traditional models of industrial "movie" production, excelling in short film forms such as documentary, animation, and experimental cinema. Alma Duncan and Audrey McLaren were mid-twentieth-century Canadian filmmakers who created, in this context, three short stop-motion animation films, and one sponsored film in Ottawa. It is outside those industrial models that Duncan's film *Folksong Fantasy* (NFB, 1951) (cat. 24, pp. 118–121) and those created by Dunclaren Productions (her company founded with partner Audrey McLaren in 1951) would be produced in the 1950s, a period in which very few Canadian feature films were being made, and even fewer were being screened.[2] Only 18 features were produced from 1939 to 1959 in English-speaking Canada, while literally thousands of short films such as theirs were produced.[3] From the 1950s and 1960s onward, filmmaking in Canada would evolve out of a combination of state-supported cultural institutions and a tenacious independent sector largely working in short-film formats. Lacking access to its own screens, and therefore less commercially driven, Canadian postwar cinema, in all its many forms, is surprisingly formally freewheeling, æsthetically daring, and, occasionally, politically provocative.

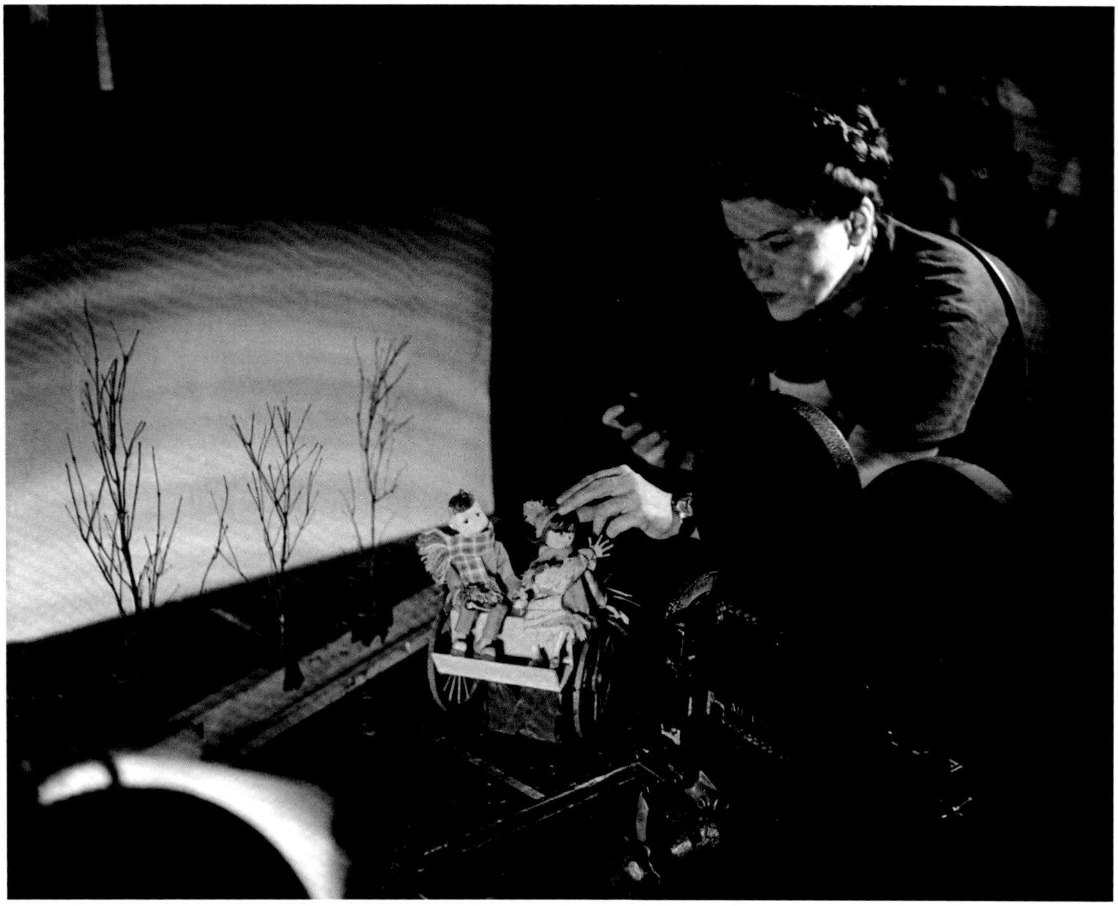

Alma Duncan working on the making of the film *Folksong Fantasy*, 1951
Alma Duncan travaillant à la réalisation du film *Fantaisie folklorique*, 1951

Paradoxically, this evolution of a cinema of experimentation and provocation brings us to the doors of another government institution set up in Canada's capital city. The National Film Board of Canada (NFB) was established in Ottawa in 1939 to produce informational and propaganda films — documentaries and animated films — about Canada's war effort, under the fierce stewardship of documentary film legend, John Grierson. In the period after the war and before television, the NFB was re-imagined to be an instrument of national education, and its films were rooted in didactic discourses of civic duty, national unity, and the ongoing project of Canadian nation building. After the arrival of television in 1952, the NFB would adjust its distribution and exhibition activities, but continue to expand its film-as-education mandate. Moreover, it would yield much more experimental work, in both documentary and animation. These were films that questioned — like so

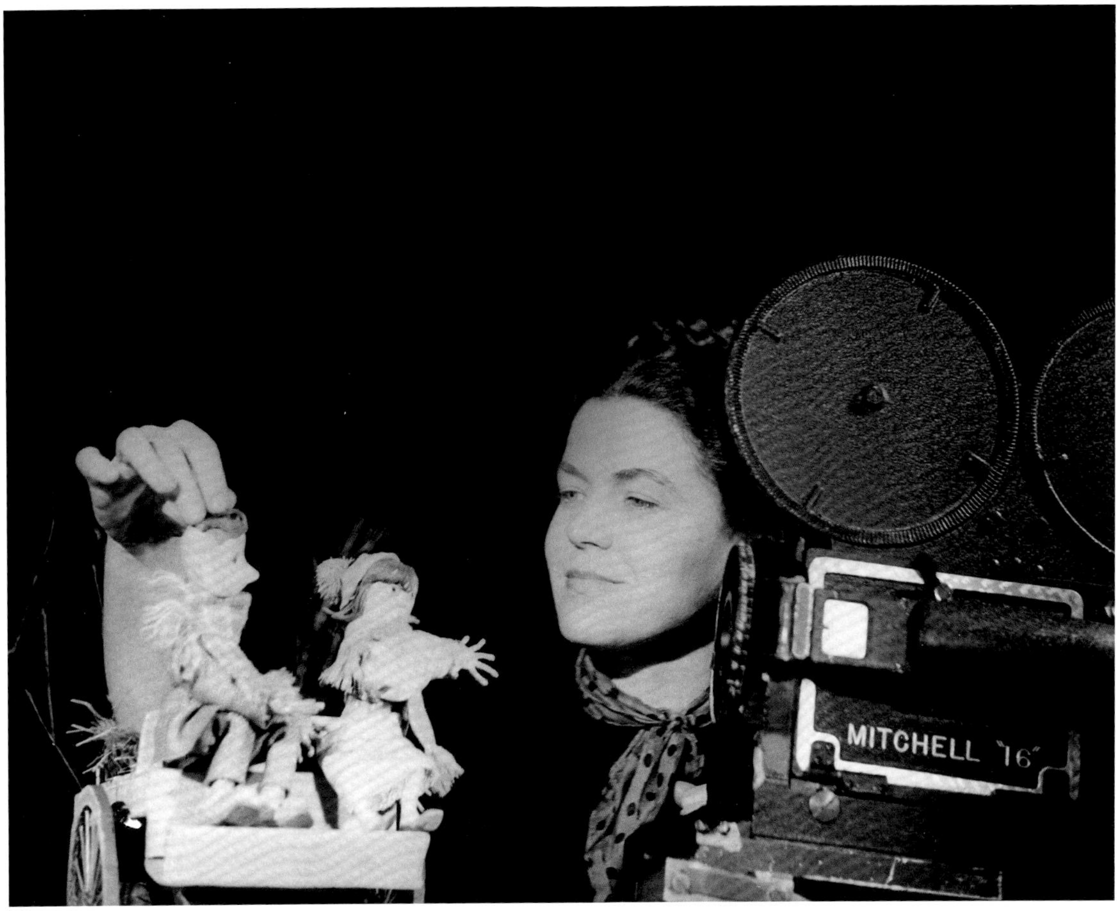

Alma Duncan working on the making of the film *Folksong Fantasy*, 1951
Alma Duncan travaillant à la réalisation du film *Fantaisie folklorique*, 1951

many other cultural forms in the newly arrived atomic age—old certainties and old æsthetic codes that now seemed anachronistic in anxious Cold War times.

It is unimaginable for us today, in our radically decentralized country, to understand the importance of Ottawa itself in mid-century Canadian cinematic history. While sporadic private sector production was happening in other cities, especially Montreal and Toronto, Ottawa was for a time the epicentre of film production in Canada (certainly from 1939 to 1956, when the NFB was moved to Montreal). Not only was it home to the NFB, but also to a prolific private-sector film company, Crawley Films, also founded in 1939, which was by 1952 producing an astonishing 23% of all non-theatrical short educational and "sponsored films" (films funded by industries and private companies to introduce and promote a product or service) in Canada. After producing hundreds of sponsored films and educational documentaries in the 1940s and 1950s, in the 1960s Crawley Films even began to expand into that very risky venture of making Canadian feature fiction films.[4] Dunclaren also produced one such film in 1958 for Steep Rock Iron Mine in Atikokan, ON. Entitled *Friendly Interchange* (cat. 34, p. 127), it advertised the mining industry and promoted the importance of open trade relations across the Canadian-American border.

Ottawa? A film capital? Fyodor Dostoevsky once observed that his Russian capital, St. Petersburg, was a "premeditated city," where the social atmosphere was dominated by silent strategies of identity control, careful attention to social behaviour, and a paranoiac concern with regulating individual passion. In many ways, Ottawa is similar: it has a decidedly cautious personality with an abiding obsession with discretion. Beneath this surface, however, as in Dostoevsky's capital, there are dark fissures and anarchic, bohemian energies in the ordered city. How else to account for an Ottawa-based institution that spawned Canada's storied and, in the 1950s, searching documentary tradition of "direct cinema," and, within those same walls, in the gifted hands of animator Norman McLaren, launched Canada's equally fabled animation and avant-garde and experimental film practices. In Ottawa? Conservative, repressed, careful, "premeditated" Ottawa; city of bureaucrats, briefcases, minor conspiracies and hidden agendas? Yes, Ottawa.

For many Canadians, Ottawa is an abstraction: the capital, a tourist town, a place to send your taxes, and the seat of government corruption. Ottawa is all that, but it is also a border town, where Quebec bristles against Ontario and vice-versa; a former lawless lumber town filled with working class Irish and French who drank and brawled their way out of the nineteenth century; a place where one of Canada's few political assassinations took place; a city where a longstanding prime minister consorted regularly with prostitutes and spoke to his dead mother and his dog; a place where secrecy and repression strain against insatiable appetites for revelation and scandal. There is even a tourist walking tour of "haunted Ottawa." In many senses, Ottawa is a very peculiar place. Perhaps this quiet peculiarity has something to do with the creation in Ottawa of two of cinema's most experimental and explosive animated films: Norman McLaren's *Begone Dull Care* (1949) and *Neighbours* (1952). The former is a groundbreaking improvisational animation drawn and painted directly on celluloid (a "cameraless" film, as McLaren dubbed the process) to accompany a jazz soundtrack by Oscar Peterson; the latter, an Academy Award-winning pixilated parable of human bestiality and Cold War fears of mutually assured nuclear destruction.

Reflecting this dangerous decade of the Korean Conflict, of Senator Joe McCarthy and his communist witch hunts, of the shadows of Stalin, and of accelerated nuclear arms testing, McLaren had created a new poetics of uncertainty. For a decade often recalled as conservative and orthodox, there was plenty of angst and just as much doubt. His NFB colleagues in documentary section, for example, were embracing the emerging "direct cinema" documentary style of the mid-1950s. It was an approach that rejected didacticism in favour of more self-reflexively subjective and sceptical forms of filmic observation, and is evident in such works as *Corral* (Colin Low, 1954), *City of Gold* (Colin Low, Wolf Keonig, 1957), and *Les Raquetteurs* (Gilles Groulx, Michel Brault, 1958). If 1950s Canadian cinema in the feature-fiction-film form was moribund, its documentary and animation film practices, of which Dunclaren's production was a part, were richly creative and decidedly experimental.

This startling zeitgeist of experimentation, which challenged orthodoxies of documentary cinema and figurative, representational animation, coincides with the increased presence of women in Canadian filmmaking from 1939 to the late 1950s. During the war, many women were hired at the NFB, working as editors, scriptwriters, and directors. Pioneering Canadian women filmmakers, such as Jane Marsh, Gudrun Bjerring (Parker), and Laura C. Boulton, worked in the NFB's documentary department, while animator Evelyn Lambart worked closely with Norman McLaren as a co-director on many of his films and later emerged as one of the most accomplished, inventive animators in Canadian film history. Poet P.K. Page also worked at the Board in this era. Alma Duncan herself worked in the graphic arts and film divisions of the NFB from 1943 to 1951, moving from Montreal to Ottawa to do so. This is also where she met Audrey McLaren, who was employed there as a photographic technician. In the private sector, meanwhile, throughout the 1950s, Crawley Films engaged Judith Sparks (later the wife of company founder, F.R. Crawley) as screenwriter and director on over 30 films, including the Canadian Film Award-winning *Loon's Necklace* (1949). Sally MacDonald directed 14 sponsored films for the company from 1954 to 1970. Elsewhere, as more private companies arrived on the scene in the early 1960s to feed the infinite programming appetite of television, filmmakers such as Evelyn Spice, Margaret Perry, and Beryl Fox arrived as major and prodigious producers of work in Canada's fragmented and marginalized film sector.

In addition to Alma Duncan's other impressive modes of artistic expression, the engaging animated films that she and Audrey McLaren produced offer further evidence of the fluidity of the ever-tenuous filmmaking enterprise in mid-twentieth century Canada. Such fluidity emerged in their straddling of public- and private-sector modes of production, as well as in their engagement at various levels with public education and edification.[5] Their short animated films, and especially their use of stop-motion in them, are significant for their creative anticipation and articulation of the coming changes in Canadian society in relation to technology. And, as discussed by Jaclyn Meloche, they foreshadow the changing understanding of gender and interpretation of Aboriginal cultures in Canada. Duncan and McLaren's film work also underscores the important and unjustly ignored contributions of women to the history of Canadian cinema in the 1950s, an era of impressive æsthetic experimentation, the beginning of seismic social and political shifts, as well as considerable and ever-increasing global Cold War anxiety.

1 Cited in Carlos Fuentes, *Latin America: At War With The Past.* Toronto: Anansi Press, 1984, 3. **2** While Alma Duncan produced *Folksong Fantasy* (1951) for the National Film Board of Canada, the two women quit the NFB that same year and founded Dunclaren Productions. Working from an attic in Ottawa, they produced the animated short films *Kumak the Sleepy Hunter* (1953), *Hearts and Soles* (1955), and *Friendly Interchange* (1958) before moving on to other creative endeavours. **3** Feature filmmaking in Quebec evolved in a much different way than in English-speaking Canada, with support for feature film production and consumption coming from both the Catholic church and the provincial government as a way of preserving linguistic identity and resisting assimilation into English-speaking North America. See D. John Turner, *Canadian Feature Film Index 1913–1985* (Ottawa: Ministry of Supply and Services Canada,1987), 780–81. **4** These include *Amanita Pestilens* (1962) and *The Luck of Ginger Coffey* (1965). In 1975 the company won the Academy Award for Best Documentary with *The Man Who Skied Down Everest.* See Gary Evans, *In The National Interest: A Chronicle of the National Film Board from 1949–1989* (Toronto: University of Toronto Press,1991), 28. **5** Indeed, their work reveals the didactic ethos that characterized most NFB films and even sponsored films, which were made primarily as advertisements or public service announcements.

Further Reading: Armitage, Kay, Kass Banning, Brenda Longfellow, and Janine Marchessault, eds. *Gendering the Nation: Canadian Women's Cinema.* Toronto: University of Toronto Press, 1999. **Fetherling**, Douglas ed. *Documents in Canadian Film.* Peterborough: Broadview Press, 1988. **Magder**, Ted. *Canada's Hollywood: The Canadian State and Feature Films.* Toronto: University of Toronto Press, 1993. **Morris**, Peter. *Embattled Shadows: A History of Canadian Cinema 1895–1939.* Montreal: McGill-Queen's University Press, 1992.

Tom McSorley is Executive Director of the Canadian Film Institute, an Adjunct Research Professor of Film Studies at Carleton University, and film critic for CBC Radio One's Ottawa Morning. He is editor of *Rivers of Time: The Films of Philip Hoffman* (2008), *Life Without Death: The Cinema of Frank Cole* (2009), *Elective Identities: The Moving Images of Gariné Torossian* (2010), *Entre Nous: The Cinema of Denis Côté* (2011), *Intimacies: The Cinema of Ingrid Veninger* (2012), *Forms of Light: The Films of Malcolm Sutherland* (2012), *Time Being: The Moving Images of Daniel Cockburn* (2013), and *Dark Mirror: The Films of Theodore Ushev* (2014). He is the author of the book *Atom Egoyan's The Adjuster* (2009).

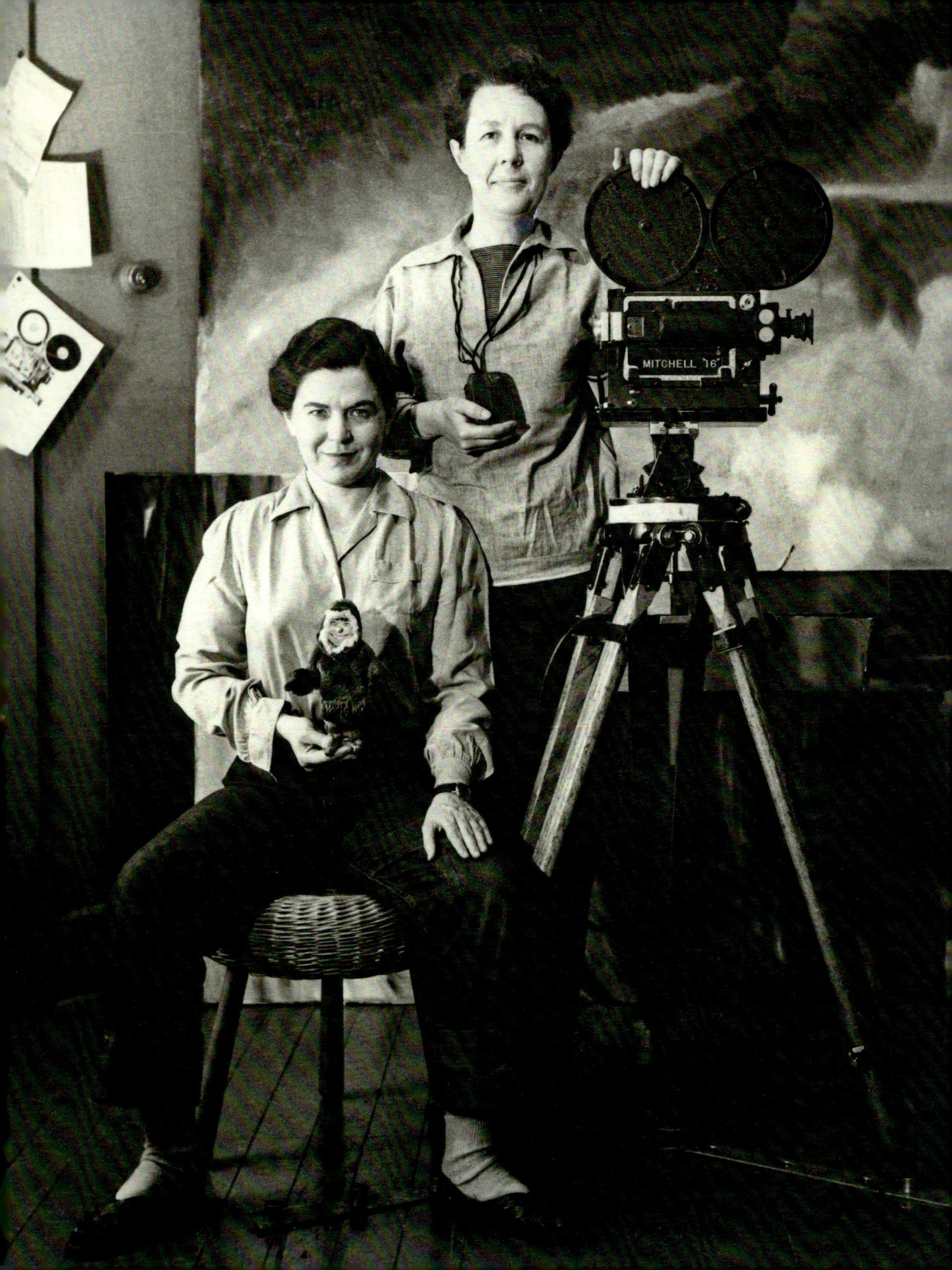
MITCHELL 16

Expériences marginales

Le cinéma canadien de 1939 à 1959

Tom McSorley

Aussi étrange que cela puisse paraître, il faut retourner au Mexique du XIXe siècle, avant le cinéma et avant la Révolution, pour bien comprendre l'histoire du cinéma canadien. C'est là que Porfirio Díaz, dictateur de l'époque, fit une célèbre déclaration au sujet de son pays, laquelle pourrait s'appliquer aussi au Canada et en particulier au film canadien : « Pauvre Mexique ! Si loin de Dieu et si près des États-Unis »[1]. Le Canada a beau être riche et privilégié, et donc pas du tout, même métaphoriquement, « loin de Dieu », il est effectivement très près des États-Unis. Le film canadien, dominé économiquement et culturellement par ce voisin du sud puissant et attrayant, lutte fort pour se distinguer face à la présence envahissante de Hollywood. Depuis l'origine du cinéma au Canada, au début du XXe siècle, les histoires que nous avons imaginées à notre sujet se démarquent largement des récits brillants, farouchement individualistes et victorieux du cinéma américain. Dans le cinéma canadien, on rêve, mais différemment. Pour les gens évoluant dans cette industrie, le rêve prédominant au siècle dernier était de quitter le Canada afin de connaître le succès à Hollywood; des milliers de cinéastes et d'interprètes talentueux quittèrent donc le pays. Le Canada est ainsi amplement représenté sur le marché du film le plus

Alma Duncan and Audrey McLaren working on the making of the film *Kumak the Sleepy Hunter*, 1953
Alma Duncan et Audrey McLaren travaillant à la réalisation du film *Kumak le chasseur somnolent*, 1953

puissant du monde, mais le déploiement du sien a été très lent. La cause principale : la possession continue, depuis les années 1920, des systèmes de distribution et de présentation du cinéma par des sociétés d'affaires américaines. Aujourd'hui, comme à l'époque, plus de 95 % des œuvres cinématographiques vues au Canada sont produites à Hollywood, et notre absence de nos propres écrans est un symptôme persistant du fait d'être « si près ».

Le cinéma a fait son arrivée au Canada à la fin du XIXe siècle, avec des images faites ailleurs et portant sur l'« ailleurs ». La première projection devant public au pays – une bobine de courts métrages des frères Lumière de France et par la compagnie Edison des États-Unis – a eu lieu à Montréal en juin 1896. Ces films ont été montrés par la suite à Ottawa avant de se rendre vers l'ouest; une campagne de charme, et, en quelque sorte de colonisation, que ces images en mouvement. Jusqu'à maintenant, en effet, c'est la consommation d'images produites ailleurs qui définit largement, pour les Canadiens et les Canadiennes, la pratique culturelle qui consiste à aller au cinéma. Ce qui ne veut pas dire qu'aucun film n'était produit ici. Au début du siècle dernier, des films de voyage vantant les merveilles de la nature canadienne étaient réalisés par le Chemin de fer Canadien Pacifique. En 1918, le gouvernement canadien reconnut la capacité potentielle d'éducation publique et de développement national du cinéma et forma, en 1923, le Bureau de cinématographie du gouvernement canadien. L'objectif de ces établissements de cinéma de l'État était de présenter de courts documentaires didactiques truffés d'informations afin d'éduquer les Canadiens et les Canadiennes; on ne contemplait pas encore l'idée du cinéma comme moyen de divertissement. Cette tendance canadienne, jumelée à l'émergence de l'hégémonie de l'industrie cinématographique hollywoodienne, a contribué à la marginalisation quasi complète de la réalisation de longs métrages canadiens.

Cette situation lamentable a cependant permis l'apparition de pratiques et d'esthétiques filmiques alternatives. En raison de son statut marginal au sein de ses propres frontières, le cinéma canadien s'est développé à l'extérieur des modèles traditionnels de la production industrielle et a brillé plutôt dans les courts métrages documentaires, les films d'animation et le cinéma expérimental. C'est d'ailleurs dans ce contexte que les cinéastes du milieu du siècle Alma Duncan et Audrey McLaren créèrent à Ottawa trois courts métrages d'animation image par image et un film commandité. C'est en dehors des modèles industriels que le film *Fantaisie folklorique* (ONF, 1951) (cat. 24, p. 118–121) de Duncan et les films de la compagnie Dunclaren Productions (qu'elle a fondée avec sa partenaire Audrey McLaren en 1951) ont été réalisés dans les années 1950, époque durant laquelle très peu de longs métrages canadiens étaient réalisés et encore moins visionnés[2]. De 1939 à 1959, 18 longs métrages ont été produits au Canada anglais, alors que des milliers de courts métrages comme les leurs ont été réalisés[3]. À partir des années 1950 et 1960,

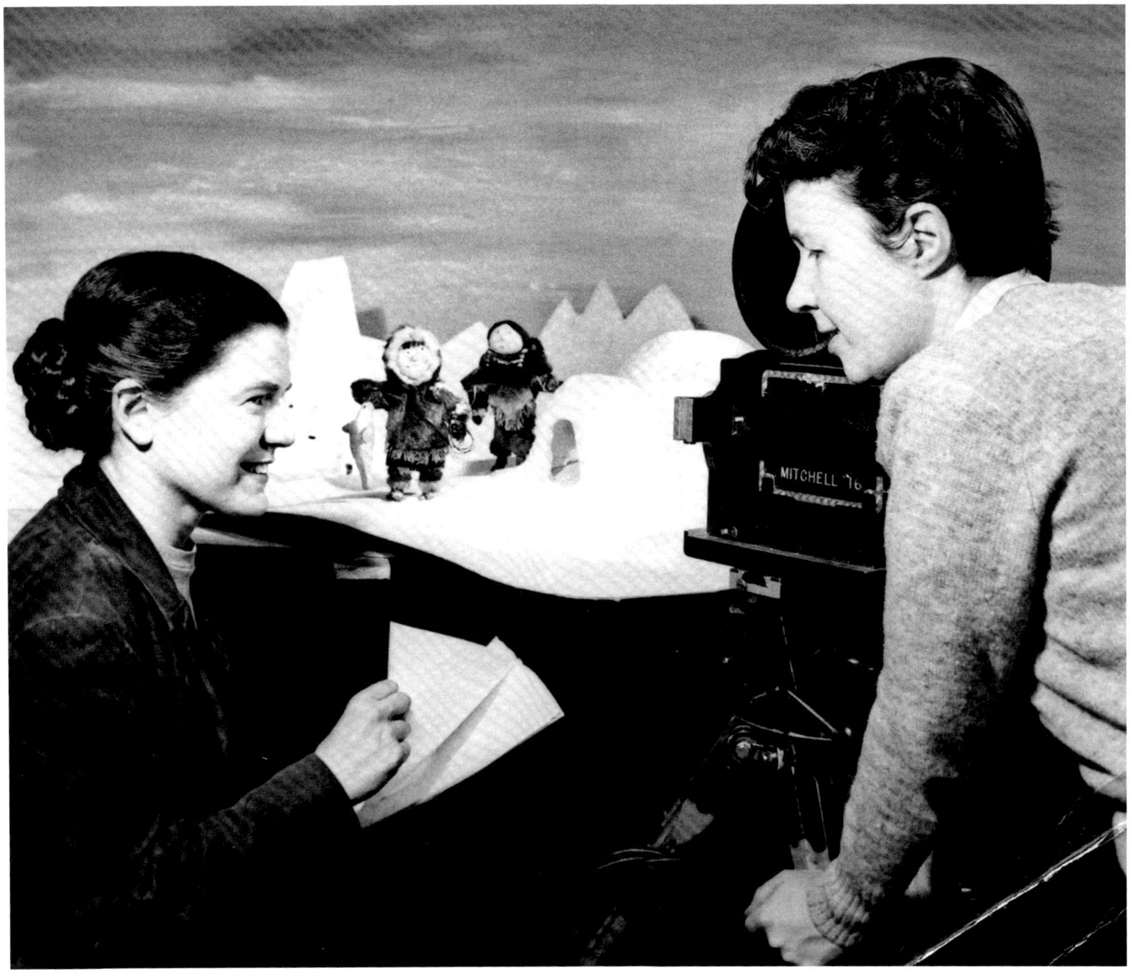

Alma Duncan and Audrey McLaren working on the making of the film *Kumak the Sleepy Hunter*, 1953
Alma Duncan et Audrey McLaren travaillant à la réalisation du film *Kumak le chasseur somnolent*, 1953

l'activité cinématographique au Canada a évolué grâce à une combinaison d'établissements culturels subventionnés par l'État et d'un secteur indépendant persévérant qui œuvrait surtout dans le court métrage. N'ayant pas accès aux écrans commerciaux, le cinéma canadien d'après-guerre, dans toute sa variété, se montre étonnamment débridé sur le plan formel, aventureux sur le plan esthétique et, parfois, provocant sur le plan politique.

Paradoxalement, l'évolution de ce cinéma d'expérimentation et de provocation nous conduit aux portes d'un autre établissement gouvernemental établi dans la capitale canadienne. L'Office national du film du Canada (ONF) est fondé à Ottawa en 1939 afin de produire des films (documentaires et d'animation) d'information et de propagande sur l'effort de guerre du pays. Le légendaire réalisateur de documentaires John Grierson en assure la gestion de manière ferme et acharnée. Après la guerre, et avant l'arrivée de la télévision, l'ONF se réinvente en instrument d'éducation nationale, et ses films sont ancrés dans un discours didactique prônant le devoir civique, l'unité nationale et l'éternel projet de construction de la nation canadienne. Après l'arrivée de la télévision en 1952, l'ONF ajuste ses activités de distribution et de présentation, mais continue d'exploiter son mandat de création de films comme outils éducatifs. L'Office génère en outre des œuvres encore plus expérimentales tant dans le domaine documentaire que de l'animation. Ces films, comme de nombreux autres produits culturels dans la nouvelle ère atomique, remettaient en question les vieilles certitudes et les codes esthétiques désuets qui, à cette époque angoissante de guerre froide, paraissaient désormais anachroniques.

Il nous est difficile aujourd'hui, dans notre pays complètement décentralisé, de saisir l'importance d'Ottawa dans l'histoire du cinéma canadien au milieu du siècle dernier. Quelques réalisations du secteur privé étaient produites ici et là, surtout à Montréal et à Toronto, mais Ottawa fut le point central de la production au Canada pour un certain temps (assurément de 1939 à 1956, date à laquelle l'ONF déménage à Montréal). À part les quartiers généraux de l'ONF, Ottawa hébergeait aussi Crawley Films, une compagnie de production privée prolifique, elle aussi fondée en 1939. En 1952, la compagnie avait réalisé la quantité surprenante de 23 % de tous les courts métrages éducatifs et autres films commandités (ces films financés par des compagnies privées et des industries souhaitant présenter ou promouvoir leurs produits ou services) non destinés aux salles de cinéma au Canada. Après avoir réalisé des centaines de films commandités et de documentaires éducatifs dans les années 1940 et 1950, Crawley Films commença même, dans les années 1960, à s'aventurer dans le territoire assez périlleux de la production de longs métrages canadiens de fiction[4]. La compagnie Dunclaren a elle aussi réalisé un film commandité, en 1958, pour la mine de fer de Steep Rock à Atikokan, en Ontario; ce film, *Échange amical* (cat. 34, p. 127), fait la promotion de l'industrie minière et prône l'importance des relations commerciales ouvertes entre le Canada et les États Unis.

Ottawa, capitale du cinéma ? Fiodor Dostoïevski a dit de sa capitale russe de Saint Pétersbourg qu'elle était une « ville préméditée », où l'atmosphère était empreinte de stratégies discrètes de contrôle des identités, d'attention particulière au comportement social et de souci paranoïaque de réglementer les passions individuelles. Ottawa est semblable de plusieurs façons : elle a une personnalité prudente, et une obsession de la discrétion. Cependant, sous cette surface ordonnée se trouvent, à Ottawa comme à Saint Pétersbourg, des fissures obscures et des énergies anarchiques et bohèmes. C'est la seule façon d'expliquer la fondation, dans cette ville, de l'institution qui a généré, dans les années 1950, la légendaire et pénétrante tradition documentaire canadienne du cinéma-vérité; cette même boîte qui a lancé, grâce aux compétences remarquables du cinéaste d'animation Norman McLaren, des pratiques d'animation d'avantgarde et expérimentales tout aussi célèbres. Oui, Ottawa, ville refoulée et conventionnelle, prudente et « préméditée », ville de bureaucrates, de portedocuments, de petites intrigues et d'intentions cachées. Cette ville là.

Pour plusieurs Canadiens et Canadiennes, Ottawa relève de l'abstraction : c'est la capitale, une ville touristique, l'endroit où l'on envoie nos taxes, et le siège de la corruption gouvernementale. Oui, Ottawa remplit toutes ces fonctions. Mais c'est aussi : une ville frontalière où le Québec se hérisse contre l'Ontario (et vice versa); une ancienne ville de bûcherons Français et Irlandais sans foi ni loi qui accueillirent le XXe siècle dans la beuverie et la bagarre; l'endroit où a eu lieu l'un des rares assassinats politiques au pays; une ville où un premier ministre longtemps en poste fréquentait des prostituées et discutait avec sa mère et son chien décédés; un endroit où le secret et l'autocensure se heurtent à une insatiable soif de révélations et de scandales. Il existe même une « promenade hantée » de la ville pour les touristes. Ottawa est, de plusieurs façons, un endroit très étrange. Cette discrète étrangeté explique peut-être pourquoi c'est là qu'ont été créés deux des films d'animation les plus expérimentaux et fougueux de l'histoire du cinéma : *Caprice en couleur* (1949) et *Voisins* (1952) de Norman McLaren. Le premier est une animation novatrice improvisée, dessinée et peinte directement sur la pellicule (un film « sans caméra », dira McLaren) accompagnée d'une bande sonore d'Oscar Peterson; le second, récompensé d'un Oscar, est une parabole fantaisiste traitant de la brutalité humaine sur fond de guerre froide et de crainte de destruction nucléaire mutuelle assurée.

En parfait témoin de cette décennie dangereuse marquée par la guerre de Corée, la chasse aux sorcières communistes du sénateur Joe McCarthy, l'ombre de Staline et l'accélération des essais d'armes nucléaires, McLaren a créé une nouvelle poétique de l'incertitude. Cette décennie, qu'on qualifie souvent de conventionnelle et conservatrice, avait néanmoins sa part d'angoisse et de doute. Les collègues de McLaren dans la section documentaire de l'ONF, par exemple, intégraient le style émergent du « cinémavérité » du milieu des années 1950. Cette approche rejetait le didactisme pour favoriser des formes d'observations filmiques empreintes de réflexivité, de subjectivité et de scepticisme, comme on peut le voir dans les œuvres *Corral* (Colin Low, 1954), *Capitale de l'or* (Colin Low, Wolf Keonig, 1957) et *Les Raquetteurs* (Gilles Groulx, Michel Brault, 1958). Si le long métrage de fiction canadien ne se porte pas très bien dans les années 1950, le domaine du documentaire et de l'animation, dont faisaient partie les productions Dunclaren, était riche de créativité et incontestablement expérimental.

Ce stupéfiant esprit d'expérimentation qui régnait à l'époque, qui a mis au défi les conventions du cinéma documentaire et de l'animation figurative et représentationnelle, coïncide avec la présence accrue de femmes dans le cinéma canadien, de 1939 jusqu'à la fin des années 1950. Plusieurs femmes furent embauchées à l'ONF pendant la guerre, travaillant comme monteuses, scénaristes et réalisatrices. Des pionnières du cinéma canadien telles que Jane Marsh, Gudrun Bjerring (Parker) et Laura C. Boulton travaillaient au département des documentaires, alors que l'animatrice Evelyn Lambart travaillait de près avec Norman McLaren en tant que coréalisatrice de plusieurs de ses films. Elle deviendra plus tard l'une des cinéastes d'animation les plus accomplies et ingénieuses de l'histoire du cinéma canadien. La poète P.K. Page travaillait aussi à l'Office à cette époque. Quant à Alma Duncan, elle quitte Montréal pour s'installer à Ottawa afin d'occuper des postes aux départements des arts graphiques et des films de l'ONF de 1943 à 1951. C'est là qu'elle rencontra Audrey McLaren, qui était technicienne en photographie. Pendant ce temps, dans le secteur privé, Crawley Films engage Judith Sparks (qui épousera plus tard le fondateur de la compagnie, F.R. Crawley) comme scénariste et réalisatrice de plus de 30 films, notamment *Le Collier magique* (1949), film récompensé au Palmarès du film canadien. Sally MacDonald quant à elle a produit pour Crawley Films 14 films commandités de 1954 à 1974. Ailleurs, au début des années 1960, alors que de plus en plus de sociétés privées entrent en scène afin de combler la demande grandissante de programmation télévisuelle, des cinéastes telles que Evelyn Spice, Margaret Perry et Beryl Fox se démarquent en tant que productrices importantes et prodigieuses dans le marché du film canadien fragmenté et marginalisé.

Outre les multiples autres modes d'expression artistique d'Alma Duncan, les films d'animation attachants qu'elle et Audrey McLaren ont réalisés sont une démonstration supplémentaire de la fluidité qui existe dans le monde fragile du cinéma canadien au milieu du siècle dernier. On constate cette fluidité dans la position intermédiaire, entre secteurs public et privé, de leurs modes de production, ainsi que dans leur manière d'aborder à divers niveaux la question de l'éducation et de l'instruction publiques[5]. Leurs courts métrages d'animation, particulièrement par l'utilisation qu'elles font de l'animation image par image, sont importants, car ils anticipent et illustrent de façon créative les changements qui apparaissent alors dans le domaine de la technologie au Canada. Comme le mentionne Jaclyn Meloche dans son essai, ces œuvres laissent aussi présager les changements qui se produiront dans la perception des genres et dans l'interprétation des cultures autochtones au Canada. Les œuvres cinématographiques de Duncan et McLaren témoignent aussi de la contribution importante et injustement passée sous silence des femmes dans l'histoire du cinéma canadien dans les années 1950, une époque marquée par des expérimentations esthétiques extraordinaires, par l'amorce de changements politiques et sociaux fulgurants, ainsi qu'une angoisse généralisée, considérable et croissante, face à la guerre froide.

1 Cité dans Carlos Fuentes, *Latin America: At War With the Past* (L'Amérique latine. En guerre contre le passé), Toronto, Anansi Press, 1984, p. 3. **2** Alma Duncan a réalisé *Fantaisie folklorique* (1951) pour l'ONF, mais les deux femmes ont quitté l'Office la même année et ont fondé Dunclaren Productions. Elles réalisèrent les courts métrages d'animation *Kumak le chasseur somnolent* (1953), *L'amour pas-à-pas* (1955) et *Échange amical* (1958) dans un grenier à Ottawa avant de passer à d'autres projets créatifs. **3** Au Québec, la production de longs métrages évolue bien différemment qu'au Canada anglais; l'Église catholique et le gouvernement provincial appuient la création et la consommation de films, car le cinéma est vu comme une manière de conserver l'identité linguistique et de combattre l'assimilation à l'anglais de l'Amérique du Nord. Voir D. John Turner, *Canadian Feature Film Index 1913–1985* (Index des longs métrages canadiens, 1913–1985), Ottawa, Ministère des approvisionnements et services, 1987, p. 780–81. **4** On retrouve parmi ces films *Amanita Pestilens* (1962) et *The Luck of Ginger Coffey* (La chance de Ginger Coffey) (1965). La compagnie remporte l'Oscar du meilleur documentaire pour *The Man Who Skied Down Everest* (L'homme qui a descendu l'Everest en ski) en 1975. Voir Gary Evans, *In The National Interest: A Chronicle of the National Film Board from 1949–1989* (Dans l'intérêt national. Chronique de l'Office national du film de 1949 à 1989), Toronto, University of Toronto Press, 1991, p. 28. **5** En effet, leur travail révèle la philosophie didactique qui était l'apanage de la majorité des films de l'ONF, voire des films commandités, créés surtout en guise de publicités ou de messages d'intérêt public.

Lectures complémentaires: Armitage, Kay, Kass Banning, Brenda Longfellow et Janine Marchessault (directrices). *Gendering the Nation: Canadian Women's Cinema* (Sexuer la nation. Le cinéma des femmes canadiennes). Toronto, University of Toronto Press, 1999. **Fetherling**, Douglas (dir.). *Documents in Canadian Film* (Documents du film canadien). Peterborough, Broadview Press, 1988. **Magder**, Ted. *Canada's Hollywood: The Canadian State and Feature Films* (Le Hollywood canadien. L'État canadien et les longs métrages). Toronto, University of Toronto Press, 1993. **Morris**, Peter. *Embattled Shadows: A History of Canadian Cinema 1895–1939* (Ombres en bataille. Une histoire du cinéma canadien 1895–1939). Montréal, McGill-Queen's University Press, 1992.

Tom McSorley est directeur de l'Institut du film canadien, professeur de recherche auxiliaire d'études cinématographiques à l'Université Carleton, et critique de film à l'émission *Ottawa Morning* de CBC Radio One. Il a dirigé la publication de *Rivers of Time: The Films of Philip Hoffman* (Rivières de temps. Les films de Philip Hoffman) (2008), *Life Without Death: The Cinema of Frank Cole* (La vie sans la mort. Le cinéma de Frank Cole) (2009), *Elective Identities: The Moving Images of Gariné Torossian* (Identités facultatives. L'œuvre cinématographique de Gariné Torossian) (2010), *Entre Nous: The Cinema of Denis Côté* (2011), *Intimacies: The Cinema of Ingrid Veninger* (Intimités. Le cinéma d'Ingrid Veninger) (2012), *Forms of Light: The Films of Malcolm Sutherland* (Formes de lumière. Les films de Malcolm Sutherland) (2012), *Time Being: The Moving Images of Daniel Cockburn* (Pour l'instant. L'œuvre cinématographique de Daniel Cockburn) (2013) et *Dark Mirror: The Films of Theodore Ushev* (Sombre miroir. Les films de Theodore Ushev) (2014). Il est l'auteur du livre *Atom Egoyan's The Adjuster* (L'ajusteur de Atom Egoyan) (2009).

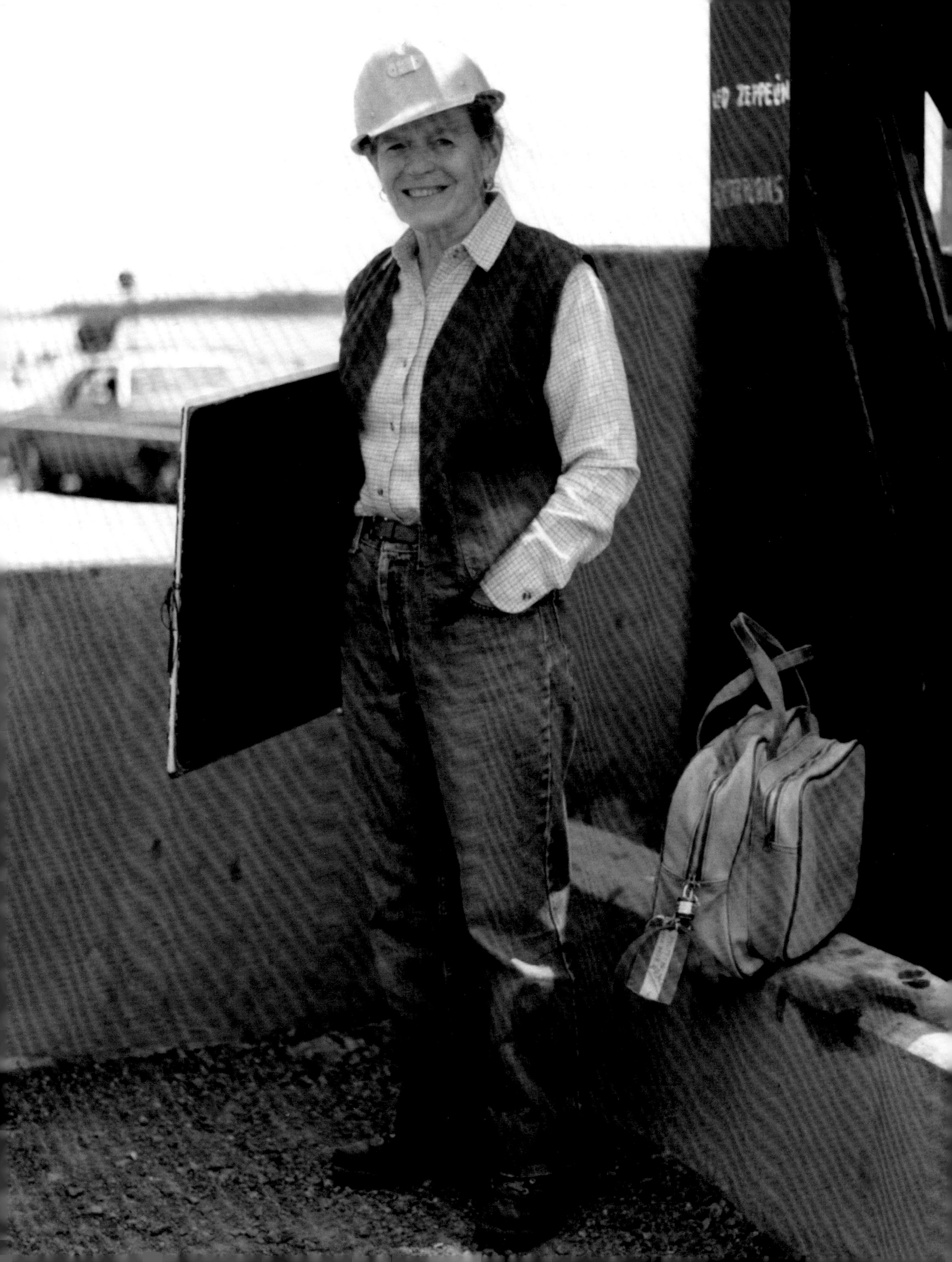

A is for ALMA

Artist, Acrobat, Animal Lover, Adopted and Adored Grandmother

Anne Maheux

One of the greatest pleasures of being an art conservator is the privilege of becoming intimate with works of art. Even more satisfying is the occasional opportunity to establish a rapport with the artist. Such was my experience with Alma Duncan. One day in early spring of 1985, Rosemarie Tovell, then curator of Canadian prints and drawings at the National Gallery of Canada, walked into my small conservation laboratory with a petite, elegant woman with sparkling blue eyes, sporting a beret and carrying a large portfolio. She pulled out a pastel scene of an open-pit mine on two pieces of joined paper. Could I offer advice on how best to re-adhere the partially detached sheets? She drew from life, having travelled to the site and perched on the edge of the open mine with her box of pastels to capture the scene. It had drizzled that day; small rain droplets were scattered throughout the work. I was instantly enchanted. After explaining the most archival way of reattaching the sheets, I melted under her warm gaze, and offered to do it myself. Thus began one of the most cherished friendships of my life.

Invitations to spirited parties at the Froggery, the beautiful property in Cumberland that Alma shared with her NFB colleague and dear friend Babs McLaren, soon followed. In springtime, the drive up the curved lane

Alma Duncan, 1985, Stelco Inc., Nanticoke, ON

to the house opened up to a vast field of brilliant daffodils ringing the frog pond. Alma and Babs loved to entertain; many of their friends came from a broad cross-section of Ottawa's artistic community. Babs kept a journal of guest lists and menus from year to year. These were the people who made up their extended family.

As our friendship with Alma and Babs grew, my husband, Greg, and I spent time in Cumberland, where visits included walks through the nine acres of undisturbed forest that surrounded the sprawling fieldstone house, inspecting fiddleheads pushing up through pine needles and traversing the small brook that ran through the property. At relaxed Sunday brunches, we sat around the dining table by the large picture window where we were entertained by the plentiful wildlife and the beloved family dogs, Pepper and Daisy. After the meal was the time I loved most: out came the portfolios of drawings, pastels and paintings, carefully organized chronologically and by theme. Portraits of friends from the National Film Board days, pen-and-ink sketches from a trip to the Middle East, oil sketches of the Laurentians, colourful abstracts from the 1960s. The monumental pastels and black chalk drawings of industrial scenes were my favourites; imagine fearless Alma in a hardhat perched on a catwalk high above huge vats of molten metal, or sketching in a factory of screaming wood saws in a cloud of sawdust. The broad body of her work demonstrated the breadth of her talent, boundless experimentation, and sense of adventure.

Alma studied ballet as a young girl and remained forever flexible; at the age of 75, a somersault over the back of the sofa after one of our brunches in Cumberland proved the point. As a follower of transcendental meditation, Alma was able to sit in a perfect lotus position for hours. She and Babs were introduced to the practice during one of the Maharishi's early trips to North America. From them we learned the benefits of practice: reduced stress, increased focus, an eternally youthful attitude, and the secret to sustaining a physical wellbeing that belies age.

Our lives eventually became further entwined. Alma's failing health prompted a move back to Ottawa, and she and Babs relocated to a property in our neighbourhood—literally down the street. Renovations included a bright studio, and although she was surrounded by her art materials and had started a painting, she was not able to continue as the dementia progressed. Brunch at Claire de Lune, tea parties with our daughter Madeleine, and Saturday movie nights at the townhouse became part of our life. Alma and Babs had amassed a collection of some 700 movies over the years, and she never tired of watching anything with Katharine Hepburn, Audrey Hepburn, and Miss Marple. Muskoka was a common summer destination; we shared visits to Norway Point on Lake Rosseau, to the rambling McLaren summer retreat dating back to 1889, and to Greg's family cottage on Lake Muskoka. We shared friends, and Christmas and Thanksgiving now included our adopted grandmothers, too. One could not imagine better role models for our daughter: strong, independent, creative and loving spirits. The absence of our own parents made their role in our lives even more special.

The occasion of this exhibition has brought me closer than ever to Alma. In my current position as Conservator at Library and Archives Canada, I have gained renewed appreciation for her draughtsmanship, playfulness, and love of experimentation through an intimate examination of her works: from the jewel-like maple-leaf watercolours produced for stamps and the delightful handmade puppets that peopled the Dunclaren stop-motion animation films, to the powerful black-chalk abstracts of totemic women figures. How fitting that her accomplishments are being celebrated at the Ottawa Art Gallery, in the cultural community that she so loved and enthusiastically supported. And how lucky we were to have counted Alma as family.

Anne Maheux moved to Ottawa in 1982 to work at the National Gallery of Canada (NGC) after completing her studies in art conservation at the Center for Conservation and Technical Studies at Harvard University, and Queen's University. She first met Alma Duncan in her capacity as Paper Conservator at the NGC in 1985. She participated in the NGC *Degas* exhibition of 1988 as part of the team that conducted research into Edgar Degas's pastels. In 1996 she was a Rome Prize recipient at the American Academy in Rome, where she continued her research in pastels, exploring the relationship of Degas and the Italian artist Giuseppe de Nittis. Since 2009 she has been employed at Library and Archives Canada, as Head of Conservation of Maps, Manuscripts, and Fine Art on Paper. Anne has published extensively on the use of pastel by Degas and his Italian contemporaries, as well as on various conservation treatments.

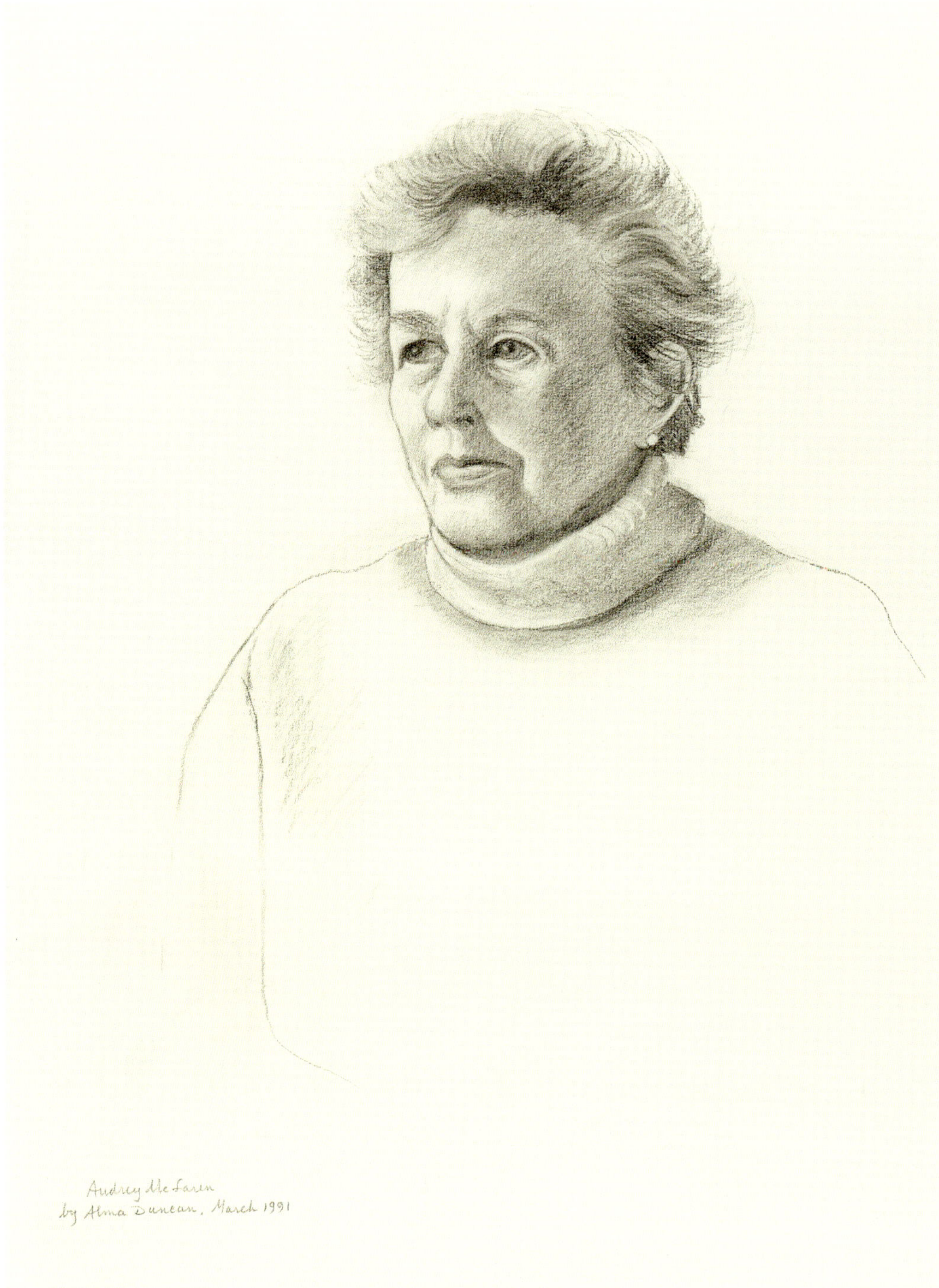

Audrey McLaren 1991 (cat. 81)
Library and Archives Canada | Bibliothèque et Archives Canada

A comme dans ALMA

Artiste, acrobate, amie des animaux, grand-mère adoptive et adorée

Anne Maheux

Avoir le privilège de se lier étroitement avec des œuvres d'art, voilà un des grands plaisirs du métier de conservateur d'art. Encore plus satisfaisant : l'occasion – assez rare – d'entrer en relation avec l'artiste. J'ai eu cette chance avec Alma Duncan. Un jour de printemps 1985, Rosemarie Tovell, qui était à l'époque la conservatrice des dessins et estampes canadiens au Musée des beaux-arts du Canada, s'est présentée dans mon petit laboratoire de conservation accompagnée d'une femme menue et élégante aux yeux bleus étincelants, coiffée d'un béret et transportant un grand portfolio. La femme en retira un dessin d'une mine à ciel ouvert, exécuté au pastel sur deux morceaux de papier joints. Elle cherchait à recoller les deux morceaux partiellement détachés; pourrais-je lui porter conseil ? Elle dessinait d'après nature et s'était rendue sur le site, perchée avec sa boîte de pastels sur le bord de la mine, afin de croquer le lieu. Il avait bruiné cette journée-là, et des gouttelettes de pluie ponctuaient le dessin. Je suis immédiatement tombée sous le charme. Après avoir expliqué la méthode la plus permanente de joindre les feuilles, j'ai fondu sous son doux regard et j'ai fini par lui offrir de faire moi-même le travail. C'est ainsi qu'a débuté une des amitiés les plus précieuses de ma vie.

S'ensuivirent des invitations à des fêtes animées à la Froggery (la Grenouillère), la belle propriété de Cumberland qu'Alma partageait avec Babs McLaren, sa chère amie et collègue à l'ONF. Au printemps, la route sinueuse qui menait à la maison donnait sur un grand champ de jonquilles éclatantes bordant l'étang à grenouilles. Alma et Babs aimaient recevoir; Babs notait dans un journal de bord le nom des invités et les menus servis au fil des ans. Leurs amis formaient un échantillon bien représentatif de la communauté artistique d'Ottawa, et ces gens étaient les membres de leur famille élargie.

Notre amitié avec Alma et Babs a grandi au fur et à mesure des séjours que mon mari Greg et moi avons faits à Cumberland. Lors de ces visites, on se baladait dans les neuf acres de forêt qui entouraient la vaste maison de pierres, on inspectait les crosses de fougères qui perçaient à travers les aiguilles de pin, on traversait le ruisseau qui parcourait la propriété. Aux brunchs décontractés du dimanche, assis autour de la table près des grandes fenêtres, on était divertis par la faune ainsi que par Pepper et Daisy, les chiens adorés de la famille. Mon moment préféré était après le repas : c'est alors que les portfolios apparaissaient, minutieusement organisés par ordre chronologique ou par thèmes, remplis de dessins, de pastels et de peintures. Des portraits d'amis de l'époque de l'Office national du film, des esquisses à la plume et à l'encre réalisées lors d'un voyage au Moyen-Orient, des esquisses à la peinture à l'huile dépeignant les Laurentides, des œuvres abstraites colorées des années 1960. Mais ce sont les prodigieux dessins de scènes industrielles faits à la pierre noire et aux pastels qui étaient mes préférés – imaginez Alma-la-brave, casque sur la tête, perchée sur une passerelle au-dessus d'immenses cuves de métal fondu, ou dessinant dans une usine parmi les cris perçants des scies dans un nuage de sciure de bois. Son vaste corpus démontrait l'étendue de son talent, de son expérimentation sans bornes et de son sens de l'aventure.

Alma avait étudié le ballet dans sa jeunesse et demeurait très souple; à 75 ans bien sonnés, après un de nos brunchs, elle a même effectué une culbute par-dessus le divan pour le prouver. Elle pratiquait aussi la méditation transcendantale et pouvait rester immobile, assise en parfaite posture du lotus, pendant des heures. Elle et Babs s'étaient initiées à la pratique de la méditation lors d'une des premières visites nord-américaines du Maharishi. Elles nous ont enseigné, à Greg et à moi, les bienfaits d'une telle pratique : une réduction du stress, un accroissement de la concentration, une attitude jeune à perpétuité, et le secret du maintien d'un bien-être physique qui fait mentir le calendrier.

Lorsque la santé dépérissante d'Alma les poussa à retourner habiter à Ottawa, nos vies se sont trouvées encore plus unies : elle et Babs emménagèrent dans une maison de notre quartier, à quelques portes de chez nous. Elles rénovèrent la maison pour y ajouter un studio lumineux, mais, bien qu'entourée de ses matériaux et ayant commencé un tableau, Alma ne put continuer, car la démence gagnait du terrain. Des brunchs au restaurant

Clair de lune, des thés en compagnie de notre fille Madeleine et des soirées cinéma à la maison le samedi faisaient désormais partie de nos rituels. Alma et Babs avaient collectionné au fil des ans quelque 700 titres, et Alma ne se lassait pas de regarder Katharine Hepburn, Audrey Hepburn et Miss Marple. On se rendait aussi à Muskoka, séjournant ensemble à Norway Point au lac Rosseau, dans l'immense résidence d'été des McLaren datant de 1889, ou au chalet familial de Greg au lac Muskoka. Nous avions des amis en commun, et ces grands-mères adoptives étaient désormais invitées à nos fêtes de Noël et de l'Action de grâce. On ne pourrait imaginer de meilleurs modèles pour notre fille : des esprits forts, indépendants, créatifs et aimants. Vu l'absence de nos propres parents, le rôle qu'elles jouaient était d'autant plus important.

Cette exposition m'a permis de me rapprocher plus que jamais d'Alma. À titre de conservatrice à Bibliothèque et Archives Canada, j'ai dû examiner soigneusement ses œuvres, et mon estime pour son talent de dessinatrice, pour son caractère enjoué et pour son amour de l'expérimentation a été renouvelée à la vue de ces petites aquarelles de feuilles d'érable destinées à devenir des timbres, de ces charmantes marionnettes faites à la main pour les films d'animation image par image produits par Dunclaren, ou de ces puissantes figures abstraites de femmes totémiques exécutées à la pierre noire. Il est on ne peut plus approprié de célébrer ses réussites à la Galerie d'art d'Ottawa, dans la communauté culturelle qu'elle affectionnait tant et appuyait si ardemment. Et comme nous avons été chanceux de compter Alma parmi les membres de notre famille.

Anne Maheux s'est établie à Ottawa en 1982 afin de travailler au Musée des beaux-arts après avoir fait des études en conservation de l'art au Centre for Conservation and Technical Studies de l'Université Harvard, et à l'Université Queen's. Sa première rencontre avec Alma Duncan a eu lieu en 1985, alors qu'elle était conservatrice des œuvres sur papier au Musée des beaux-arts du Canada (MBAC). Elle a participé à l'exposition *Degas* du MBAC en 1988 en tant que membre de l'équipe de recherches sur les œuvres au pastel de l'artiste. Elle a remporté en 1996 le Prix de Rome décerné par l'American Academy à Rome, qui lui a permis de poursuivre ses recherches sur les pastels et la relation entre Degas et l'artiste italien Giuseppe de Nittis. Depuis 2009, elle est chef de la conservation des cartes, manuscrits et œuvres d'art sur papier à Bibliothèque et Archives Canada. Anne a publié de nombreux articles sur l'utilisation du pastel par Degas et ses confrères italiens, ainsi que sur diverses méthodes de conservation des œuvres d'art.

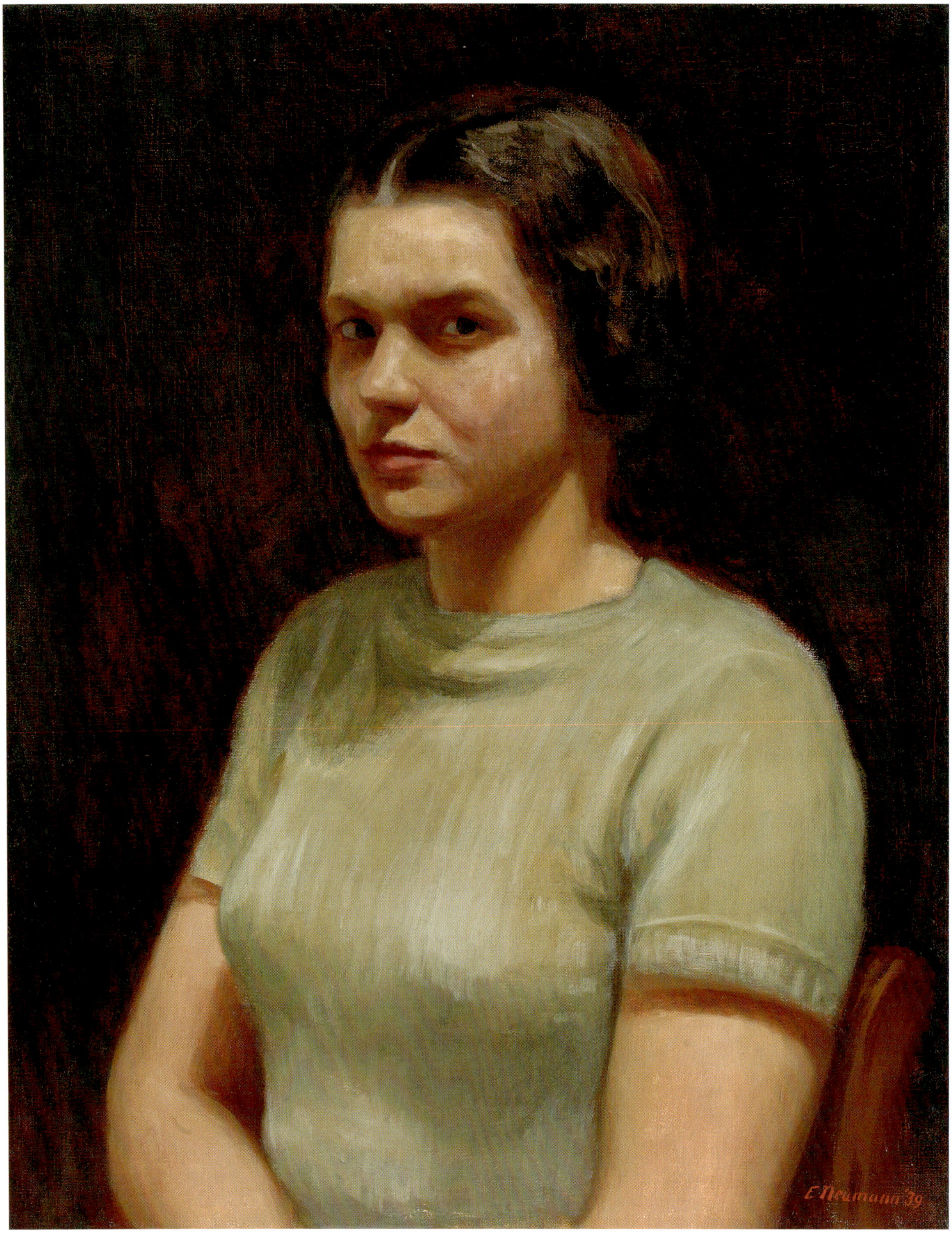

Ernst Neumann, *Alma Duncan*, 1939 (cat. 4)

Library and Archives Canada | Bibliothèque et Archives Canada

Alma Mary Duncan

1917–2004

1917

Born October 2, in the southwestern Ontario town of Paris, only child of John Alexander Duncan and Eleanor Georgina (née Stewart).

—

Née le 2 octobre à Paris, ville du sud-ouest de l'Ontario; fille unique de John Alexander Duncan et Eleanor Georgina (née Stewart).

1923

Father, a textile engineer, transfers the family to Philadelphia, PA, for three years.

—

Son père, un ingénieur en textiles, déménage la famille à Philadelphie (Pennsylvanie) pour trois ans.

1926

The family returns to Canada, settling in Hamilton, ON, where Duncan attends middle and high school.

—

La famille Duncan retourne en Ontario et s'installe à Hamilton, où Alma fréquente l'école intermédiaire et secondaire.

1935

Studies painting and drawing with Adam Sheriff Scott in Montreal.

—

Étudie la peinture et le dessin avec Adam Sheriff Scott à Montréal.

1936

Moves to Montreal, age 19.

Enrolls full time at McGill University to study Political Economy, then continues part time until 1943.

Works in advertising in Montreal until 1943.

—

Déménage à Montréal à 19 ans.

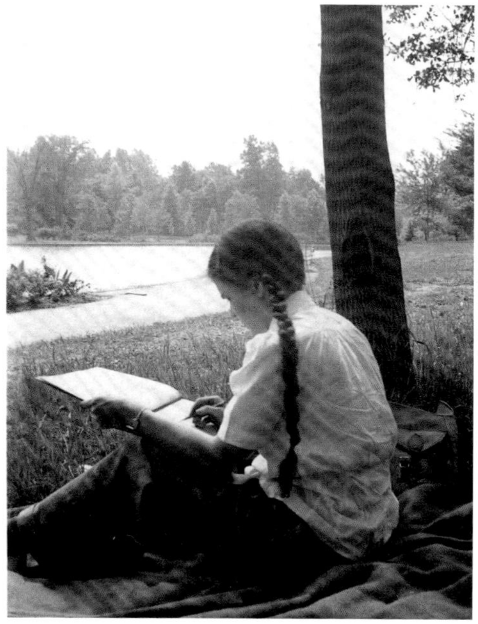

Alma Duncan, c.|v. 1935

S'inscrit à temps plein à l'Université McGill pour y étudier l'économie politique, et poursuit ensuite ses études à temps partiel jusqu'en 1943.

Travaille en publicité à Montréal jusqu'en 1943.

1937

First public exhibition of her work, in the Art Association of Montreal's Annual Spring Exhibition.

Exhibits regularly at AAM's Spring Exhibitions to 1944.

—

Première exposition publique de son travail, au Salon du Printemps de la Art Association of Montréal (AAM).

Expose régulièrement ses œuvres aux Salons du Printemps de la AAM jusqu'en 1944.

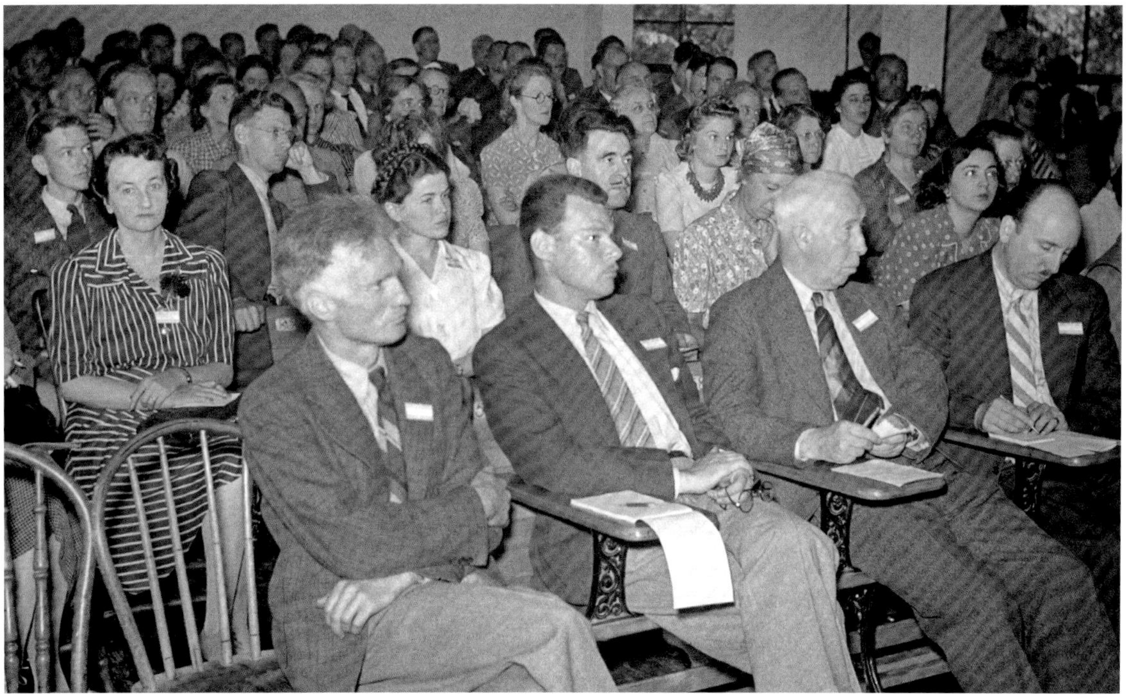

1st Conference of Canadian Artists at Queen's University. Front row, from left to right: André Biéler, Michael Forster, A.Y. Jackson, Lowrie Warrener. Second row: Alma Duncan (white dress) and Tom Stone. Third row: Miller Brittain, Walter Abell, June 1941. Courtesy of Library and Archives Canada, a151359

1re conférence des artistes canadiens à l'Université Queen's. 1re rangée, de gauche à droite : André Biéler, Michael Forster, A.Y. Jackson, Lowrie Warrener. 2e rangée : Alma Duncan (en robe blanche) et Tom Stone. 3e rangée : Miller Brittain, Walter Abell; juin 1941. Gracieuseté de Bibliothèque et Archives Canada, a151359

1938

Attends weekly classes in Ernst Neumann's Montreal studio to further her interest in life drawing.

—

Assiste à des classes hebdomadaires au studio d'Ernst Neumann à Montréal afin de développer son intérêt pour le dessin d'après modèle.

1941

Attends the seminal Kingston Conference held at Queen's University in Kingston, ON, along with approximately 150 artists, curators, and art enthusiasts.

—

Assiste, avec près de 150 artistes, commissaires et amateurs d'art, à la productive conférence des artistes de Kingston (Ontario), qui se tient à l'Université Queen's.

1942

Awarded with an honourable mention in New York's Museum of Modern Art United Hemisphere Poster Competition for her poster entitled *Hands off the Americas* (1942).

Attends morning life-drawing classes with Goodridge Roberts at the Art Association of Montreal.

Served on the executive of the Montreal branch of the Federation of Canadian Artists (FDA) (1942–43), formed as a result of the Kingston Conference.

—

Reçoit une mention honorable au concours d'affiches United Hemisphere (Hémisphère uni) du Museum of Modern Art de New York pour son affiche *Hands off the Americas* (Pas touche aux Amériques) (1942).

Assiste à des cours matinaux de dessin d'après modèle avec Goodridge Roberts à la Art Association of Montreal (prédécesseur du Musée des beaux-arts de Montréal).

Devient membre exécutif de la branche montréalaise de la Fédération des artistes canadiens (FAC) (1942–1943), organisme formé à la suite de la conférence de Kingston.

1943

Treasurer of the Writers', Artists' and Broadcasters' War Council, Montreal.

Receives permission to create drawings inside industrial plants, shipyards, arms factories and factories around Montreal such as Canadian Vickers Ltd. and Canadian Industries Ltd., along with artists Louis Muhlstock and Fritz Brandtner. Also sketches the Canadian Women's Army Corps (CWAC). Sends drawings to National Gallery of Canada director Harry McCurry and advisor A.Y. Jackson for consideration for the war art program. Does not gain the commission.

Moves to Ottawa, age 26, to work in the Graphics Division at the National Film Board of Canada (NFB).

—

Trésorière du Writers', Artists' and Broadcasters' War Council à Montréal (Conseil de guerre des auteurs, artistes et radiodiffuseurs).

Reçoit la permission d'exécuter des dessins à l'intérieur des fabriques industrielles, des chantiers navals et des usines d'armements autour de Montréal, tels que la Canadian Vickers Limited et Canadian Industries Limited, avec les artistes Louis Muhlstock et Fritz Brandtner. Dessine aussi le Service féminin de l'Armée canadienne (CWAC). Envoie des dessins à Harry McCurry, le directeur de la Galerie nationale du Canada (ancien nom du Musée des beaux-arts du Canada) et le conseiller A.Y. Jackson afin d'être considérée pour le programme d'art de guerre. N'obtient pas la commission.

Déménage à Ottawa à l'âge de 26 ans, afin de travailler au département des arts graphiques de l'Office national du film du Canada (ONF).

1944

The artist's father, John Duncan (born January 19, 1895), dies under tragic circumstances on June 18.

—

Le père de l'artiste, John Duncan (né le 19 janvier 1895), meurt dans des circonstances tragiques le 18 juin.

1945

Sets up and directs a department at the NFB making travelling displays.

—

Créé et dirige à l'ONF un département chargé de fabriquer des étalages d'exposition itinérants.

1947

After the Graphics Division at the NFB disbands, becomes part of their Animation Department.

Continues work on industrial drawings at Algoma Steel Corp., Sault Ste. Marie and E.B. Eddy Paper plant, Hull, QC.

First solo show (*Industrial Drawings*) held at The Gallery, Ottawa.

Solo exhibition at the University of Ottawa Academic Hall, of sixty-nine sketches and drawings made during the Marian Congress, a four-day Catholic conference held in Ottawa.

—

Se joint au département d'animation de l'ONF après la suppression du département des arts graphiques.

Continue de produire des dessins industriels aux Aciers Algoma Ltée de Sault Ste. Marie et à la papeterie E.B. Eddy à Hull (Québec).

Première exposition solo (*Industrial Drawings* [Dessins industriels]) à The Gallery, à Ottawa.

Exposition solo, au Hall académique de l'Université d'Ottawa, de soixante-neuf dessins et croquis exécutés au Congrès marial, une conférence catholique de quatre jours tenue à Ottawa.

1949

Teaches the course "Visual Presentation of Ideas" at Camp Laquemac (Laval University [Quebec, QC] and Macdonald College [Sainte-Anne-de-Bellevue, QC]).

—

Enseigne le cours « Visual Presentation of Ideas » (La présentation visuelle des idées) au Camp Laquemac (Université Laval [Québec, Québec] et Collège Macdonald [Sainte-Anne-de-Bellevue, Québec]).

1950

Produces her first film, entitled *Folksong Fantasy*, which she completes the following year for the NFB.

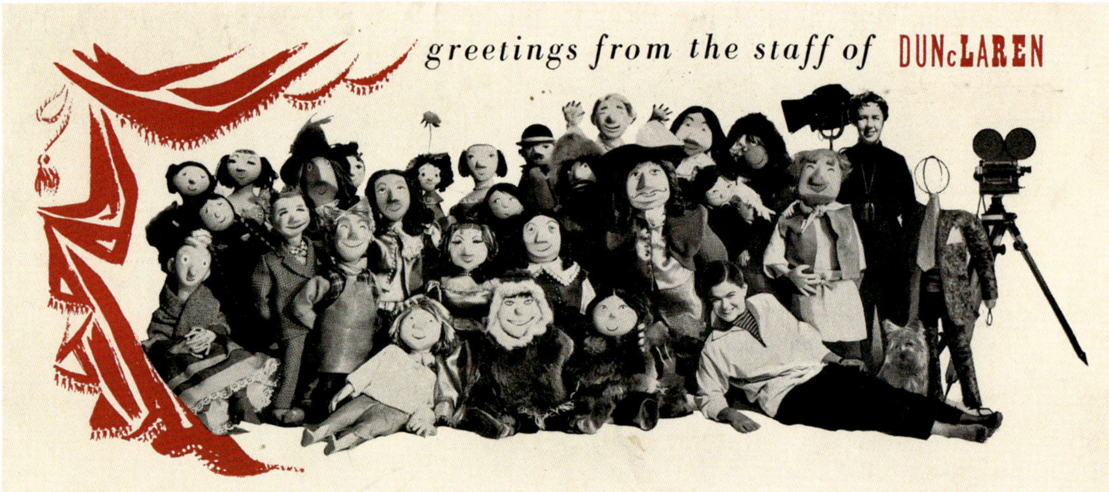

Dunclaren Productions Christmas card, c. 1950, Library and Archives Canada, e011083943
Carte de Noël de Dunclaren Productions, v. 1950, Bibliothèque et Archives Canada, e011083943

Lectures on " The Art of Animation" to the Advertising Club in Montreal.

—

Produit son premier film, *Fantaisie folklorique*, qu'elle terminera l'année suivante à l'ONF.

Donne une conférence sur l'art de l'animation au Advertising Club de Montréal

1951

Folksong Fantasy is shown at the Edinburgh International Film Festival, Edinburgh, UK.

Travels to Italy, France, Switzerland and Britain with Audrey McLaren for research into animation film trade and production.

Leaves the NFB to form Dunclaren Productions, an independent film company situated in an Ottawa attic, in partnership with Audrey McLaren.

—

Fantaisie folklorique est présenté au Festival international du film d'Édimbourg (RU).

Se rend en Italie, en France, en Suisse et en Grande-Bretagne avec Audrey McLaren pour faire de la recherche sur l'industrie et la production de films d'animation.

Quitte l'ONF afin de former la compagnie indépendante de film Dunclaren Productions, dans un grenier à Ottawa, en partenariat avec Audrey McLaren.

1953

Dunclaren Productions produces their first film, entitled *Kumak the Sleepy Hunter*, with music by Frederick Karam. Selected for exhibition at the International Edinburgh Film Festival.

Time Magazine Canada runs a short article highlighting Dunclaren and the creation of *Kumak*, featuring a photograph of Duncan and McLaren with their puppets (November 9).

—

Dunclaren Productions produit son premier film, *Kumak le chasseur somnolent* sur une musique de Frederick Karam. Le film est présenté au Festival international du film d'Édimbourg.

La revue *Time Magazine Canada* publie un court article sur Dunclaren et la création de *Kumak*, agrémenté d'une photographie de Duncan et McLaren avec leurs marionnettes (9 novembre).

1954

Kumak the Sleepy Hunter nominated for a British Academy of Film and Television Arts (BAFTA) Award, in the category of documentary film.

—

Kumak le chasseur somnolent est en lice pour un prix de la British Academy of Film and Television Arts (BAFTA), dans la catégorie du film documentaire.

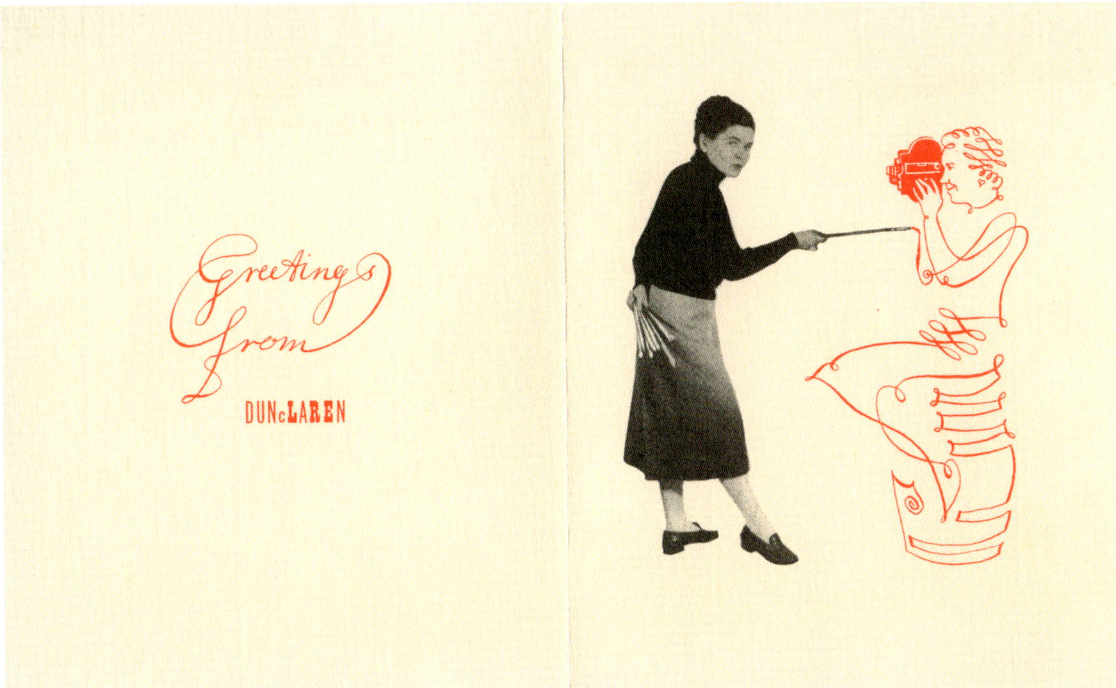

Dunclaren Productions Christmas card, c. 1950, Library and Archives Canada, e011083944
Carte de Noël de Dunclaren Productions, v. 1950, Bibliothèque et Archives Canada, e011083944

1955

Kumak the Sleepy Hunter receives a Recognition of Merit by the American Film Assembly at the Golden Reel Film Festival, New York.

—

Kumak le chasseur somnolent reçoit une Récompense pour le mérite lors du Golden Reel Film Festival (Festival de film Bobine d'or) de la American Film Assembly (Assemblée américaine du film) à New York.

1956

Dunclaren Productions produces *Hearts and Soles*, their second animated film , with music by Frederick Karam. Premiered by the Ottawa Film Council at the NFB, Ottawa, March 18. Included in the Venice Biennale (Venice International Film Festival) in the experimental and avant-garde section of the International Exhibition of Documentary Film and Short Films. Also included in the Vancouver International Film Festival.

Continues *Industrial Drawings* series at Steep Rock Iron Mine at Atikokan, ON, due to a contract received from the mine to produce a promotional film, as well as at Ore Docks at Prince Arthur.

—

Dunclaren Productions produit *L'amour pas-à-pas*, son deuxième film d'animation, sur une musique de Frederick Karam. Montré en première par le Ottawa Film Council (Conseil cinématographique d'Ottawa) à l'ONF à Ottawa le 18 mars. Est compris dans la section expérimentale et avant-garde de l'Exposition internationale du film documentaire et du court-métrage de la Biennale de Venise (Festival international d'art cinématographique de Venise). Aussi présenté au Festival international du film de Vancouver.

Continue de produire des dessins industriels à la mine de fer de Steep Rock à Atikokan, qui lui octroie un contrat de film promotionnel, ainsi qu'aux quais minéraliers de Prince Arthur.

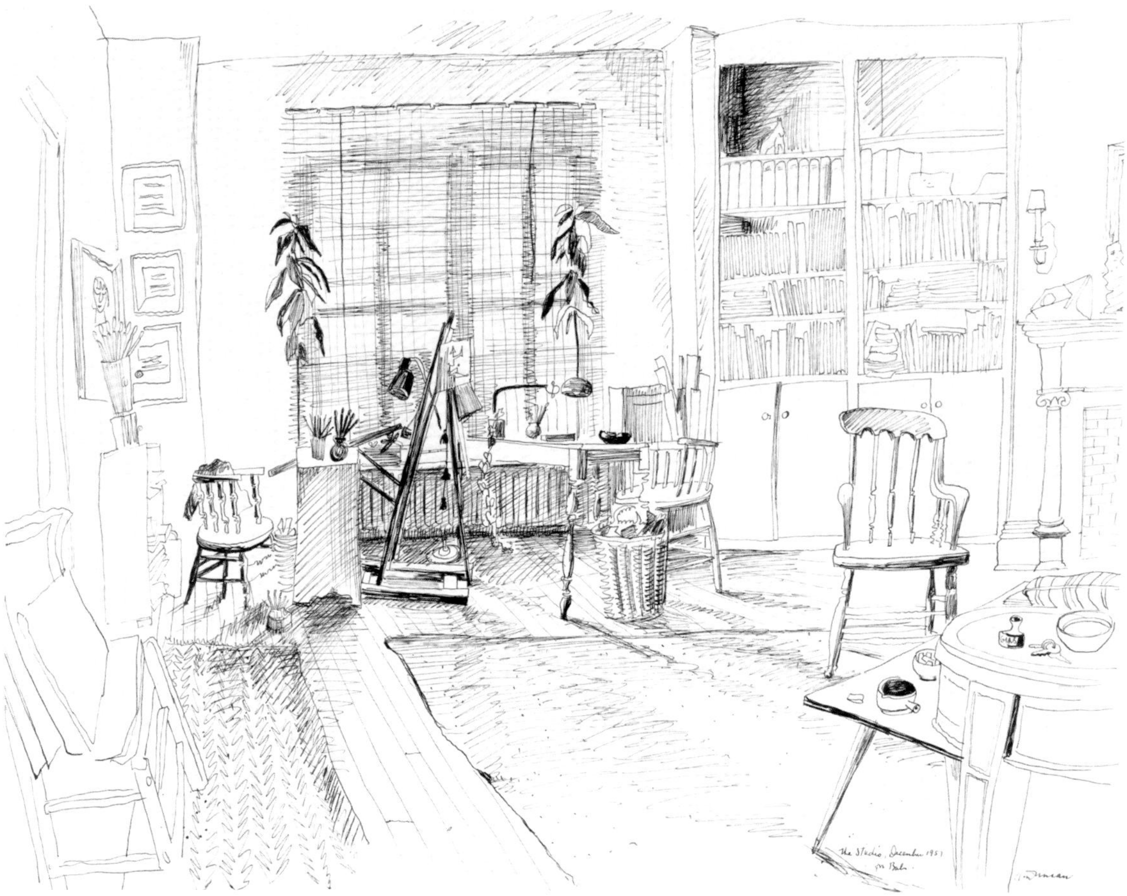

The Studio | L'atelier 1957 (cat. 31)
Library and Archives Canada | Bibliothèque et Archives Canada

1957

Illustrates the French textbook *Le francais vivant* by Dora Stock, Marie Stock and F.C.A. Jeanneret (Mississauga, ON: Copp Clark, 1957).

Kumak the Sleepy Hunter selected for exhibition at the British International Animated Film Festival.

—

Exécute les illustrations du manuel scolaire *Le français vivant* de Dora Stock, Marie Stock et F.C.A. Jeanneret (Mississauga, Ontario, Copp Clark, 1957).

Kumak le chasseur somnolent est choisi par le British International Animated Film Festival (Festival britannique international de film d'animation).

1958

Dunclaren Productions completes their last film, a promotional film entitled *Friendly Interchange* for Steep Rock Iron Mine, with music by Frederick Karam.

Again travels to Atikokan to draw interior of processing plant at Steep Rock Iron Mine.

—

Dunclaren Productions produit son dernier film, *Échange amical*, un film d'animation promotionnel pour la compagnie d'exploitation minière Steep Rock, sur une musique de Frederick Karam.

Se rend à nouveau à Atikokan pour dessiner l'intérieur de l'usine de traitement Steep Rock.

1962

Begins a three-year teaching position in painting and drawing at the Ottawa Municipal Art Centre (now the Ottawa School of Art).

—

Commence à enseigner la peinture et le dessin au Ottawa Municipal Art Centre (ancien nom de l'École d'art d'Ottawa), un poste qu'elle occupera trois ans.

1964

Untitled No. 1 (1964), one of her first conceptual "dot" pen-and-ink drawings, is accepted by the National Gallery of Canada (NGC) into their *Canadian Water Colours, Drawings and Prints 1964* exhibition. William S. Lieberman, Curator of Prints and Drawings of the Museum of Modern Art, particularly notes this work, and the NGC purchases it the same year, making it the first of 19 the NGC would eventually acquire.

Friendly Interchange (1958) is given an Award of Merit by the International Labor and Industrial Film Triennial, Antwerp, Belgium.

Work wins President's Award for Best in Show at the 4th Annual Rodman Hall Annual Exhibition.

—

Sans titre nº 1 (1964), un de ses premiers dessins conceptuels « en pointillé » réalisé à la plume et à l'encre, fait partie de l'exposition *Aquarelles, estampes et dessins canadiens, 1964* à la Galerie nationale du Canada. William S. Lieberman, le conservateur des dessins et estampes du Museum of Modern Art, remarque spécialement cette œuvre de Duncan. La Galerie l'acquiert la même année; 19 autres œuvres seront acquises au fil de la carrière de Duncan.

Échange amical reçoit un Prix du mérite décerné par le La Triennale internationale de films ouvriers et industriels à Anvers (Belgique).

Une œuvre remporte le prix du président de la meilleure œuvre lors de la 4e exposition annuelle du Rodman Hall Arts Centre.

1965

Teaches painting and drawing at the Rockcliffe Public School Art Club, Ottawa.

Lectures on "The Art of Animation" to the National Gallery Association.

Included in the exhibition *Focus on Drawings: Canada/Great Britain/Italy/Spain* (an exhibition and sale of drawings presented by the Women's Committee of the Art Gallery of Toronto (now the Art Gallery of Ontario [October 15–November 7, 1965]).

—

Enseigne la peinture et le dessin au club d'art de la Rockcliffe Public School à Ottawa.

Donne une conférence sur l'art de l'animation à l'Association de la Galerie nationale.

Une de ses œuvres fait partie de *Focus on Drawings: Canada/Great Britain/Italy/Spain* (Cap sur le dessin : Canada/Grande-Bretagne/Italie/Espagne), une exposition et vente de dessins présentées par le Comité féminin de la Art Gallery of Toronto (ancien nom du Musée des beaux-arts de l'Ontario), du 15 octobre au 7 novembre 1965.

1966

Joins the Canadian Society of Graphic Arts.

Teaches painting and drawing to young children at the After Four Centre, Ottawa.

Lectures on "The Art of Collage," National Gallery Association, Ottawa.

Donna della Serie 42 (c. 1965) earns the Purchase Prize at the Ninth Annual International Exhibition of Drawings and Engravings in Lugano, Switzerland, is illustrated in the catalogue, and is subsequently purchased for the collection of the regional contemporary art museum, Il Museo d'arte.

Woman (1964) and *Woman Series–Bouquet* (1965), are included in the exhibition *Canadian Water Colours, Drawings and Prints 1966*, held at the NGC and then circulated across Canada. Una E. Johnson, Curator of Prints and Drawings at the Brooklyn Museum, juries the exhibition and purchases *Black Butterfly–Woman Series* (1966) for their Collection, as well as *Nude–Woman Series* for her personal collection. The Brooklyn Museum Collection of Prints and Drawings, established by Johnson, is still considered one of the best in the United States.

The Family, No. 2 (1966) and *Primavera '67* (1967) are included in the Royal Canadian Academy (RCA) 88th annual exhibition at the Montreal Museum of Fine Arts (MMFA).

—

Se joint à la Société canadienne des arts graphiques.

Enseigne la peinture et le dessin aux jeunes enfants au centre After Four, à Ottawa.

Donne des conférences sur l'art du collage à l'Association de la Galerie national, à Ottawa.

Donna della Serie 42 (v. 1965) remporte le prix pour l'achat d'une œuvre à la neuvième Exposition internationale de dessins et de gravures de Lugano, en Suisse. L'œuvre est aussi comprise dans le catalogue de l'exposition et est ensuite acquise afin d'intégrer la collection du musée régional d'art contemporain Il Museo d'arte.

Femme (1964) et *Série Femme–Bouquet* (1965) sont incluses dans *Aquarelles, estampes et dessins canadiens, 1966*, une exposition présentée à la Galerie nationale du Canada et ensuite à travers le pays. Un membre du jury qui sélectionne les œuvres de cette exposition, la conservatrice des dessins et estampes du Brooklyn Museum Una E. Johnson, acquiert *Papillon noir–Série Femme* (1966) pour le musée et *Nue–Série Femme* pour sa collection privée. La collection de dessins et d'estampes du Brooklyn Museum, établie par Johnson, est encore aujourd'hui perçue comme étant une des meilleures aux États-Unis.

La famille n° 2 (1966) et *Primavera '67* (1967) sont comprises dans la 88e exposition annuelle de l'Académie royale des arts du Canada (ARC) au Musée des beaux-arts de Montréal (MBAM).

1967

Solo exhibition of *Lady's Series* at Isaacs Gallery, Toronto.

—

Exposition solo de la série *Dame* à la Isaacs Gallery, Toronto.

1968

With the help of a Canada Council Grant, Duncan and McLaren travel throughout Spain, North Africa, Lebanon, Iran, and Turkey to study Islamic art.

—

Grâce à une bourse du Conseil des arts, Duncan et McLaren se rendent en Espagne, en Afrique du Nord, au Liban, en Iran et en Turquie pour y étudier l'art islamique.

1970

Duncan and McLaren travel throughout Japan, Hong Kong, and Hawaii.

Invited by Canada Post to design a series of four postage stamps of the maple leaf in all four seasons.

Work included in the *IX Joan Miró International Show of Drawings* in Barcelona, and selected for an American tour

—

Duncan et McLaren font un grand voyage au Japon, à Hong Kong et à Hawaï.

La Société canadienne des postes invite Duncan à créer une série de quatre timbres-poste représentant la feuille d'érable dans les quatre saisons.

Son travail est compris dans le « IX Joan Miró International Show of Drawings » à Barcelone, et aussi sélectionné pour une tournée américaine.

1971

Maple Leaf in Four Seasons stamp series are issued by Canada Post, and *Autumn* is selected as the "stamp of the month" by the *Scott Monthly Journal*, a New York-based philately journal.

Teaches painting and drawing at the Lindenlea Community Centre in Ottawa (until 1973).

Three munitions drawings purchased by the Canadian War Museum.

—

La série de timbres *La feuille d'érable dans les quatre saisons* est émise. Le timbre *Automne* reçoit la mention « timbre du mois » par le *Scott Monthly Journal*, un journal de philatélie de New York.

Enseigne la peinture et le dessin au centre communautaire Lindenlea à Ottawa jusqu'en 1973.

Trois de ses dessins de munitions sont acquis par le Musée canadien de la guerre.

1972

Leaf-in-snow drawing is reproduced by Unicef.

Department of External Affairs purchases drawings from *Forest Floor* series.

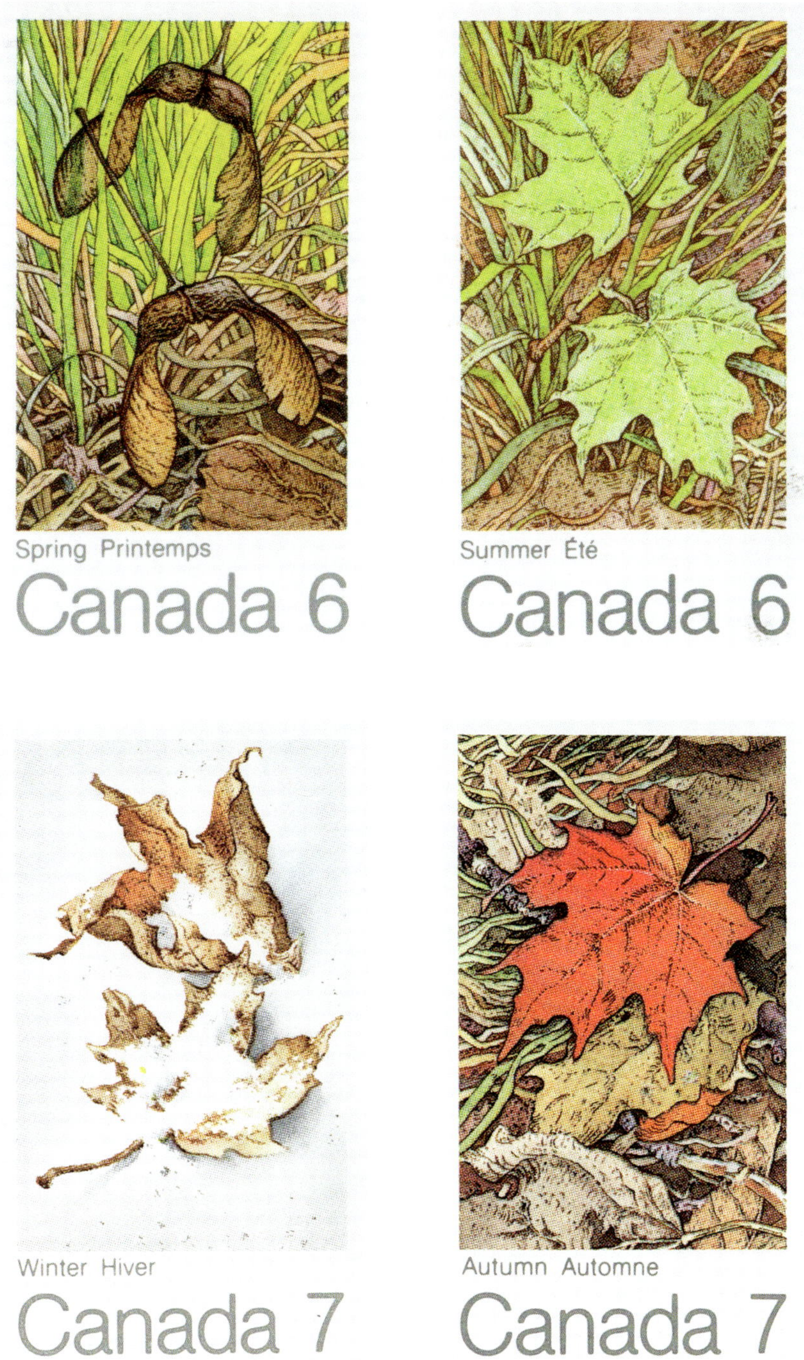

Maple Leaf in Four Seasons | Feuille d'érable dans les quatre saisons 1971 (cat. 65)
Private Collection and the Canada Post Corporation | Collection privée et de la Société canadienne des postes

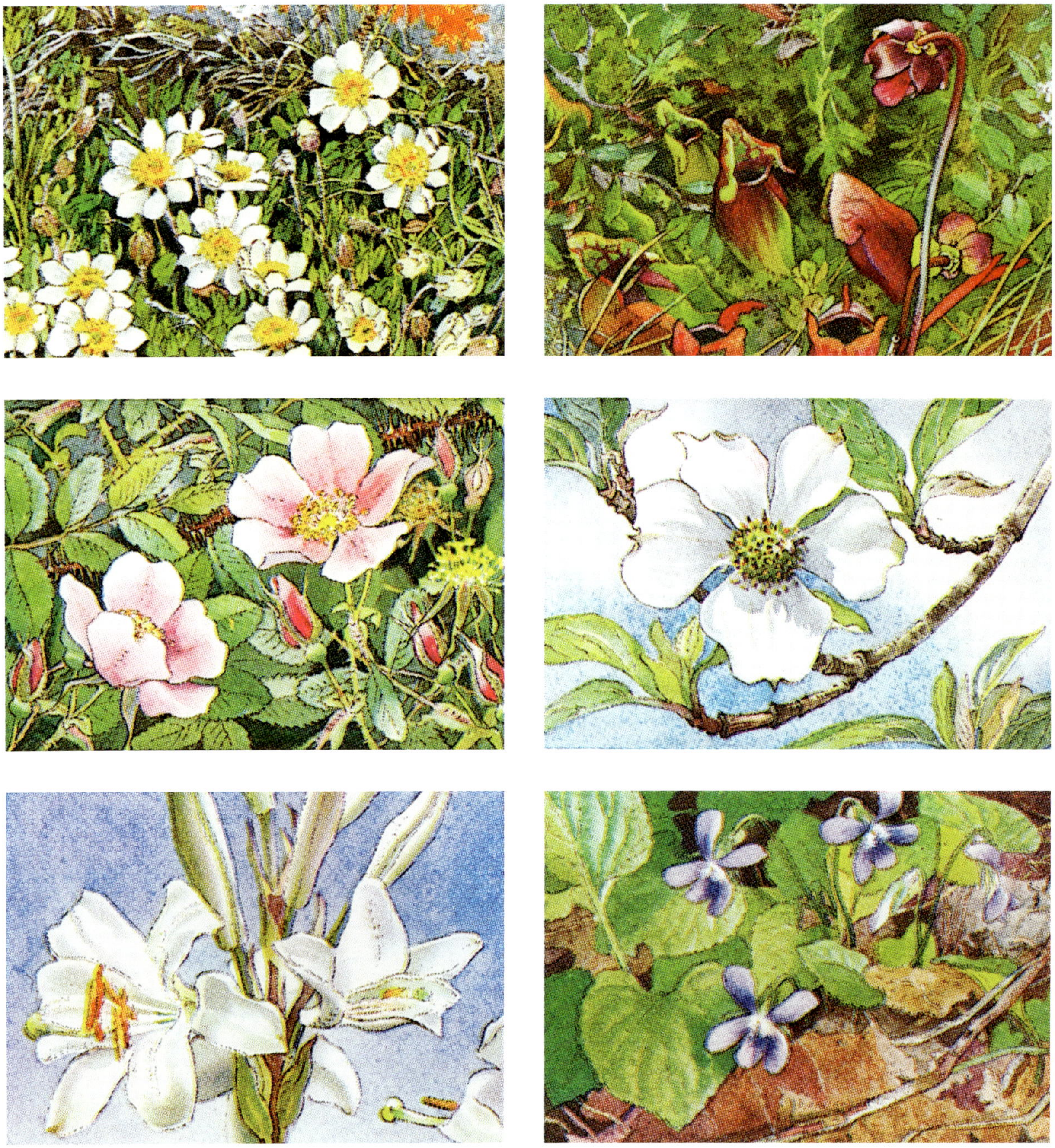

Floral Aerogrammes (details) | **Aérogrammes floraux** (détails) 1973 (cat. 66)

Private Collection and the Canada Post Corporation | Collection privée et de la Société canadienne des postes

Un de ses dessins de feuille dans la neige est reproduit par l'Unicef.

Le ministère des Affaires extérieures achète des dessins de la série *Sol de la forêt*.

1973

Second postal series, *Floral Aerogrammes*, is released. Each of these twelve "domestogrammes" represents the official flower of Canada's provinces and territories.

—

Une deuxième série postale, *Aérogrammes floraux*, est émise. Les fleurs qui ornent les douze « domestogrammes » représentent les emblèmes floraux officiels des provinces et territoires du Canada.

1974

Becomes a Board Member of ATAI Arctic Creative Development Foundation.

—

Devient membre du conseil d'administration de la « ATAI Arctic Creative Development Foundation » (Fondation pour le développement créatif arctique).

1975

Travels to Pangnirtung and other areas of the Eastern Arctic (now Nunavut) for two months to sketch the landscape, with the help of a grant from the Canada Council for the Arts.

—

Se rend à Pangnirtung et dans d'autres endroits de l'Arctique de l'Est (aujourd'hui le Nunavut) pour deux mois grâce à une bourse du Conseil des arts du Canada afin de faire des croquis du paysage.

1976

Joins the Print and Drawing Council of Canada.

—

Se joint au Conseil canadien de gravure et de dessin.

1978

Teaches painting and drawing at the Arnprior Art Club (until 1981).

Joins the Canadian Artists Representation.

—

Enseigne la peinture et le dessin au Arnprior Art Club (jusqu'en 1981).

Se joint au Front des artistes canadiens.

1979

Enrolls in the Correspondence Programme at the University of Waterloo; studies Fine Arts 110: *Introduction to World Art 1: Prehistoric, Ancient and Non-Western Art* and *Introduction to World Art 2: Western Art from Classical to Modern*.

Following a visit, Mimi Cazort and Rosemarie Tovell, curators of prints and drawings at the NGC select six *Industrial Drawings* for the Gallery's collection. Tovell subsequently shows these drawings to Joan Murray (The Robert McLaughlin Gallery, Oshawa, ON), Christine Boyanoski (Art Gallery of Ontario), Andrew Oko (Art Gallery of Hamilton), and other visiting curators to Ottawa.

Two *Woman Series* drawings and an ink on paper landscape purchased by the Canada Council Art Bank.

—

S'inscrit au programme par correspondance de l'Université de Waterloo; suit le cours Beaux-arts 110 : *Introduction à l'art du monde 1 : Art préhistorique, ancien et non occidental* et *Introduction à l'art du monde 2 : Art occidental de l'époque classique à l'époque moderne*.

Après lui avoir rendu visite, les conservatrices des dessins et estampes du Musée des beaux-arts du Canada, Mimi Cazort et Rosemarie Tovell, choisissent six *Dessins industriels* afin de les intégrer à la collection du Musée. Tovell montre ensuite ces dessins à Joan Murray (The Robert McLaughlin Gallery, Oshawa, Ontario), Christine Boyanoski (Musée des beaux-arts de l'Ontario), Andrew Oko (Art Gallery of Hamilton) et d'autres commissaires en visite à Ottawa.

Deux dessins de la *Série Femme* ainsi qu'un paysage à l'encre sur papier sont achetés par la Banque d'œuvres d'art du Conseil des arts du Canada.

1980

Solo exhibition at Gallery Graphics (Ottawa).

Work included in the exhibition *Canadian Artists of the Second World War* (17 October – 30 November 1981), curated by Joan Murray for The Robert McLaughlin Gallery, resulting in purchases of her work for their collection.

—

Exposition solo à la galerie Gallery Graphics (Ottawa).

Son travail est compris dans l'exposition *Canadian Artists of the Second World War* (Artistes canadiens de la Deuxième Guerre mondiale) (du 17 octobre au 30 novembre 1981), organisée par Joan Murray pour The Robert McLaughlin Gallery. Acquisition de certaines œuvres pour la collection de la galerie.

1981

Solo exhibition at Gallery Ann Doran (Ottawa).

—

Exposition solo à la Gallery Ann Doran (Ottawa).

1982

Moves to Cumberland, ON, age 65. Duncan and McLaren chose this location to be closer to the artist's mother, Eleanor Duncan. In the lower Ottawa Valley, the artist works on various series inspired by the country landscape.

—

Déménage à Cumberland, en Ontario, à l'âge de 65 ans. Duncan et McLaren choisissent ce lieu pour sa proximité à la mère de l'artiste, Eleanor Duncan. Dans le bas de la vallée de l'Outaouais, Duncan travaille à plusieurs séries inspirées des paysages campagnards.

1985

Makes drawings at Stelco Inc. at Nanticoke, ON.

—

Exécute des dessins à la Stelco Inc., à Nanticoke, Ontario.

1986

Drawings made at James MacLaren Industries Inc at Thurso, QC.

—

Dessins faits aux Industries James MacLaren Inc à Thurso, Québec.

1987

Joan Murray curates the retrospective exhibition *Alma Duncan and Men at Work: 1943–1986* for The Robert McLaughlin Gallery (Oshawa, ON), which subsequently tours to Rodman Hall Arts Centre (St. Catharines, ON) the Macdonald Stewart Art Centre (Guelph, ON), the Art Gallery of Greater Victoria (Victoria, BC), the Art Gallery of York University (Toronto), the Sarnia Public Library and Art Gallery (Sarnia, ON), and the Gallery at Arts Court (Ottawa).

Industrial Drawings included in the survey exhibition *Industrial Images*, and reproduced in the catalogue, curated by Rosemary Donegan for the Art Gallery of Hamilton and circulated to the Vancouver Art Gallery.

—

Murray monte l'exposition rétrospective *Alma Duncan and Men at Work: 1943–1986* (Alma Duncan et Hommes au travail. 1943–1986) pour The Robert McLaughlin Gallery (Oshawa, Ontario); l'exposition se rendra aussi au Rodman Hall Arts Centre (St. Catharines, Ontario), au Macdonald Stewart Art Centre (Guelph, Ontario), à la Art Gallery of Greater Victoria (Victoria, Colombie-Britannique), à la Art Gallery of York University (Toronto), à la Sarnia Public Library and Art Gallery (Sarnia, Ontario) et à La Galerie à la Cour des arts (Ottawa).

Des *Dessins industriels* sont compris dans l'exposition survol *Images industrielles* ainsi que publiés dans le catalogue de cette exposition organisée par Rosemary Donegan pour la Art Gallery of Hamilton et ayant ensuite été présentée à la Vancouver Art Gallery.

1989

Two munitions drawings and *Self-Portrait with Blue Handkerchief* (1941) purchased by the Art Gallery of Ontario.

—

Deux dessins de munitions et *Autoportrait avec mouchoir bleu* (1941) sont acquis par le Musée des beaux-arts de l'Ontario.

1991

The artist's mother, Eleanor Duncan, dies November 29, at the Élisabeth Bruyère Continuing Care Center in Ottawa.

—

La mère de l'artiste, Eleanor Duncan, meurt le 29 novembre au Centre de santé Élisabeth-Bruyère à Ottawa.

1993

Travels to Europe.

—

Se rend en Europe.

1994

Donates papers and artwork to the National Archives of Canada (now Library and Archives Canada).

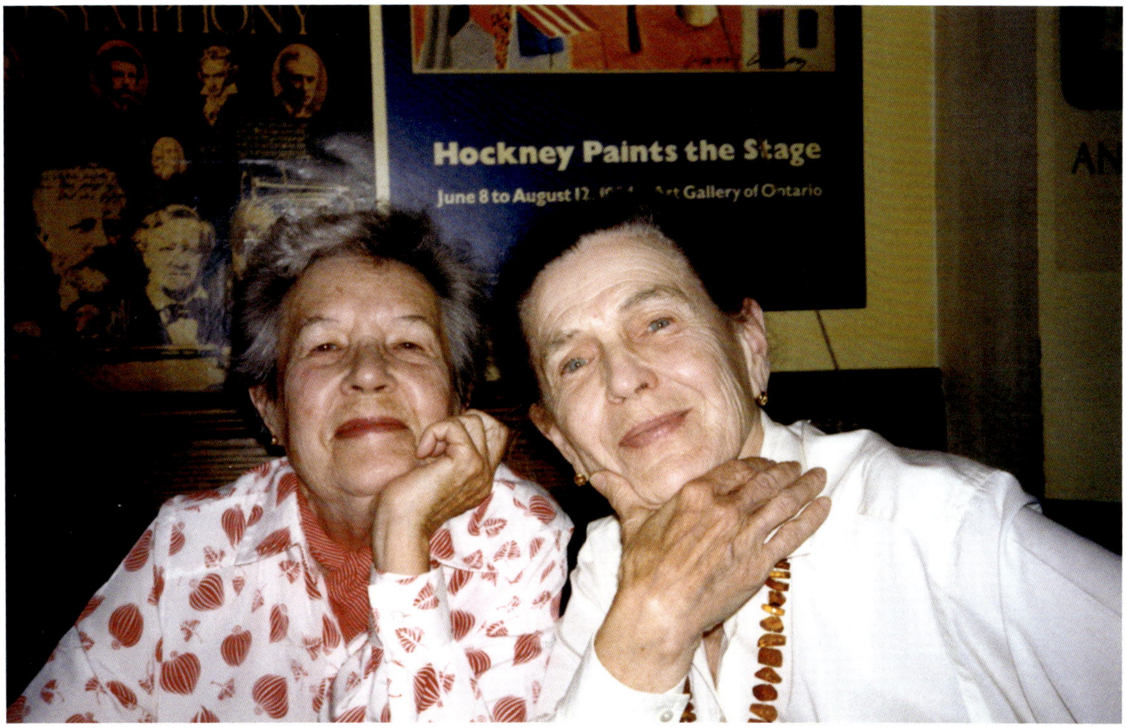

Audrey (Babs) McLaren and Alma Duncan, 1993
Audrey (Babs) McLaren et Alma Duncan, 1993

Lègue des archives et des œuvres aux Archives nationales du Canada (ancien nom de Bibliothèque et Archives Canada).

1995

Work included in *Part III (1946–1970)* of *History of Art and Artists of Ottawa and Surroundings, 1790–1970*, curated by Jim Burant for the Ottawa Art Gallery.

Army Women in Warehouse (1943), from the collection of the National Gallery of Canada, included in *The View from Here: A Canadian Picture Show in Nine Acts*, an NFB documentary film. Duncan's work is particularly noted by author Anne Newlands, alongside the work of Fritz Brandtner, as an example of a Canadian artist depicting workers in the field.

Diagnosed with Alzheimer's disease and moves into a nursing home in Ottawa, age 77

—

Son travail est inclus dans *Histoire de l'art et des artistes d'Ottawa et des environs de 1790 à 1970: troisième partie, 1946–1970*, organisé par Jim Burant pour la Galerie d'art d'Ottawa.

Femmes de l'armée dans un entrepôt (1943), de la collection du Musée des beaux-arts du Canada, est comprise dans *The View from Here: A Canadian Picture Show in Nine Acts* (Ce que l'on voit d'ici. Une image du Canada en neuf actes), un documentaire de l'ONF. Le travail de Duncan est souligné, avec celui de Fritz Brandtner, par l'auteure Anne Newlands comme une représentation exemplaire d'ouvriers.

Reçoit un diagnostic de maladie d'Alzheimer; emménage dans une maison de soins infirmiers à Ottawa à l'âge de 77 ans.

2004

Passes away on December 15, age 86.

—

Décède le 15 décembre, à l'âge de 86 ans.

Eleanor Audrey (Babs) McLaren

1916–2014

Eleanor Audrey (Babs) McLaren was born in the town of Hythe in Kent, England in 1916. She relocated to Hamilton, Ontario with her mother soon after her father Richard J. McLaren, who served with the 1st West York Regiment, was killed in action in 1918. McLaren received her schooling in Hamilton, Switzerland, and Florence, Italy. After her social debut in 1934 which included many "dull parties," McLaren spent several years travelling in England, the United States and the Caribbean before joining the Red Cross Transport Corps as a driver in 1940. She enlisted in the Royal Canadian Armed Forces (RCAF) the following year as a driver and was posted to the Western Air Command in Victoria, British Columbia, where she obtained her commission in 1943. After discharge in 1946, McLaren took a job at the National Film Board (NFB), where she met Alma Duncan. In 1950 she left the NFB and a year later, the two formed Dunclaren Productions. Together they toured animation studios in Europe, then returned to make their first film, *Kumak the Sleepy Hunter* (1953). From 1952 to 1963, they made various films and advertising campaigns with puppets, garnering international recognition. After touring the Middle East for four and a half months in 1968, the women returned to their country home in Arnprior, Ontario. McLaren loved the country and soon established huge vegetable plots that produced ample quantities for the whole year that they pickled, froze and dried. They eventually settled in Cumberland, Ontario at what they called their idyllic "Froggery" property. A move back to Ottawa in 1995 was prompted by Duncan's declining health, where McLaren resided until her death in 2014.

Eleanor Audrey « Babs » McLaren est née à Hythe, dans le Kent (Angleterre), en 1916. Elle et sa mère retournent à Hamilton, en Ontario, lorsque son père, le soldat Richard J. McLaren du régiment 1st West York, meurt au combat. McLaren reçoit son éducation à Hamilton, puis en Suisse et à Florence, en Italie. Elle fait son entrée dans le monde en 1934 et, après maintes « soirées mornes », passe plusieurs années à voyager en Angleterre, aux É.-U. et dans les Caraïbes, avant de se joindre au Corps de la Croix-Rouge canadienne comme conductrice en 1940. Elle s'enrôle l'année suivante dans l'Aviation royale canadienne, encore en tant que conductrice, et est affectée au commandement aérien de l'ouest à Victoria, en C.-B., où elle obtient sa commission en 1943. Après son retour à la vie civile en 1946, Babs trouve du travail à l'Office national du film (ONF), où elle rencontre Alma Duncan. Elle quitte l'ONF en 1950 et, l'année suivante, Alma et elle fondent les productions Dunclaren. Elles visitent des studios d'animation en Europe et retournent au Canada pour créer leur premier film, *Kumak le chasseur somnolent*. Elles créent, de 1952 à 1963, plusieurs films et campagnes publicitaires avec des marionnettes qui leur méritent une renommée internationale. Après un voyage de quatre mois et demi au Moyen-Orient en 1968, elles retournent à leur maison de campagne à Arnprior. Babs adore la campagne et s'empresse de cultiver d'immenses parcelles de terre qui produisent suffisamment de légumes pour toute l'année, une fois marinés, congelés ou séchés. Plusieurs déménagements plus tard, elles s'installent à Cumberland, dans leur « Froggery » (Grenouillère) idyllique. La santé dépérissante d'Alma force un retour à Ottawa en 1995, où McLaren habite jusqu'à son décès en 2014.

Catalogue

All works are reproduced courtesy of the Alma Duncan Estate. | Ces œuvres sont reproduites avec l'aimable autorisation de la succession d'Alma Duncan.[1]

1. *The Striped Kimono* | *Le kimono rayé*, 1935
Oil on canvas | Huile sur toile
41 × 33 cm
Courtesy of Brian Oickle | Gracieuseté de Brian Oickle

2. *Self-Portrait* | *Autoportrait*, 1939
Oil on canvas | Huile sur toile
30.2 × 22.5 | 30,2 × 22,5 cm
Courtesy of a Private Collection | Gracieuseté d'une collection privée

3. *Mother in Ribbon Hat (Eleanor Duncan)* | *Mère coiffée d'un chapeau à ruban (Eleanor Duncan)*, 1938
Charcoal (or conté crayon) on laid paper | Fusain (ou crayon conté) sur papier vergé
63.5 × 48.6 | 63,5 × 48,6 cm
Library and Archives Canada, Major Lender | Bibliothèque et Archives Canada, prêteur important, e011083809

4. Ernst Neumann
Alma Duncan, 1939
Oil on canvas | Huile sur toile
41 × 33 cm
Library and Archives Canada, Major Lender | Bibliothèque et Archives Canada, prêteur important, e011080203

5. *Canada Carries On Presents Look to the North* | *En avant Canada présente « Look to the North »*, 1939
Serigraph Poster | Affiche sérigraphiée
121.9 × 91.4 | 121,9 × 91,4 cm
Beaverbrook Collection of War Art, Canadian War Museum, CWM 20010129-0541 | Collection Beaverbrook d'art militaire, Musée canadien de la guerre, MCG 20010129-0541

6. *Self-Portrait with Braids* | *Autoportrait avec tresses*, 1940
Oil on masonite | Huile sur masonite
51 × 39.8 | 51 × 39,8 cm
Library and Archives Canada, Major Lender | Bibliothèque et Archives Canada, prêteur important, c146139

7. *Young Black Girl* | *Jeune fille noire*, 1940
Oil on multi-ply paper-board | Huile sur carton fort multicouches
41.5 × 33 cm
Collection of the Art Gallery of Ontario | Collection du Musée des beaux-arts de l'Ontario, Toronto; Gift of the artist | Don de l'artiste, Ottawa, 1999, 99/38

8. *Self-Portrait with Blue Handkerchief* | *Autoportrait avec mouchoir bleu*, 1941
Oil and egg-oil tempera on canvas | Huile et tempéra à l'œuf sur toile
63.5 × 50.9 | 63,5 × 50,9 cm
Collection of the Art Gallery of Ontario | Collection du Musée des beaux-arts de l'Ontario, Toronto; Purchase | Achat, Ottawa, 1989, 89/3

9. *Joan Wilkie*, 1942
Oil over egg tempera on masonite | Huile et tempéra à l'œuf sur toile
63.6 × 50.8 | 63,6 × 50,8 cm
Library and Archives Canada, Major Lender | Bibliothèque et Archives Canada, prêteur important, c150809

10. *Ernst Neumann*, 1942
Charcoal on paper | Fusain sur papier
35.2 × 27.4 | 35,2 × 27,4 cm
Courtesy of The Robert McLaughlin Gallery | Gracieuseté de The Robert McLaughlin Gallery, Oshawa; Gift of the artist | Don de l'artiste, 1985

11. *Self-Portrait* | *Autoportrait*, 1943
Oil on masonite | Huile sur masonite
61 × 61 cm
Collection of the Ottawa Art Gallery; Gift of the artist | Collection de la Galerie d'art d'Ottawa; don de l'artiste, 1997

12. *Rosie with Badminton Racquet* | *Rosie avec une raquette de badminton*, 1943
Ink and oil on canvas | Encre et huile sur toile
63.6 × 50.8 | 63,6 × 50,8 cm
Collection of the Art Gallery of Ontario | Collection du Musée des beaux-arts de l'Ontario, Toronto; Gift of the artist | Don de l'artiste, Ottawa, 1999, 99/39

13. *Shaping Hot Metal Under Hammer (Ship Building)* | *Forgeant du métal chaud sous un marteau-pilon (Construction de navire)*, 1943
Charcoal on paper | Fusain sur papier
50.7 × 66.3 | 50,7 × 66,3 cm
Beaverbrook Collection of War Art, Canadian War Museum, CWM 19710261-5927 | Collection Beaverbrook d'art militaire, Musée canadien de la guerre, MCG 19710261-5927

14. *Army Girl in Warehouse* | *Jeune soldate dans un entrepôt*, 1943
Tempera on masonite | Tempéra sur masonite
50.8 × 58.6 | 50,8 × 58,6 cm
Library and Archives Canada, Major Lender | Bibliothèque et Archives Canada, prêteur important, c107016

15. *Army Women in Warehouse | Femmes de l'armée dans un entrepôt*, 1943
Oil on masonite | Huile sur masonite
58.5 × 71.5 | 58,5 × 71,5 cm
National Gallery of Canada | Musée des beaux-arts du Canada, Ottawa; Purchase | Achat, 1985

16. *Riveters in Boiler Shop | Riveurs dans un atelier de montage de chaudières*, 1943
Black chalk on paper | Pierre noire sur papier
50.7 × 66.3 | 50,7 × 66,3 cm
Courtesy of The Robert McLaughlin Gallery | Gracieuseté de The Robert McLaughlin Gallery, Oshawa; Gift of the artist | Don de l'artiste, 1981

17. *Isabel Jordon*, 1947
Oil on masonite | Huile sur masonite
41 × 33 cm
Library and Archives Canada, Major Lender | Bibliothèque et Archives Canada, prêteur important, c149239

18. *Papermakers, E.B. Eddy Company | La papetière E.B. Eddy*, 1947
Black conté crayon on wove paper | Crayon conté noir sur papier vélin
51 × 66 cm
Library and Archives Canada, Major Lender | Bibliothèque et Archives Canada, prêteur important, e011083815

19. *Grant Munro*, 1947
Oil on masonite | Huile sur masonite
63.5 × 50.8 | 63,5 × 50,8 cm
Collection of the Ottawa Art Gallery; Gift of the artist | Collection de la Galerie d'art d'Ottawa; don de l'artiste, 1997

20. *Norman McLaren*, 1947
Oil on masonite | Huile sur masonite
63.6 × 50.8 | 63,6 × 50,8 cm
Library and Archives Canada, Major Lender | Bibliothèque et Archives Canada, prêteur important, c146244

21. *P.K. Page*, 1947
Oil on masonite | Huile sur masonite
41 × 33 cm
Library and Archives Canada, Major Lender | Bibliothèque et Archives Canada, prêteur important, c107299

22. *Audrey (Babs) McLaren | Audrey « Babs » McLaren*, 1949
Oil on masonite | Huile sur masonite
41.1 × 33.1 | 41,1 × 33,1 cm
Library and Archives Canada, Major Lender | Bibliothèque et Archives Canada, prêteur important, e011092623

23. *UNO by EACH for all* film poster | Affiche de film *UNO : par chacun pour tous*, c.|v. 1950s
Conté and gouache on wove paper-faced illustration board | Fusain et gouache sur un carton à dessin recouvert de papier vélin
54.5 × 41.8 | 54,5 × 41,8 cm
Library and Archives Canada, Major Lender | Bibliothèque et Archives Canada, prêteur important, e011083816

24. *Folksong Fantasy | Fantaisie folklorique*, 1951
16 mm film | Film 16 mm
7 min 10 s
Animation | Dessins : Alma Duncan
Camera | Caméra : Lyle Enright
Song | Chanson : Emma Caslor
© 2007 National Film Board of Canada. All rights reserved. Printed in Canada. | © Office national du film du Canada. Tous droits réservés. Imprimé au Canada.

25. *Kumak the Sleepy Hunter | Kumak le chasseur somnolent*, 1953
16 mm film | Film 16 mm
13 min
Production | Réalisation : Alma Duncan and/et Audrey McLaren
Animation | Dessins : Alma Duncan
Photography | Photographie : Audrey McLaren
Music | Musique : Frederick Karam
Narration : Moira Dunbar
Courtesy of Dunclaren Productions (Alma Duncan Estate and Audrey McLaren) | Gracieuseté de Dunclaren Productions (la succession d'Alma Duncan et Audrey McLaren)

26. *Hearts and Soles | L'amour pas-à-pas*, 1955
16 mm film | Film 16 mm
5 min
Production | Réalisation : Alma Duncan and/et Audrey McLaren
Music | Musique : Frederick Karam
Courtesy of Dunclaren Productions (Alma Duncan Estate and Audrey McLaren) | Gracieuseté de Dunclaren Productions (la succession d'Alma Duncan et Audrey McLaren)

27. Puppets and film props | Marionnettes et accessoires de films
From | De :
Folksong Fantasy | Fantaisie folklorique, 1951
Kumak the Sleepy Hunter | Kumak le chasseur somnolent, 1953
Hearts and Soles | L'amour pas-à-pas, 1955
Dimensions variable | Dimensions variées
Library and Archives Canada, Major Lender | Bibliothèque et Archives Canada, prêteur important

28. *Open Pit Mine and Lake in Shower | Mine à ciel ouvert et lac sous l'orage*, 1956
Pastel on calendered wove paper | Pastel sur papier vélin calandré
49.5 × 64.7 | 49,5 × 64,7 cm
National Gallery of Canada | Musée des beaux-arts du Canada, Ottawa; Purchase | Achat, 1981

29. *Open Pit and Skipway | Mine ouverte et passerelle*, 1956

Pastel on paper | Pastel sur papier
49.5 × 95.9 | 49,5 × 95,9 cm
Courtesy of The Robert McLaughlin Gallery | Gracieuseté de The Robert McLaughlin Gallery, Oshawa; Gift of the artist | Don de l'artiste, 1991

30. *Mother's Room, Christmas* | *La chambre de ma mère, Noël*, 1957
Watercolour over pen and ink drawing on paper | Aquarelle sur dessin à la plume et à l'encre sur papier
35.5 × 50.8 | 35,5 × 50,8 cm
Courtesy of | Gracieuseté de D & E Lake Ltd. Fine Arts, Toronto

31. *The Studio* | *L'atelier*, 1957
Pen and black ink on wove paper | Plume et encre noire sur papier vélin
35.4 × 49.9 | 35,4 × 49,9 cm
Library and Archives Canada, Major Lender | Bibliothèque et Archives Canada, prêteur important, e011073159

32. *Self-Portrait with Red Stripes* | *Autoportrait avec rayures rouges*, 1958
Oil on masonite | Huile sur masonite
50.8 × 63.5 | 50,8 × 63,5 cm
Courtesy of | Gracieuseté de D & E Lake Ltd. Fine Arts, Toronto

33. *Giant Spiral, Processing Ore* | *Spirale géante, traitement du minerai*, 1958
Pastel on paper | Pastel sur papier
49.5 × 95.9 | 49,5 × 95,9 cm
Courtesy of a Private Collection | Gracieuseté d'une collection privée

34. *Friendly Interchange* | *Échange amical*, 1958
16 mm film | Film 16 mm
10 min
Production | Réalisation : Alma Duncan
Camera | Caméra : Audrey McLaren
Music | Musique : Frederick Karam
Narration : Raymond Peter
Scriptwriter | Scénariste : James Cowan
Courtesy of Dunclaren Productions (Alma Duncan Estate and Audrey McLaren) | Gracieuseté de Dunclaren Productions (la succession d'Alma Duncan et Audrey McLaren)

35. *Grass, August 1* | *Herbe 1er août*, 1962
Pen and black ink on thin wove card | Plume et encre noire sur carton vélin mince
21.6 × 28.2 | 21,6 × 28,2 cm
Library and Archives Canada, Major Lender | Bibliothèque et Archives Canada, prêteur important, e011083786

36. *Grass, August 2* | *Herbe 2 août*, 1962
Pen and black ink on thin wove card | Plume et encre noire sur carton vélin mince
21.6 × 28.2 | 21,6 × 28,2 cm
Library and Archives Canada, Major Lender | Bibliothèque et Archives Canada, prêteur important, e011083788

37. *Grass I* | *Herbe I*, 1962
Pen and black ink on thin wove card | Plume et encre noire sur carton vélin mince
21.6 × 28.2 | 21,6 × 28,2 cm
Library and Archives Canada, Major Lender | Bibliothèque et Archives Canada, prêteur important, e011083787

38. *Grass II* | *Herbe II*, 1962
Pen and black ink on thin wove card | Plume et encre noire sur carton vélin mince
21.6 × 28.2 | 21,6 × 28,2 cm
Library and Archives Canada, Major Lender | Bibliothèque et Archives Canada, prêteur important, e011083785

39. *Untitled No. 1* | *Sans titre nº 1*, 1964
Pen and black ink on wove paper | Plume et encre noire sur papier vélin
75.9 × 58.2 | 75,9 × 58,2 cm
National Gallery of Canada | Musée des beaux-arts du Canada, Ottawa; Purchase | Achat, 1964

40. *Untitled 3* | *Sans titre 3*, 1965
Pen and ink on paper | Plume et encre sur papier
74 × 58 cm
Courtesy of Renato Albino | Gracieuseté de Renato Albino

41. *The Tangled Web* | *La toile enchevêtrée*, 1965
Pen and black ink on wove paper | Plume et encre noire sur papier vélin
18.2 × 14.6 | 18,2 × 14,6 cm
Library and Archives Canada, Major Lender | Bibliothèque et Archives Canada, prêteur important, e011083784

42. *Woman Series – II* | *Série Femme – II*, 1965
Conté on heavy wove paper | Fusain sur papier vélin épais
50.6 × 50.6 | 50,6 × 50,6 cm
Library and Archives Canada, Major Lender | Bibliothèque et Archives Canada, prêteur important, e011073159

43. *Woman Series – Torso* | *Série Femme – Torse*, 1965
Conté on heavy wove paper | Fusain sur papier vélin épais
50.6 × 50.6 | 50,6 × 50,6 cm
Library and Archives Canada, Major Lender | Bibliothèque et Archives Canada, prêteur important, e011083808

44. *Woman Series – Square Torso* | *Série Femme – Torse carré*, 1965
Conté on heavy wove paper | Fusain sur papier vélin épais
50.5 × 50.5 | 50,5 × 50,5 cm
Library and Archives Canada, Major Lender | Bibliothèque et Archives Canada, prêteur important, e011083804

45. *Woman Series – Maiden* | *Série Femme – Demoiselle*, 1965
Conté on heavy wove paper | Fusain sur papier vélin épais
50.5 × 50.5 | 50,5 × 50,5 cm
Library and Archives Canada, Major Lender | Bibliothèque et Archives Canada, prêteur important, e011083805

46. *Woman Series – Matron* | *Série Femme – Madame*, 1965
Conté on heavy wove paper | Fusain sur papier vélin épais
50.4 × 50.4 | 50,4 × 50,4 cm
Library and Archives Canada, Major Lender | Bibliothèque et Archives Canada, prêteur important, e011083807

47. *The Family* | *La famille*, 1966
Canvas collage on masonite | Collage de toile sur masonite
60.4 × 103 | 60,4 × 103 cm
Courtesy of a Private Collection | Gracieuseté d'une collection privée

48. *The Family* | *La famille*, 1966
Canvas collage on masonite | Collage de toile sur masonite
60.4 × 112 | 60,4 × 112 cm
Courtesy of a Private Collection | Gracieuseté d'une collection privée

49. *Coloured Lady* | *Dame de couleur*, 1966
Watercolour : collage on heavy wove paper adhered to illustration board | Aquarelle : collage de papier vélin épais fixé sur du carton à dessin
40.6 × 35.5 | 40,6 × 35,5 cm
Library and Archives Canada, Major Lender | Bibliothèque et Archives Canada, prêteur important, e011083798

50. *Lady in Bed* | *Dame au lit*, 1966
Watercolour : collage on heavy wove paper adhered to illustration board | Aquarelle : collage de papier vélin épais fixé sur du carton à dessin
40.6 × 35.5 | 40,6 × 35,5 cm
Library and Archives Canada, Major Lender | Bibliothèque et Archives Canada, prêteur important, e011083799

51. *Lady at a Picnic* | *Dame en pique-nique*, 1967
Watercolour and gouache on heavy wove paper | Aquarelle et gouache sur papier vélin épais
40.6 × 35.5 | 40,6 × 35,5 cm
Library and Archives Canada, Major Lender | Bibliothèque et Archives Canada, prêteur important, e011080221

52. *Lady in Bed* | *Dame au lit*, 1967
Watercolour on paper | Aquarelle sur papier
40.6 × 35.5 | 40,6 × 35,5 cm
Courtesy of Brian Oickle | Gracieuseté de Brian Oickle

53. *A Round, II* | *Un cercle, II*, 1966
Pen and black ink on wove paper | Plume et encre noire sur papier vélin
73.7 × 58.6 | 73,7 × 58,6 cm
Library and Archives Canada, Major Lender | Bibliothèque et Archives Canada, prêteur important, e011083811

54. *Landing* | *Atterissage*, 1966–1967
Pen and black ink on wove paper | Plume et encre noire sur papier vélin
73.7 × 58.6 | 73,7 × 58,6 cm
Courtesy of Brian Oickle | Gracieuseté de Brian Oickle

55. *Untitled (Blue Tilt)* | *Sans titre (Inclinaison bleue)*, 1967
Acrylic on canvas | Acrylique sur toile
68.7 × 89 | 68,7 × 89 cm
Courtesy of Renato Albino | Gracieuseté de Renato Albino

56. *Tilt I* | *Inclinaison I*, 1967
Black ink applied with pen and spray on wove paper | Encre noire appliquée à la plume et au jet sur papier vélin
58 × 73.5 | 58 × 73,5 cm
Library and Archives Canada, Major Lender | Bibliothèque et Archives Canada, prêteur important, e011083812

57. *Untitled (Blue Circle)* | *Sans titre (Cercle bleu)*, 1967
Acrylic on canvas | Acrylique sur toile
69 × 88.8 | 69 × 88,8 cm
Courtesy of a Private Collection | Gracieuseté d'une collection privée

58. *Untitled (Target)* | *Sans titre (Cible)*, 1967
Acrylic on canvas | Acrylique sur toile
68.7 × 89 | 68,7 × 89 cm
Courtesy of a Private Collection | Gracieuseté d'une collection privée

59. *Untitled (Purple Circle)* | *Sans titre (Cercle violet)*, 1967
Acrylic on canvas | Acrylique sur toile
68.7 × 89.2 | 68,7 × 89,2 cm
Courtesy of Renato Albino | Gracieuseté de Renato Albino

60. *Milkweed* | *Laiteron*, 1967
Pen and black ink on wove paper | Plume et encre noire sur papier vélin
58.4 × 78.7 | 58,4 × 78,7 cm
National Gallery of Canada | Musée des beaux-arts du Canada, Ottawa; Gift of the artist | Don de l'artiste, 1998

61. *Canada 67*, 1967
Pen and ink on paper | Plume et encre sur papier
39.4 × 29.2 | 39,4 × 29,2 cm
Courtesy of Brian Oickle | Gracieuseté de Brian Oickle

62. *Female Nude Study* | *Étude de nu – Femme*, 1969
Pen and black ink on wove paper | Plume et encre noire sur papier vélin
29.3 × 18.2 | 29,3 × 18,2 cm
Library and Archives Canada, Major Lender | Bibliothèque et Archives Canada, prêteur important, e011083783

63. *Male Nude Study* | *Étude de nu – Homme*, 1970
Pen and black ink on thin wove card | Plume et encre noire sur carton vélin mince
28.2 × 21.6 | 28,2 × 21,6 cm
Library and Archives Canada, Major Lender | Bibliothèque et Archives Canada, prêteur important, e011083782

64. *Feathers and Grass* | *Plumes et pelouse*, 1971
Pen and black ink on wove paper | Plume et encre noire sur papier vélin
28.5 × 19 | 28,5 × 19 cm
National Gallery of Canada | Musée des beaux-arts du Canada, Ottawa; Gift of the artist | Don de l'artiste, 1998

65. *Maple Leaf in Four Seasons* | *Feuille d'érable dans les quatre saisons*, 1971
Postage stamps: photo-lithographs | Timbre-poste : photolithographies
4 × 2.4 cm each | 4 × 2,4 cm chacun
Courtesy of a Private Collection and the Canada Post Corporation | Gracieuseté d'une collection privée et de la Société canadienne des postes

66. *Floral Aerogrammes* | *Aérogrammes floraux*, 1973
Offset lithograph | Lithographie offset
13.5 × 21 cm each | 13,5 × 21 cm chacune
Collection and the Canada Post Corporation | Gracieuseté d'une collection privée et de la Société canadienne des postes

67. *Hepatica Leaves* | *Feuilles d'hépatique*, 1974
Pen and ink on paper | Plume et encre sur papier
19.1 × 29.2 | 19,1 × 29,2 cm
Courtesy of Brian Oickle | Gracieuseté de Brian Oickle

68. *From Dawn to Dusk* | *De l'aube au crépuscule*, 1977
Ink on paper | Encre sur papier
29.3 × 78.6 | 29,3 × 78,6 cm
Collection of the Art Gallery of Ontario | Collection du Musée des beaux-arts de l'Ontario, Toronto; Gift of the artist | Don de l'artiste, Ottawa, 1999, 99/40

69. *Small World* | *Le monde est petit*, 1977
Pen and black ink on wove paper | Plume et encre noire sur papier vélin
57.9 × 57.9 | 57,9 × 57,9 cm
National Gallery of Canada | Musée des beaux-arts du Canada, Ottawa; Gift of the artist | Don de l'artiste, 1998

70. *Progression from Red and Blue* | *Progression de rouge et bleu*, 1977
Watercolour on paper | Aquarelle sur papier
28 × 37.6 | 28 × 37,6 cm
Courtesy of a Private Collection | Gracieuseté d'une collection privée

71. *Untitled (Circles and Squares)* | *Sans titre (Cercles et carrés)*, 1977
Ink on paper | Encre sur papier
17.2 × 12.7 | 17,2 × 12,7 cm
Courtesy of Brian Oickle | Gracieuseté de Brian Oickle

72. *Progression in Blue Box* | *Progression dans une boîte bleue*, 1977
Watercolour on wove paper | Aquarelle sur papier vélin
17.2 × 12.7 | 17,2 × 12,7 cm
Library and Archives Canada, Major Lender | Bibliothèque et Archives Canada, prêteur important, e011083780

73. *Pink Box* | *Boîte rose*, 1977
Watercolour on wove paper | Aquarelle sur papier vélin
17.2 × 12.7 | 17,2 × 12,7 cm
Library and Archives Canada, Major Lender | Bibliothèque et Archives Canada, prêteur important, e011083779

74. *Progression with Green* | *Progression avec vert*, 1977
Watercolour on paper | Aquarelle sur papier
37.1 × 27.6 | 37,1 × 27,6 cm
Courtesy of Renato Albino | Gracieuseté de Renato Albino

75. *Untitled* | *Sans titre*, 1977
Colour pencil on paper | Crayon de couleur sur papier
29.7 × 26.7 | 29,7 × 26,7 cm
Courtesy of Renato Albino | Gracieuseté de Renato Albino

76. *Progession with Three Colours* | *Progression avec trois couleurs*, 1979
Watercolour on paper | Aquarelle sur papier
37.8 × 28.2 | 37,8 × 28,2 cm
Courtesy of Renato Albino | Gracieuseté de Renato Albino

77. *Progession in Orange* | *Progression en orange*, 1979
Watercolour on paper | Aquarelle sur papier
38 × 28.3 | 38 × 28,3 cm
Courtesy of Renato Albino | Gracieuseté de Renato Albino

78. *Edge of Woods* | *Lisière d'une forêt*, 1979
Pen and black ink on wove paper | Plume et encre noire sur papier vélin
29 × 37 cm
National Gallery of Canada | Musée des beaux-arts du Canada, Ottawa; Gift of the artist | Don de l'artiste, 1998

79. *Winter Woods* | *Forêt d'hiver*, 1979–80
Conté crayon on wove paper | Crayon conté sur papier vélin
58.7 × 73.7 | 58,7 × 73,7 cm
National Gallery of Canada | Musée des beaux-arts du Canada, Ottawa; Bequest of Alma Duncan | Legs d'Alma Duncan, 2005

80. *Self-Portrait* | *Autoportrait*, 1978
Pen, ink and coloured pencils on paper | Plume, encre et crayons de couleur sur papier
38.8 × 35.8 | 38,8 × 35,8 cm
Library and Archives Canada, Major Lender | Bibliothèque et Archives Canada, prêteur important, e011083727

81. *Audrey McLaren*, 1991
Charcoal on laid paper | Fusain sur papier vergé
63.7 × 47.8 | 63,7 × 47,8 cm
Library and Archives Canada, Major Lender | Bibliothèque et Archives Canada, prêteur important, e011080758

1 With the exception of the work *Alma Duncan* by Ernst Neumann, public domain. | Dans le domaine public, à l'exception de l'œuvre *Alma Duncan* d'Ernst Neumann.

Acknowledgements

I would sincerely like to acknowledge my partner in crime, Jaclyn Meloche. Her enthusiasm for Alma Duncan's work is infectious, and she brought such amazing research and analysis to this project. Jaclyn, thank you! I am also beyond thankful for the support of the late Audrey McLaren (Babs) who provided us with countless resources to help this all happen, as well as Anne Maheux who made this support possible. Babs' passing this year saddened us all and hearkened the end of an era — we are so thankful to have had the time we did with her and that she was aware of the project. I would also like to mention thanks to the incredible team at Library and Archives Canada, including Anne Maheux, Myriam Godin, Karine Brisson, and Mary-Margaret Johnson Miller. Your organization is impeccable and dedication to Alma Duncan's legacy is heartwarming. You went over and above for us. I am so grateful to the generosity of the private lenders and institutions who have let their works go for two years to facilitate this exhibition tour. Special thanks to Stephanie Germano, our Interim Collections Manager at the OAG for her untiring spirit, and Jen Gilliland Collections Manager, for all their help with the borrowing and shipping. Big props to my intern Teodora Dimitrova for a summer full of copyright requests, and to both Marie-Camille Lalande and Mark Timmings for their extraordinary eye for detail and patience. My thanks to the writers, through whose words Alma's work has been brought to life and given context. I would like to thank Anik Glaude, Curator of the Varley Art Gallery of Markham, Catharine Mastin, Director/Curator of the Windsor Art Gallery, and Lisa Daniels, Director/Curator of the Judith & Norman Alix Art Gallery, for your enthusiastic support from the get-go. Gratitude to OAG's Director, Alexandra Badzak, as well as to Ola Wlusek, Curator of Contemporary Art, for your constant support. Thanks to my wonderful unofficial editors, Amanda Cockburn and Matt Harrison. Last but not least, special shout-out to my family, Matt and Belle, who give me a soft place to land, patiently endure my late-night writing, and are my constant joy.

Catherine Sinclair

I would like to thank, first and foremost, Catherine Sinclair for her collaboration, cooperation, support, and most of all her shared interest in Alma Duncan. I would also like to thank the Ottawa Art Gallery for this opportunity. When I started my research on Duncan in 2001, I never imagined that my work would materialize into a comprehensive exhibition of the artist's life and work. Moreover, to be complemented by such an inspired publication is a dream come true. Many thanks go to the late Audrey (Babs) McLaren, Anne Maheux, Rosemarie Tovell, and Tom McSorley for their generous contributions. Their stories and histories have helped to shape the narrative of this exhibition. I cannot overlook the support from my family, Colleen Meloche and James Meloche, who continue to encourage me in my artistic and professional pursuits. Without them my work would not be possible. Lastly, I would like to dedicate my work on Alma Duncan to the late Natalie Luckyj, who introduced me to the artist, and who continues to inspire the ways in which I practice feminism in my research, my writing, my art, and my everyday life.

Jaclyn Meloche

Remerciements

J'aimerais remercier chaleureusement ma complice Jaclyn Meloche. Son enthousiasme pour l'œuvre d'Alma Duncan est contagieux, et ses recherches et son analyse de grande envergure ont contribué magnifiquement au projet. Jaclyn, merci ! Je suis aussi très reconnaissante à la regrettée Audrey « Babs » McLaren de nous avoir fourni maintes ressources nécessaires à la réalisation du projet, ainsi qu'à Anne Maheux, qui a rendu cet appui possible. Le décès de Babs cette année nous a tous attristés, et a marqué la fin d'une époque. Nous sommes si heureux d'avoir pu passer ce temps avec elle et qu'elle ait été au courant du projet. J'aimerais aussi exprimer ma gratitude envers la formidable équipe de Bibliothèque et Archives Canada : Anne Maheux, Myriam Godin, Karine Brisson et Mary-Margaret Johnson Miller. Vous avez fait preuve d'un sens de l'organisation impeccable et d'un dévouement très touchant à l'égard du legs artistique d'Alma Duncan. Merci de vous être dépassées pour nous. Je tiens à remercier de leur générosité les individus et les établissements qui ont prêté leurs œuvres pour deux ans afin de permettre la tournée de cette exposition. Un merci tout particulier à Stephanie Germano, la gestionnaire intérimaire des collections de la GAO, et Jen Gilliland, la gestionnaire des collections, de leur aide avec les emprunts et les envois. Des gros mercis à ma stagiaire Teodora Dimitrova, pour son été passé à remplir des demandes de droits d'auteur, et à Marie Camille Lalande et Mark Timmings, pour leur sens du détail et leur patience. Je remercie les auteurs, grâce à qui l'œuvre d'Alma a été ranimée et mise en contexte. J'aimerais remercier Anik Glaude, commissaire à la Varley Art Gallery de Markham, Catharine Mastin, directrice et commissaire de la Art Gallery of Windsor, et Lisa Daniels, directrice et commissaire de la Judith & Norman Alix Art Gallery, de leur appui enthousiaste dès le départ. Merci énormément à la directrice de la GAO Alexandra Badzak et la commissaire de l'art contemporain Ola Wlusek, qui m'appuient sans cesse. Merci à mes merveilleux réviseurs non officiels Amanda Cockburn et Matt Harrison. Et finalement, une mention toute spéciale aux membres de ma famille, Matt et Belle, qui m'offrent un nid douillet où atterrir, endurent patiemment mes longues nuits de rédaction, et sont une source de joie inépuisable.

Catherine Sinclair

J'aimerais tout d'abord remercier Catherine Sinclair de sa collaboration, de sa coopération et de son appui, mais surtout de son intérêt pour Alma Duncan, que je partage. Je remercie aussi la Galerie d'art d'Ottawa de cette occasion. Lorsque j'ai commencé mes recherches sur Duncan en 2001, je n'aurais jamais imaginé que mon travail prendrait la forme d'une exposition exhaustive sur la vie et l'œuvre de l'artiste. Que l'exposition s'accompagne d'un catalogue aussi captivant est, de surcroît, un rêve. Mille mercis à la regrettée Audrey « Babs » McLaren, Anne Maheux, Rosemarie Tovell et Tom McSorley de leurs contributions si généreuses; leurs récits et recherches ont aidé à former la trame de l'exposition. Je ne peux passer sous silence l'appui de ma famille, Colleen Meloche et James Meloche, qui appuient sans relâche mes activités artistiques et professionnelles. Je ne pourrais faire mon travail sans eux. Enfin, j'aimerais dédier mes travaux sur Alma Duncan à la regrettée Natalie Luckyj, qui m'a fait connaître cette artiste, et qui inspire toujours ma façon de pratiquer le féminisme dans mes recherches, mes écrits, mon art et ma vie quotidienne.

Jaclyn Meloche

Catalogue of an exhibition organized by, and held at the Ottawa Art Gallery, Ottawa (2 October 2014 – 11 January 2015) and toured to the Varley Art Gallery, Markham, ON (January 24 – May 3, 2015); Judith & Norman Alix Art Gallery, Sarnia, ON (June 5 – August 3, 2015); and the Art Gallery of Windsor, Windsor, ON (15 April – 12 June 2016).

Lenders to the Exhibition

Renato Albino
Art Gallery of Ontario
D & E Lake Ltd. Fine Arts, Toronto
Canadian War Museum
Library and Archives Canada
National Gallery of Canada
National Film Board of Canada
Brian Oickle
The Robert McLaughlin Gallery
Various Private Collections

Publication Coordination: Catherine Sinclair
Editorial Assistance: Malcolm Sutton, Geneviève Letarte
French Translation: Marie-Camille Lalande
Design: Mark Timmings
Image preparation: Trevor Mills
Printed in Canada by Friesens

Front Cover: *Self Portrait with Red Stripes* (detail), 1958, Courtesy of D & E Lake Ltd. Fine Arts, Toronto (cat. 32)

Front Endleaves: *Grass, August 1* (detail), 1962, Library and Archives Canada (cat. 34); Alma Duncan, c. 1940

Frontispiece: *Coloured Lady* (detail), 1966, Library and Archives Canada (cat. 49); *Lady in Bed* (detail), 1966, Library and Archives Canada (cat. 50)

Title page: Alma Duncan, c. 1950

Back endleaves: Alma Duncan at work in the Gatineau Hills, c. 1960; *Grass I* (detail), 1962, Library and Archives Canada (cat. 36)

Back cover: Alma Duncan working on the making of the film *Folksong Fantasy*, 1951

All photos are reproduced courtesy of the lending institutions, with the exception of: David Barbour (front cover, pp. 27, 32, 40, 46–47, 65–69, 74, 80–81, 85–87, 95, 99, 102–104, 161, 162); Anne Maheux (p. 165); Audrey (Babs) McLaren (front endleaf [ii], pp. 4, 6, 128, 131, 132, 136, 139, 177, back cover); © National Gallery of Canada (pp. 24, 26, 31, 36–38, 52–53); Hazen Sise (p. 154); photographer unknown (pp. 15, 144, 153).

Library and Archives Canada Cataloguing in Publication

Alma : the life and art of Alma Duncan (1917–2004) / texts by Tom McSorley, Anne Maheux, Jaclyn Meloche, Catherine Sinclair, Rosemarie L. Tovell = Alma : la vie et l'œuvre d'Alma Duncan (1917–2004) / textes par Tom McSorley, Anne Maheux, Jaclyn Meloche, Catherine Sinclair, Rosemarie L. Tovell.

Co-published by the Judith & Norman Alix Art Gallery.
Includes bibliographical references.
Text in English and French.
Catalogue of an exhibition held at the Ottawa Art Gallery.
ISBN 978-1-894906-49-4 (bound)

1. Duncan, Alma—Exhibitions. I. McSorley, Tom, writer of added commentary II. Ottawa Art Gallery, issuing body, host institution III. Judith & Norman Alix Art Gallery, issuing body IV. Title: Alma. French.

NC143.D85A4 2014 759.11 C2014-904129-2E

Ottawa Art Gallery

2 Daly Avenue, Ottawa, ON, Canada K1N 6E2
613-233-8699
www.ottawaartgallery.ca

Distributed by ABC Art Books Canada
230-372, rue Sainte-Catherine Ouest
Montréal, QC H3B 1A2
www.ABCartbookscanada.com

Catalogue d'une exposition organisée par et présentée à la Galerie d'art d'Ottawa, Ottawa (2 octobre 2014–11 janvier 2015) et présentée en tournée à la Varley Art Gallery, Markham (Ontario) (24 janvier–3 mai 2015), à la Judith & Norman Alix Art Gallery, Sarnia (Ontario) (5 juin–3 août 2015) et la Art Gallery of Windsor, Windsor (Ontario) (15 avril–12 juin 2016).

Prêteurs de l'exposition

Renato Albino
Musée des beaux-arts de l'Ontario
D & E Lake Ltd. Fine Arts, Toronto
Musée canadien de la guerre
Bibliothèque et Archives Canada
Musée des beaux-arts du Canada
Office national du film du Canada
Brian Oickle
Robert McLaughlin Gallery
Divers collectionneurs privés

Coordination de la publication : Catherine Sinclair
Aide à la revision : Malcolm Sutton, Geneviève Letarte
Traduction française : Marie-Camille Lalande
Conception graphique : Mark Timmings
Préparation d'images : Trevor Mills
Imprimée au Canada par Friesens

Couverture avant : *Autoportrait avec rayures rouges* (détail), 1958, Gracieuseté de D & E Lake Ltd. Fine Arts, Toronto (cat. 32)

Pages de gardes avant : *Herbe, 1er août* (détail), 1962, Bibliothèque et Archives Canada (cat. 34); Alma Duncan, v. 1940

Frontispice : *Dame de couleur* (détail), 1966, Bibliothèque et Archives Canada (cat. 49); *Dame au lit* (détail), 1966, Bibliothèque et Archives Canada (cat. 50)

Page titre : Alma Duncan, v. 1950

Pages de gardes arrière : Alma Duncan au travail dans les collines de la Gatineau, v. 1960; *Herbe I* (détail), 1962, Bibliothèque et Archives Canada (cat. 36)

Couverture arrière : Alma Duncan travaillant à la réalisation du film *Fantaisie folklorique*, 1951

Toutes les photographies sont reproduites avec l'aimable autorisation des organismes prêteurs à l'exception de : David Barbour (couverture avant, p. 27, 32, 40, 46–47, 65–69, 74, 80–81, 85–87, 95, 99, 102–104, 161, 162); Anne Maheux (p. 165); Audrey (Babs) McLaren (page de garde avant [ii], p. 4, 6, 128, 131, 132, 136, 139, 177, couverture arrière); © Musée des beaux-arts du Canada (p. 24, 26, 31, 36–38, 52–53); Hazen Sise (p. 154); photographe inconnu (p. 15, 144, 153).

Catalogage avant publication de Bibliothèque et Archives Canada

Alma : the life and art of Alma Duncan (1917–2004) / texts by Tom McSorley, Anne Maheux, Jaclyn Meloche, Catherine Sinclair, Rosemarie L. Tovell = Alma : la vie et l'œuvre d'Alma Duncan (1917–2004) / textes par Tom McSorley, Anne Maheux, Jaclyn Meloche, Catherine Sinclair, Rosemarie L. Tovell.

Publié en collaboration avec la Judith & Norman Alix Art Gallery.
Comprend des références bibliographiques.
Texte en anglais et en français.
Catalogue d'une exposition présentée à la Galerie d'art d'Ottawa.
ISBN 978-1-894906-49-4 (relié)

1. Duncan, Alma — Expositions. I. McSorley, Tom, auteur de commentaire ajouté II. Galerie d'art d'Ottawa, organisme de publication, institution hôte III. Judith & Norman Alix Art Gallery, organisme de publication IV. Titre : Alma. Français.

NC143.D85A4 2014 759.11 C2014-904129-2F

Galerie d'art d'Ottawa

2, avenue Daly, Ottawa (Ontario) Canada K1N 6E2
613-233-8699
www.ottawaartgallery.ca

Distribué par ABC Art Books Canada
230-372, rue Sainte-Catherine Ouest
Montréal (Québec) H3B 1A2
www.ABCartbookscanada.com

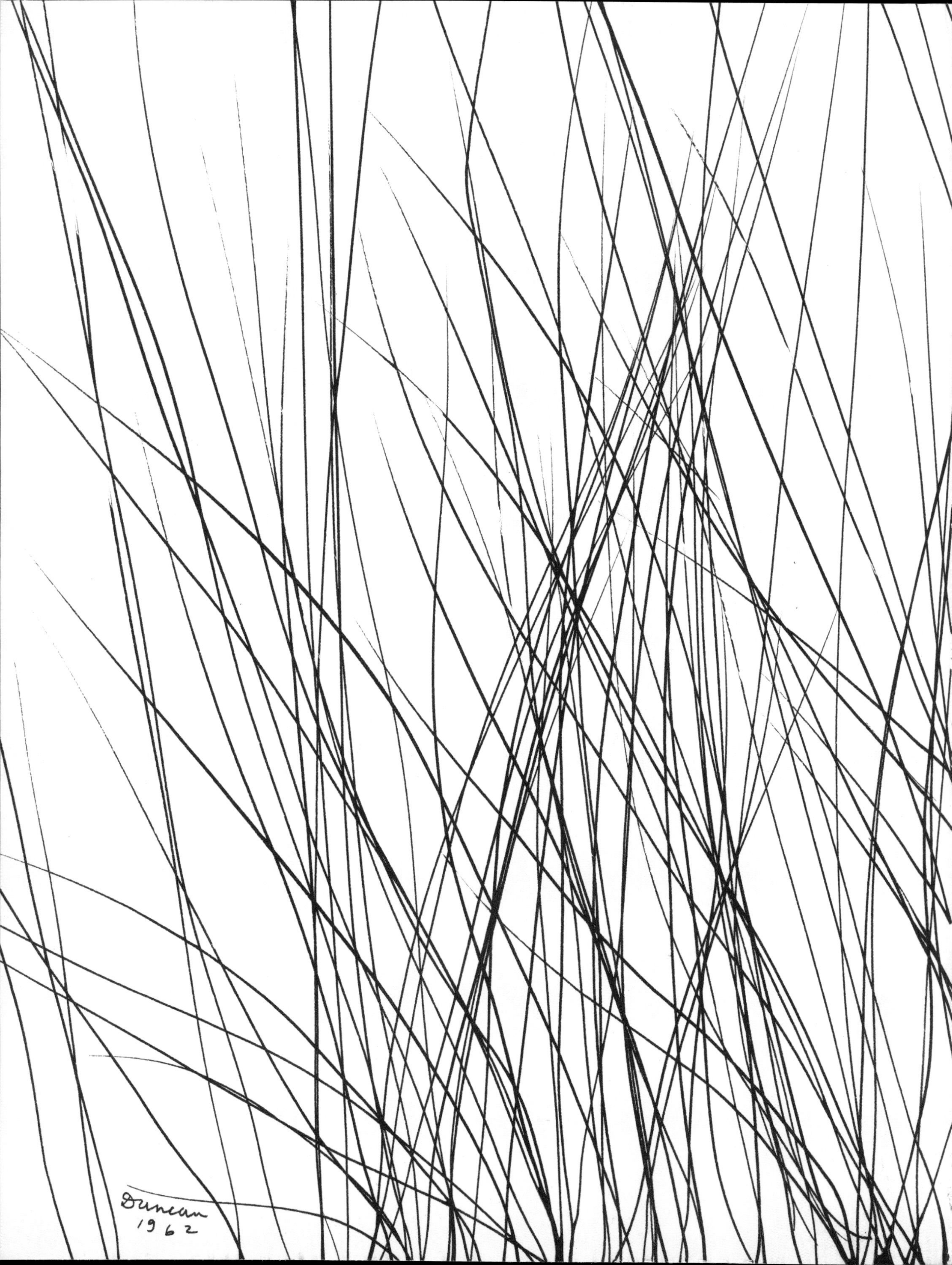
Duncan
1962